A 12-Step Approach
to the
Sunday Readings

A 12-Step Approach to the Sunday Readings

Jim Harbaugh, S.J.

SHEED & WARD

Lanham, Maryland
Chicago, Illinois

Scripture quotations are from the New Revised Standard Version of the Bible, copyright 1946, 1952, 1971 by the Division of Christian Education of the National Council of the Churches of Christ in the USA. Used by permission. All rights reserved.

Published by Sheed & Ward
An imprint of Rowman & Littlefield Publishers, Inc.
4720 Boston Way
Lanham, MD 20706

12 Hid's Copse Road
Cumnor Hill, Oxford OX2 9JJ, England

Library of Congress Cataloging-in-Publication Data

Harbaugh, Jim, 1945-
    A 12-step approach to the Sunday readings / Jim Harbaugh.
      p. cm.
    Includes bibliographical references
    ISBN 1-58051-128-7 (pbk.)
        1.Bible-Meditations. 2.Twelve-step programs—Religious aspects—
          Christianity—Meditations. 3.Church year meditations. I.Title:
    Twelve-step approach to the Sunday readings. II.Title.

BS483.5 .H28 2002
242'.3—dc21

                  2002073427

1 2 3 4 5   05 04 03 02

Contents

Dedication

*To my nephew and godson, Matt,
and to Matt's nephews and godsons,
my grand-nephews, Alexander and Nicolas—
for all they have taught me about God.*

*And to Matt's wife, Jennifer,
and to the parents of Alexander and Nicolas,
my niece Lisa and her husband Stanley—
for the care they all take of the boys.*

✛

"For John [the Baptist] came neither eating nor drinking, and
they say, 'He has a demon'; the Son of Man came eating and
drinking, and they say, 'Look, a glutton and a drunkard, a
friend of tax collectors and sinners!' Yet wisdom is vindicated
by her deeds" (Mt 11:18–19).

"Be quick to see where religious people are right. Make use of
what they offer" (BB 87, on Step 11).

✛

Acknowledgments

Unless specified otherwise, I am using the New Revised Standard Version, Catholic Edition, translation of the Scriptures. I am also using that Bible's abbreviations of names of books of the Bible, except for a few rarely used books, like Baruch and Micah, which I spell out to save the reader time hunting in the table of contents.

· · ·

I have found the following works helpful in writing this book, and in preparing homilies for many years as well:

Raymond Brown, S.S., Joseph Fitzmyer, S.J., and Roland E. Murphy, O. Carm., eds. *The Jerome Biblical Commentary.* Englewood Cliffs, NJ: Prentice-Hall, 1968.

_____. *The New Jerome Biblical Commentary.* Englewood Cliffs, NJ: Prentice-Hall, 1990.

John Dominic Crossan. *Jesus: A Revolutionary Biography.* San Francisco: HarperCollins, 1994.

J. C. Fenton. *The Gospel of St. Matthew.* London: Penguin Books, 1963.

Reginald H. Fuller. *Preaching the New Lectionary: The Word of God for the Church Today.* Collegeville, MN: Liturgical Press, 1974.

Wilfrid Harrington, O.P. *Mark.* Wilmington, DE: Michael Glazier, 1979.

Eugene LaVerdiere, S.S.S. *Luke.* Wilmington, DE: Michael Glazier, 1980.

James McPolin, S.J. *John.* Wilmington, DE: Michael Glazier, 1979.

John Marsh. *The Gospel of St. John.* London: Penguin Books, 1968.

Sebastian Moore. *Let This Mind Be in You: The Quest for Identity through Oedipus to Christ.* New York: Harper and Row, 1986.

D. E. Nineham. *The Gospel of St. Mark.* London: Penguin Books, 1969.

George V. Wigram and Ralph D. Winter. *The Word Study Concordance.* Wheaton, IL: Tyndale House, 1978.

• • •

I am using the following 12-Step literature, all published by Alcoholics Anonymous World Services, Inc., New York City:

Alcoholics Anonymous, a.k.a. The Big Book, 3rd ed. (1976), abbreviated BB.
Twelve Steps and Twelve Traditions (1953), abbreviated 12 X 12.
Alcoholics Anonymous Comes of Age (1957), abbreviated AACA.
As Bill Sees It (1967), abbreviated ABSI.

This material is reprinted with the permission of Alcoholics Anonymous World Services, Inc. Permission to reprint this material does not mean that A.A. has reviewed or approved the contents of this publication. A.A. is a program of recovery from alcoholism *only*—use of this material in any other non-A.A. context does not imply otherwise.

Additionally, although A.A. is a spiritual program, it is not a religious program. Hence, A.A. is not allied with any sect, denomination, or specific spiritual belief.

• • •

The following reference books on A.A. literature and history were also very helpful:

Alcoholics Anonymous World Services, Inc. *Dr. Bob and the Good Oldtimers: A Biography, with Recollections of Early A. A. in the Midwest.* New York: A.A. World Services, 1980.
_____. *Pass It On: The Story of Bill Wilson and How the A. A. Message Reached the World.* New York: A.A. World Services, 1984.
Stewart C. *A Reference Guide to the Big Book of Alcoholics Anonymous.* Seattle: Recovery Press, 1986.

Ernie Kurtz. *Not-God: A History of Alcoholics Anonymous.* Center City, MN: Hazelden, 1979.
Bill Pittman. *A.A.: The Way It Began.* Seattle: Glen Abbey Books, 1988.
Robert Thomsen. *Bill W.* New York: Harper and Row, 1975.

• • •

In addition, I have quoted or paraphrased material from the following sources (permission has been given where material is directly quoted):

Viktor Frankl. *Man's Search for Meaning.* Rev. ed.; New York: Washington Square Press/Simon & Schuster, 1985.
Michael Himes. "Living Conversation: Higher Education in a Catholic Context," *Conversations*, Fall 1995, pp. 21–27.
William James. *The Varieties of Religious Experience: A Study in Human Nature.* 1902; rpt. New York: Macmillan, 1961.
Ernest Kurtz and Katherine Ketcham. *The Spirituality of Imperfection: Modern Wisdom from Classic Stories.* New York: Bantam, 1992.
Earnie Larsen and Janee Parnegg. *Recovering Catholics: What to Do When Religion Comes Between You and God.* San Francisco: HarperCollins, 1992.
Gerald May. *Addiction and Grace.* San Francisco: HarperCollins, 1991.
Flannery O'Connor. *The Complete Stories.* New York: Farrar, Strauss and Giroux, 1971.
M. Scott Peck. *People of the Lie: The Hope for Healing Human Evil.* New York: Simon & Schuster, 1983.
Virginia Satir. *Conjoint Family Therapy.* 3rd ed. Palo Alto, CA: Science and Behavior Books, 1983.
Richard Wilbur. "A Wedding Toast," in *New and Collected Poems*, p. 61. San Diego: Harcourt Brace Jovanovich, 1988.

• • •

Finally, a few personal acknowledgments:

To Steve Morris, director of Addiction Studies, Seattle University, an excellent boss, who has supported me in my writing.

To the Jesuits of the Oregon Province, and particularly at Seattle University, for their welcome, and especially to those who have read this work in manuscript.

To Dr. Mary Cross, my spiritual director, and to Tom Weston, S.J., for ideas and for affection.

To Karen Lutz and the other secretary/receptionists in Addiction Studies at Seattle University, for helping me get things printed and copied and mailed.

And especially to all the retreatants, on 12 Step and on Christian retreats, at Seattle University and elsewhere, over the years, for listening and responding.

✛

Introduction

This book was written with several audiences in mind. I thought first of the many people who have found the spiritual path of the 12 Steps helpful in overcoming various addictions and compulsions. Some of these people also belong to churches, including the Roman Catholic, the Episcopalian, and the Lutheran churches, all of which have for some years used the same Bible readings weekend by weekend over a repeating three-year cycle (there are minor variations between churches, but by and large, the readings on a given Sunday or big feast will be the same). There are some other 12-Step folks who may not be part of these church groups, but who do find the Hebrew and Christian Scriptures useful in working their recovery programs. Both these crossover groups will, I think, find these meditations meaningful.

There is a second large bunch who will, I hope, be intrigued by my reflections. A lot of church people who do not practice a full-fledged 12-Step program may have some interest in 12-Step principles, or be fond of 12 Steppers and want to pray in solidarity with their friends. These church members may come to understand their recovering friends better by following along with these meditations. Perhaps they may even see how 12-Step principles can apply to their own lives.

Finally, while I was writing this book, I was thinking particularly of my fellow clergypersons. Every weekend many of us have to think and pray until we can find some fresh way to carry the ancient messages of the Scripture readings assigned by our churches. In my own preaching I have often found 12-Step concepts a key to unlocking the Sunday readings. I hope that the concentrated sermons contained in this book can tickle the imaginations of other preachers.

Whichever of these audiences you belong to, you may want some instructions about how to use this book, particularly if you are unfamiliar with the three-year cycles. The particular years between 2002 and 2010 covered by each cycle are listed at the beginning of the cycles. Cycle A mostly uses Matthew's Gospel, B uses Mark's, C Luke's. Cycles begin on the First Sunday of Advent each year, usually the Sunday after Thanksgiving in the United States. Each cycle is divided into three major segments: 4 Advent Sundays leading to the Christmas season (December and early January); 6 Sundays of Lent leading to the 8-Sunday Easter season (February to May, more or less); and 34 Sundays of Ordinary Time (the rest of the year).

If you're still baffled about where we are in this church calendar, a friend who attends church regularly perhaps can help you. Some denominations issue books, which are called "missals" in the Roman church; these are available at modest prices in church-oriented bookstores. Some denominations also stock their pews with booklets that contain appropriate instructions.

Once you know where the worshipping communities are, you can go one of two ways. If you attend church yourself, you may read the meditation for that weekend either before or after you attend service (or even both). You may want to meditate on it, if meditation is part of your religious or spiritual practice. If you do not attend service, you can read the meditation on your own.

Whatever your worship arrangements, you will want to have in front of you for your personal prayer a Bible, or at any rate a copy of the full text of the readings for a given weekend, in a missal or a missalette, so you can get the point of the meditation. My meditations follow the biblical texts very closely, and often will concentrate on a single word or phrase. If you know 12-Step literature—the Big Book (*Alcoholics Anonymous*), the 12 X 12 (*Twelve Steps and Twelve Traditions*), and others—you may also want to have them handy as you read the meditations, since I quote from this literature practically every week. Each meditation is prefaced with a quotation from one of the readings, which provides a focus for what I have to say; you can return to this keynote quotation from time to time in the course of the week to be reminded of your reflections from the previous weekend.

No special knowledge of either the Bible or the 12 Steps is necessary. I like nothing better than explaining things, so as we go I will fill you in on anything I think you need to know to get the point of a particular meditation. At the beginning of the book I have listed some sources I have found helpful in preparing these meditations, sources I sometimes quote or paraphrase.

Once you have climbed onto the carousel of the cycle of readings, all you need to do is stay on. If you lose track, you may have to go back to that understanding friend I mentioned earlier. One of the advantages of attending services, in fact, is that you don't have to be beholden to friends for this kind of information. But suit yourself.

This whole exercise would be pointless if the 12 Steps and the Bible didn't have similar aims. But I deeply believe they do, for reasons that are spelled out in the Introduction to my *A 12-Step Approach to the Spiritual Exercises of St. Ignatius* (Sheed & Ward, 1997). I think the chief aim of both, and so the aim of this book, is best summed up in the words of the ancient Christian writer Irenaeus: "The glory of God is a human being fully alive." Human beings—or more specifically, human beings who become addicted, "attached" to things and people—come "fully alive," according to the Big Book, when they "find a Power greater than [themselves] which will solve [their] problem" (BB, 45). "Well, that's exactly what this book is about. . . . [T]hat One is God. May you find [God] now!" (BB, 45, 59)

CYCLE A

December 2004–2005
December 2007–2008

✣

Advent
and Christmas

First Sunday of Advent

Is 2:1–5; Rom 13:11–14; Mt 24:37–44

". . . how it is now the moment for you to wake from sleep"
(Rom 13:11).

This Sunday begins the season of Advent. Advent prepares for Christmas. The greatest preparation we recovering people can make for the holidays, the greatest gift we can give those we love and those who love us, are precisely our newfound ability to "live honorably," as St. Paul urges the group in Rome to whom he is writing. One of the things I most missed when I was drinking was the ability to be "honorable," which to me meant the same as "reliable." But how could I keep my word to people and still drink? I couldn't guarantee that I would show up; if it was during the evening, I certainly couldn't guarantee that I would be sober if I did show up.

The word Paul uses for *honorably* means "with dignity" or "gracefully," neither of them expressions that anyone would use of someone still struggling with an addiction. When we're using, we keep falling, physically and spiritually. If we want to become honorable, we have to wake up, turn on the lights, and walk down "the Road of Happy Destiny" (BB, 164). To put it in 12-Step terms, we need to have "a spiritual awakening" in order to receive "the sunlight of the spirit" (BB, 66), so that we can "walk in the light of the Lord" (Is 2:5). And we get our wake-up call as "the result of these Steps" (Step 12). Because we have tapped into a Power greater than ourselves in the course of working the Steps of recovery, we now have the ability to "live honorably as in daylight; not in carousing and drunkenness" (Rom 13:13).

Living honorably is the best present we can give to people we care about. Nevertheless, a lot of people, including recovering people, get badly stressed out at this time of year because they're afraid they won't be ready in time, that the holidays, like the thief in today's Gospel, will catch them unprepared. Addicted people often think the holidays have to be perfect, if only to make up for the rest of the year. But recovery is a matter of "spiritual progress rather than spiritual perfection" (BB, 60). Bear in mind that the word *progress* literally means "walking forward," not arrival. We won't arrive at perfection, this Christmas or any Christmas. "Arriving" isn't our job; "walking honorably" is. And we can do our job if we turn our lives over to the One who *does* arrive (the word *advent* means "arrival"). "[T]hat One is God. May you find [God] now!" (BB, 59)

Second Sunday of Advent

Is 11:1–10; Rom 15:4–9; Mt 3:1–12

"May the God of steadfastness and encouragement grant you to live in harmony with one another, in accordance with Christ Jesus"
(Rom 15:5).

Each year, the Second and Third Sundays of Advent center on the figure of John the Baptist. John was a strange figure, a "preacher" as Matthew calls him, a bit like the hollow-eyed preacher played by John Carradine in the movie version of John Steinbeck's *The Grapes of Wrath*. Like this character, John the Baptist is a prophet, denouncing contemporary social ills and predicting a great and imminent crisis. John warns people that God will forcefully intervene to save the powerless.

In the light of this approaching crisis, John has a one-word message for the people who come out to the desert to hear him: *"Metanoete!"* The New American Bible translates this as "Reform your lives!" But *metanoete,* which is very important in all the Gospels and in the book you are reading, is also very difficult to translate simply. The closest I can come is "change your attitude." John is urging the crowds to undergo the "huge emotional displacements and rearrangements [of] ideas, emotions, and attitudes" that, according to Carl Jung, have to take place for a person to begin recovery (BB, 27). This may seem like a tall order, but we need not be discouraged. The prophet Isaiah says that "on that day"—the "day" when God "arrives"—"the earth shall be filled with knowledge of the Lord." The whole point of John's message and of this season of Advent is that "that day" is *now*: we can receive "knowledge of the Lord" from every person we meet. In particular, every time we attend a meeting or contact a trusted recovering friend, we get "lessons of patience" and "words of encouragement" (Rom). Paul notes that these "lessons" and "words" can also be found in the Bible, and no wonder, since God, the brains behind the Bible, is "the source of all patience and encouragement."

This "knowledge"—which the Serenity Prayer calls "wisdom"— is exactly what we need if we are going to *metanoete*, to change the way we look at the world. The whole world looks pretty miserable the morning after a drinking bout. But after a 12-Step meeting the world looks very different: when we have seen "people who normally would not mix" gathered in "fellowship, . . . friendliness, and an understanding which is indescribably wonderful" (BB, 17), it is easier to believe in a world where lions and cows and bears (oh, my) can "be neighbors" (Is).

Third Sunday of Advent

Is 35:1–6. 10; Jas 5:7–10; Mt 11:2–11

"You also must be patient . . . for the coming of the Lord is near"
(Jas 5:8).

On this Third Sunday of Advent, we continue focusing on John the Baptist. Christians are used to thinking of John as the forerunner, as the herald, of Jesus. They may imagine that God had informed John that his task was to prepare the way for one "more powerful" than he, and that, once Jesus arrived, John calmly accepted that his job was finished. But, in fact, this concept of John's role was completely clear to the early Christian community only many years after John's death. During his lifetime, John himself was so unsure about his relationship to Jesus that, as this Sunday's Gospel relates, he sent some of his disciples to Jesus precisely to find out who Jesus was.

Jesus answers John's question about whether Jesus is "He who is to come" ("come" as in "advent") by citing our First Reading this week, from Isaiah: Jesus reminds John that anyone can know that the Lord has come when blind people start seeing the light, when those who have stumbled now walk "with dignity" (see the meditation above for the first Sunday of Advent), when the weak find courage—and when compulsive people find the power to behave in a new, freer way. And when the Lord has come, there is "joy to the world."

But it isn't only human beings who have "come to know a new freedom and a new happiness" (BB, 83), who have joyful reasons for singing. "Heaven and nature sing," too, when the Lord comes. Isaiah speaks of the desert blooming, and the ever-practical Letter of James (which Bill W. and Dr. Bob especially liked because it stresses "how it works") points to "the precious yield of the soil." Of course, as any farmer or gardener knows, things don't bloom overnight: like farmers. We have to be patient as we await the coming of the Lord.

In the meantime, we can rejoice that one sign of the presence of God that Jesus points to is happening all the time: "the poor have the good news [the Gospel] preached to them." Every time we share, at a meeting or elsewhere, the changes that a Higher Power has brought about in our lives, there's a chance that some poor woman, some poor man, will hear it as good news. Like John, we are to carry the message; and when that message is heard, even by the deaf, then the kingdom of God has arrived, that kingdom to which John, in prison, could only wistfully look forward.

Fourth Sunday of Advent

Is 7:10–14; Rom 1:1–7; Mt 1:18–24

"'Joseph, son of David, do not be afraid to take Mary as your wife'"
(Mt 1:20).

Just as the Second and Third Sundays of Advent invite us to remember the great man who prepared the way for Jesus, so the Fourth brings to mind the great woman who *was* the way: Mary, the mother of the Lord. This Sunday's Gospel focuses on the enormous problems Mary faced when the time for her child to be born drew near.

As I mentioned a couple of Sundays ago, a lot of people are badly frazzled this time of year. Why? These folks, and *even* people in recovery, have fallen into the old trap of believing that, whatever things are like the rest of the year in our homes and families, Christmas is the one day of the year when it's reasonable to expect things to be perfect. Yet that is hardly the message of the gospel accounts of the birth of Jesus. As we will see, Luke's Gospel will highlight the confusions of the first Christmas. Today we have Matthew's story about the awkward engagement of Jesus' parents.

When the time for the wedding approached, it became painfully clear to Mary's fiancé, Joseph, that she was pregnant, and not by him. In a patriarchal culture like theirs, Joseph would have had every right to hand Mary over to public scorn. But he was an "upright" man, a "*Tzaddik*," one of those quietly decent people who, in Jewish thought, keep the world from coming apart. So he thought a quiet divorce was the upright thing to do; perhaps he reasoned that Mary and the child would be happier with the child's real father, whoever that was.

But then he received a conscious (or unconscious) contact with God, in the form of a dream, and learned that God's will for him was to be a father to someone else's son. Like so many other people in the stories about Jesus' birth, Joseph is told not to be afraid. We, too, shouldn't be afraid or discouraged at this time of year because our families are different from other people's; Jesus was born into a non-traditional arrangement.

Nor should we believe that messy families are somehow inferior to tidy ones. What was remarkable about the Holy Family was not that they didn't have problems, but that, like Joseph, they dealt with them graciously. Even if our Christmases don't go as we might like, we can still, with the help of God who "arrives," "cheerfully capitalize [trouble] as an opportunity to demonstrate [God's] omnipotence" (BB, 133).

Christmas, Mass at Midnight

Is 9:1–6; Ti 2:11–14; Lk 2:1–14

"For the grace of God has appeared, bringing salvation to all"
(Ti 2:11).

". . . there were shepherds living in the fields"
(Lk 2:8).

As I pointed out last Sunday, the first Christmas was anything but perfect, or even well-organized. Matthew has described for us the anxiety that surrounded the wedding of Mary and Joseph; the turmoil continues as the time for the birth of the child draws near. Mary and Joseph will be away from home, because of some kind of confusing bureaucratic necessity. When they get to Bethlehem, they discover that there are no vacancies, and of course they're too poor to pull strings by tipping the concierge. They are directed to a makeshift shelter. Then, at the worst possible moment, Mary gives birth. So, as humans do when it gets messy, the family of Jesus improvises.

Despite Jesus' parents' best efforts, the situation stays rather messy. In Luke, the first people to hear about the birth of the One Who Is to Come, the One Who Has Arrived, the Messiah, are shepherds, very messy people. After centuries of manger scenes, we probably think of shepherds and sheep as just cute and fluffy. But, in fact, both shepherds and sheep live rough and spend so much time together that they look and smell like each other. Then, as today, "shepherd" is not a vocational goal for most school kids. Even worse, shepherds could not very well "keep kosher" (strictly observe Jewish dietary laws) living in the fields, and so they would have been looked down on by pious Jews like the Pharisees.

And that is precisely Luke's point: Jesus comes above all to riffraff, to "human trash," to the people no one thinks very highly of. This is the good news, the tidings of great joy: God comes, not to those who are perfectly worthy of receiving God, but to those whose lives are so messy that God practically *has* to come to them if they are going to make it through the night. It's shepherds—and we, if we are a bit powerless—who "have nothing to fear!" As Jesus will make clear when he grows up and begins preaching, at the beginning of his Sermon on the Mount, it's the powerless "on whom God's favor rests."

These "tidings of great joy" (Lk 2:10) are most likely to get through to those who are "as open-minded to conviction and as willing to listen as only the dying can be" (12 X 12, 24). During this holiday season, be sure to "share" your "tidings," your story, your "message" of recovery "with the whole people."

Holy Family

Sir 3:2–6, 12–14; Col 3:12–21; Mt 2:13–15, 19–23

*". . . an angel of the Lord suddenly appeared in a dream to Joseph
. . . and said, 'Get up . . .' Then Joseph got up"*
(Mt 2:19, 21).

Roman Catholics celebrate a feast in honor of the Holy Family— Jesus, Mary, and Joseph—on the Sunday between Christmas and

New Year's. To someone whose family has, for the umpteenth year in a row, made them miserable over the holidays, or to someone who has been beaten up in the name of somebody else's version of "family values," this feast may seem like the last straw. But "[d]o not be discouraged" (BB, 60). As we have seen, the actual family of Jesus had little experience with the eerie immunity from real-life problems or the glassy-eyed cheerfulness of the Brady Bunch.

In fact, the Gospel today depicts the Holy Family as going on to yet another crisis, the worst yet: now they are political refugees, one step ahead of King Herod's Gestapo. And the only way to escape is across the desert. They are poor, and can't bribe border guards or pay "coyotes" to smuggle them across. The life of this family is a relentless series of opportunities to learn that "[j]ust to the extent that we do as we think [God] would have us, and humbly rely on [God], does [God] enable us to match calamity with serenity" (BB, 68).

So what can be done in the face of all the misery in the world, misery that perhaps is no worse during the holidays, but *seems* worse? What needs to be done is what Joseph does: when the angel, God's messenger, tells him to get up and do something, he gets up and does it.

The word for *get up* is a favorite of Matthew's; he uses it thirty-three times, more often than the other Evangelists. It is, in addition to its other meanings, the word he uses to describe Jesus being raised from the dead. Much of ordinary life is about "getting up"—not usually from death, although sometimes, as at the beginning of recovery, it can feel like we are rising from a living death: "We were reborn" (BB, 63). But more often "getting up" connotes for us, "Get up, suit up, and show up for your life," an admonition we all need every day, not just during the holidays. Perhaps, if we do get up, one day at a time, we'll find it possible to deal with our families, healthy or difficult. Or perhaps we'll be able to create new ones that really are "holy" families in their ability "to match calamity with serenity" (BB, 68).

January 1, New Year's Day

Nm 6:22–27; Gal 4:4–7; Lk 2:16–21

"After eight days had passed, it was time to circumcise the child;
and he was called Jesus, the name given by the angel
before he was conceived in the womb"
(Lk 2:21).

The Roman Catholic Church has been a little unsure over the years about what to do with January 1. In secular society it is, of course, New Year's Day. But that is often associated with exuberant partying the evening before (which is why some A. A.'s call December 31 "amateur night"), so the Church mentions the new year only in a *very* soft voice in the readings for this Mass.

However, since it is also exactly a week after Christmas, the Church tries to keep reminding us of the events of the season, and especially of the part played by Mary of Nazareth. This year let's focus on the gospel reading for the feast. It mentions that Jesus, like any other Jewish boy, was circumcised, as a sign of his mother's and father's fidelity to the covenant God made with the people of Abraham and Sarah, Miriam and Moses.

On this occasion, as is the custom, Jesus is given his name, a name his mother believed had been recommended to her by God. As is often the case in the great stories of the world, Jesus' name is significant: he is named after Moses' lieutenant, Joshua, who led the people into the Promised Land after Moses' death. *Joshua*, in turn, means "savior." According to dictionaries of biblical Hebrew, the Hebrew root (*YS*) for "Joshua" connotes the experience of being taken out of a narrow, confining place—say, a prison or a coffin—and set free to roam in wide spaces, with room to move, and with a sudden increase in viable options.

Viktor Frankl, a Jewish Holocaust survivor, describes a typical *YS* experience when he tells us about taking a spring walk in the meadows near Auschwitz after the liberation by the Allied Forces (the story appears in his *Man's Search for Meaning*, p. 111). He had a powerful spiritual experience when he realized that God had brought him out of a dark, deadly, claustrophobic tomb into a light and spacious place.

Our recovery may feel a lot like this: addiction always offers too few good choices, while recovery begins with the perception that there are suddenly many ways out of the trap. On this first day of a new year, let's rejoice that God has "saved" us by blessing us with so many hopeful options and with "the power to carry [them] out" (Step 11).

Epiphany

Is 60:1–6; Eph 3:2–3, 5–6; Mt 2:1–12

"Arise, shine; for your light has come, and the glory of the LORD has risen upon you"
(Is 60:1).

Christians in the East have always celebrated this feast of Epiphany as the climax of the Christmas season (it's the "12th day of Christmas," for you partridge-in-a-pear-tree fans). We Western Christians (i.e., Western Europe and America) prefer the feast of Christmas, perhaps because we are charmed by its folksy intimacy, as opposed to the royal grandeur of Epiphany, more congenial to the stately worship of the Eastern churches.

But the two feasts are, of course, interconnected. Jesus hasn't "arrived" just for his parents or his immediate family or even for a cozy circle with shepherds added. Indeed, one of the problems with the American approach to Christmas is that we too often narrowly focus on "me and my [perhaps very crazy] family." Take, for instance, the Arnold Schwarzenegger film in which he commits mayhem on other parents in order to get for his kid the last sample of that Christmas's hot toy. No, the message of salvation in Jesus is for all women and men, even people from far away, like the *goyim* (Gentiles) who bring their gifts in today's Gospel. On these "astrologers," and on all the people of the world, a new light has dawned, "the glory of the Lord shines" (Is).

The word *epiphany* means "the shining out." The love of God and the compassion for human beings that were at the core of Jesus the Savior have illuminated a dark world. This is suggested by the lights that typify the holiday season—colored bulbs on houses and trees. Nor are Christians the only people celebrating light during this season: the Menorah, the seven-branched candlestick, is the central symbol of the Jewish winter feast of Hanukkah. Light helps during the darkest days of the year.

Hanukkah celebrates the rededication of the Jerusalem Temple. Just as the Jews rejoiced at having a "well-lighted place" to gather, tell the stories, and share gratitude, so on this feast of Epiphany we can rejoice that recovery gives us gifts of light, warmth, and companionship even in the dead of winter. The message of peace and grace from God announced to shepherds at Christmas can now "shine out" to all women and men, if we "carry [this] message" to them in what we say and do, in the way we "practice these principles in all our affairs" (Step 12).

Baptism of the Lord

Is 42:1–4, 6–7; Acts 10:34–38; Mt 3:13–17

"Here is my servant, whom I uphold"
(Is 42:1).

In the Roman Catholic Church these days, the Christmas season ends with the celebration of Jesus' baptism. It's a kind of flash-forward from his childhood, with which we have been concerned recently, to his adulthood and to his ministry, the "carrying of the message" that was the focus of his adult life. By all accounts, that ministry began with Jesus seeking baptism in the Jordan River from John the Baptist. The early church was actually rather hesitant about bringing up the fact of Jesus' baptism. Mark flatly mentions it; the later Gospel of Matthew (this year) and of Luke rather hurries over the baptism, for fear of giving the impression that John the Baptist was somehow superior to Jesus. This was more of an open question at the time, at least for disciples of the Baptist, some of whom who were still around when the Gospels were written. Matthew even has John trying to talk Jesus out of being baptized, as a step Jesus could surely avoid. Nevertheless, Jesus insists that he must receive baptism, that it's God's idea.

Matthew, like all the other gospel writers, preserved the story, despite their misgivings, because it was such a crucial event in Jesus' own spiritual growth. Mark thinks this moment of "conscious contact" of Jesus with God is so important that Mark begins his Gospel with Jesus' baptism. Matthew and Luke begin their Gospels with Jesus' childhood, but for them, too, his baptism is a crucial moment, because it signals the beginning of Jesus' adult service of God as a preacher of Abba's kingdom.

How did Jesus' baptism lead to his ministry? At Jesus' baptism he came to realize in a new, full way that he was Son of the God whom he later taught his followers to call "Abba"—a much gentler concept of God than John the Baptist's fire-breathing deity. That Jesus was a specially beloved child of such a God must have come as good news (the Greek word we translate as *gospel* means "good news") to Jesus, on the occasion of his baptism as well as all through his life.

This is the good news that Jesus will in turn spend the rest of his life carrying to others. It's as the angels proclaimed on the night he was born: God's favor rests on all women and men, not just on Jesus; God offers all of us the chance to be God's beloved children. This is particularly good news for those of us who felt, during our addictions and attachments, that we would never be at home on this earth. The truth is that, after all, we "can fit and belong in God's scheme of things" (12 X 12, 124). Jesus' ministry, which begins on this feast, will show us how people behave when they know they are loved.

✚

Lent
and Easter

First Week of Lent

Gn 2:7–9, 3:1–7; Rom 5:12–19; Mt 4:1–11

"Worship the Lord your God, and serve only him"
(Mt 4:10, quoting Dt 6:13).

Lent is the time of year when Christians try either to experience a "spiritual awakening" or to recall and stir up again a change of heart they have undergone in the past. If we received ashes on our foreheads last Wednesday, the person putting them there may have said "Repent and believe the Good News" in summoning us to spiritual renewal. Jesus began his ministry with those words, as had John the Baptist before him. In Greek *repent* is *metanoete,* an important biblical word that I've translated above as "Change your heart, your attitude, your vision."

Why do we need to undergo such radical changes of direction, whether in the form of One Big One (a "burning bush" experience) or a lot of Little Ones ("the educational variety"—BB, 569)? Because, as the story of the first humans makes clear, human beings tend to get addicted to things. The story from Genesis is not about apples. Rather it's about two typical humans struggling with the 3rd Step. They don't want to "turn their will and their lives over to the care of God," the Higher Power who has provided all the good things in the Garden. Instead, at the prompting of a "cunning" (and "baffling and powerful") creature—the snake—they decide to take matters into their own hands (for more on Adam and Eve as the father and mother of all addicts, see Meditation 6 in *A 12-Step Approach to the Spiritual Exercises*).

In today's Gospel, Jesus is tempted to do something similar. The will of God is that he should be a gentle Messiah, willing to suffer; but Jesus is tempted to skip the pain by imposing his own will on events. Love is all very well, but won't power get the job done better and faster, and less painfully to Jesus (after all, that's how things

18

get done in "all the kingdoms *of the world*")? And then there's prestige: the tempter urges Jesus to imagine the media coverage Jesus could get by jumping off the highest point of the Jerusalem Temple, the center of worship. It would be like diving off the top of St. Peter's in Rome, or the Mormon Temple in Salt Lake City. At the very least, why couldn't Jesus, who is "hungry, angry, lonely, and tired" after forty days of intense spiritual struggle, get a little food without having to do any footwork?

Unlike his human forebears in Genesis, Jesus takes a Step 3: Abba's way is best. This single, quiet act of obedience, according to St. Paul, reverses the whole human history of "self-will run riot" (BB, 62). And this is wonderful news: finally the "bone-crushing juggernaut" of human "self-sufficiency" grinds to a stop (12 X 12, 37). If we follow Jesus in his path of self-surrender, we too can be renewed by being set free of our attachments.

Second Week of Lent

Gn 12:1–4; 2 Tim 1:8–10; Mt 17:1–9

"'Go from your country . . . to the land that I will show you'"
(Gn 12:1).

Last week Jesus took a 3rd Step about the mission that he believed Abba had bestowed on him at the time of his baptism by John. Specifically, Jesus made a decision that his mission would be done the way a loving God wanted it done: without violence or trickery. This week Abba responds approvingly to Jesus' decision. Partly for the benefit of some of Jesus' followers who have joined him since his ministry began, Abba repeats what Abba had said at Jesus' baptism: he "is my beloved Son on whom my favor rests. Listen to him."

These followers, and Peter especially, need to hear these words and see the loving spirit inside Jesus that is changing him outwardly in such a dramatic way. They need this vision because—typical children of

Adam and Eve—these followers are having trouble turning Jesus over to the care of God. Just before today's passage in Matthew, Jesus has horrified them by telling them that a) yes, he is the Messiah, as Peter has guessed; but b) he is going to die a miserable death, because this is the kind of Messiah people need—as opposed to the kind of Messiah that people, including Peter, want.

As believing Jews, the disciples find it almost impossible to accept that it's God's will that Jesus-the-Messiah should suffer. To come to believe in such a difficult and disheartening concept will require a real faith journey. But then the ancestors of the Jewish people, Abraham and his wife Sarah, demonstrated their faith by making a journey to a strange land when they perceived that that was God's will for them. Furthermore, Moses and Elijah appear with Jesus: both of them knew something about journeying long distances to meet God. At the time of the Exodus, Moses led the people to Mount Sinai so they could meet God. Elijah made a similar journey to "the mountain of God" during a period of unbelief and religious confusion (1 Kgs 19).

Jesus' Transfiguration shores up the disciples' shaken faith in him as a non-traditional Messiah. As with any intense spiritual experience, the disciples would like to freeze time and place in order to preserve this moment. The overshadowing cloud may not be pink, but the spiritual mountaintop is always more exciting than the valley of the shadow of death. Nevertheless, Jesus and his disciples (and we) have to come down from the mountain and resume our trudge down "the Road of Happy Destiny" (BB, 164). As this transfiguring moment has made clear, Jesus' destiny is ultimately "Happy"; but there is much suffering to endure along the way, in a world where "pain [is] the touchstone of all spiritual progress" (12 X 12, 93–94). Let's keep this in mind as we continue to "trudge" through Lent toward Easter.

Third Week of Lent

Ex 17:3–7; Rom 5:1–2, 5–8; Jn 4:5–42

*". . . and does not disappoint us, because God's love has been
poured into our hearts . . ."*
(Rom 5:5).

A man and a woman meet by chance at a watering hole. She is a woman who has been around; perhaps that's why she's alone. He says, "Give me a drink." But she has already guessed correctly that he's a Jew, and, like everybody in her world, she doesn't like Jews, so she rebuffs him.

This may sound drearily familiar to those of us who have spent some time meeting people in bars. But as so often in the Gospel of John, where this story occurs, things take a surprising twist. Instead of meeting her insult with a counter-insult, the man stays with her. The more they talk, the more the conversation turns to spiritual matters. He even helps her to "admit . . . the exact nature of [her] wrongs" (Step 5).

It's as if a battered barfly were to run into someone in a bar who knew how to get sober. The key is that Jesus knows that the woman's thirst is spiritual, not just physical. Like many alcoholics, she has been "groping toward God" (ABSI, 323); she has been looking for love in all the wrong places. Jesus unfailingly treats her with the dignity that befits a spiritual seeker.

Jesus' 12th Step on the woman works. Why? Ernie Kurtz repeats an old Hasidic tale in his masterful work on 12-Step spirituality, *The Spirituality of Imperfection* (see pp. 64 ff.). A disciple of a great rabbi, the Baal Shem Tov, travels the world collecting and relating stories of his master. Finally this disciple meets a nobleman in Italy; after a sudden bout of amnesia, the disciple can tell the nobleman only an unfinished story, the point of which the disciple has never grasped. But the nobleman understands it perfectly; unknown to the disciple, it is the nobleman's own story, and thus a sign that God has forgiven him a great sin. The moral: When someone comes and tells you everything you have done, tells you your own story, you will know that your sins are forgiven.

This is the experience with Jesus of the woman at the well; when he tells her her own story, she "comes to believe." She in turn "12th-Steps" her little town. Her townsfolk are impressed at first, like newcomers to a 12-Step fellowship, because they hear someone else's story—the woman's. But then they have a spiritual experience of their own, and, for the first time in their lives, their thirst has been quenched. Now they too have "a fountain within" them; now they have a story to tell. Spiritual seekers whose thirst has never been quenched before by alcohol or by anything else, finally can have a similar experience: when someone tells your story, you'll know you've found the fountain.

Fourth Week of Lent

1 Sm 16:1–14, 6–7, 10–13; Eph 5:8–14; Jn 9:1–41

"Sleeper awake! Rise from the dead, and Christ will shine on you"
(Eph 5:14, quoting an ancient baptismal hymn).

The person Jesus meets in the reading from John this Sunday is like the Samaritan woman at the well last week: both are working on their 2nd Step, both are coming to believe. Like a lot of recovering people, they both have stumbled by accident onto the spiritual path, she by a chance encounter at a watering hole, he by having his blindness noticed by the disciples of Jesus in a public place.

The woman doesn't believe at first, but finally comes to believe because the One she has met tells her everything she has done. In the same way, the blind man doesn't believe in Jesus immediately just because his sight is restored. In fact, Jesus seems at first to want to remain anonymous; he doesn't stay around. What drives the man to faith in the end is that everyone in his world keeps trying to take his one and only miracle away from him.

First some of his neighbors try; they claim he isn't even the same man. (Some recovering people have run into similar disbelief from people who had known them in their addiction.) Then the ex-blind man falls into the hands of the authorities, in this case the Pharisees, who try to bully him into changing his story. Yet, the more the representatives of organized religion try to demolish his story, the more the ex-blind man clings to it. He doggedly recites what it was like ("I was blind before"), what happened ("He put mud on my eyes, I washed it off"), and what it's like now ("Now I can see").

Why do the Pharisees try to argue away the man's miracle? As their dialogue with Jesus at the end of the story makes clear, the problem of the Pharisees is that they "are constitutionally incapable of being honest with themselves" (BB, 58). They keep insisting that they are fine, they see quite well, thank you. But as Jesus tirelessly pointed out, if you see fine, if you're managing nicely, you are not "poor in spirit." And so you can never really come to believe in a Power greater than yourself. You can't really use one—you don't need to be "restore[d]" (Step 2).

The best way to come to believe, then, is to try to be rigorously honest, to say what you see, and to stick to your story. The blind man ends, like many 12 Steppers, by "bow[ing] down to worship" (Jn). Bill describes a similar process of coming-to-believe in the lives of many recovered alcoholics: "Relieved of the alcohol obsession [or whatever keeps you from seeing reality], their lives unaccountably transformed, they came to believe in a Higher Power, and most of them began to talk of God" (12 X 12, 28). It takes time and honesty to come to believe.

Fifth Week of Lent

Ez 37:12–14; Rom 8:8–11; Jn 11:1–45

*"But you are not in the flesh; you are in the Spirit, since
the Spirit of God dwells in you"*
(Rom 8:9).

In the Second Reading today, Paul talks about flesh and spirit, and about death and life. As a Jew, Paul is not thinking in Greek categories: "flesh" does not mean "body," and "spirit" does not mean "soul," as if these were separable parts of human beings, or as if "spirit" was good and pure, "flesh" bad and corrupt. In Jewish thought, *all* of a person acts fleshly or spiritually on a given occasion.

What is fleshy behavior? It's "attached" (the old spiritual word, revived by Gerald May in his *Addiction and Grace*), or "addicted," behavior. We are acting fleshy when we put a thing or a person in God's place; this is idolatry. We are also acting fleshy when we treat people (made in God's image, after all) as if they were things, or treat things as if they were people; this is immorality.

Of course, as Terry Gorski noted in a taped interview I heard some years ago, addicts confuse people and things all the time. We treat people (including ourselves) as if they were things of little value; we readily sacrifice them in order to get what we think we want, or believe we have to have. And we try to have personal relationships with things, like substances and money: people may let us down, but we always know what we'll get with good old Jack Daniels (or whatever other thing we substitute for persons).

How does fleshy behavior make us feel? As any addict can testify, it makes us feel dead; our emotions dry up, and all that's left is a monotonous desire for things that don't really fill us, and a dull rage because they don't. Like Jesus' friend Lazarus, we are "bound hand and foot" by our compulsions; like Lazarus, some of us even smell bad because of our addictions. But then someone calls our name, and commands, "Untie [them] . . . and let [them] go free." And Lazarus, having somehow heard the voice of one who loves him, lives anew.

Bill W. describes the alcoholic's "spiritual awakening" in similar terms: "As we felt new power flow in . . . ., as we became conscious of [God's] presence, we began to lose our fear of today, tomorrow or the hereafter. We were reborn" (BB, p. 63). And "having had a spiritual awakening," we will find we have a newfound power to love in our turn, with the same spirit of loving service that was in Jesus. Having risen from the deadness to which our attachments consigned us, we will return to "[our] land" after a long exile (Ez). "[N]o longer isolated and alone in self-constructed prisons, [we will have the satisfaction of knowing] that we need no longer be square pegs in round holes but can fit and belong in God's scheme of things" (12 X 12, 124). We will come home.

Palm Sunday, Procession

Mt 21:1–11; Mass: Is 50:4–7; Phil 2:6–11;
St. Matthew's Passion, Mt 26:14–27:66

"Therefore [because of Jesus' death on a cross] God also highly exalted him and gave him the name that is above every name"
(Phil 2:9).

For my fellow music-lovers, this Sunday's recitation of the Passion according to St. Matthew will be inextricably tied up with Bach's musical setting, one of the greatest pieces of music ever composed. As Leonard Bernstein pointed out many years ago, Bach surrounds the music that "Jesus" sings with a "halo" of strings everywhere, except at one point: when Jesus on the cross cries out to Abba, "My God, my God, why have you forsaken me?" At this moment, Jesus does not seem like the New Moses, or the Son of David, the usual roles in which Matthew casts him. Instead, he seems utterly human, crucified like Spartacus and his followers, but in Jesus' case, without even having struck a blow for freedom. In fact, he had forbidden his followers to strike back on his behalf.

And yet, as Paul points out by means of the early Christian hymn he quotes in the Second Reading, it is precisely at this moment, when Jesus is reaching his bottom, that he is most revealing about the identity of Abba. The pivotal phrase, the hinge at the very center of this hymn, is "Therefore": precisely because Jesus was willing, in love for God and humanity, to hit a very low bottom, God raised him above everyone and everything.

Countless Christians over the centuries, in "every season of grief or suffering, when the hand of God seemed heavy or even unjust" (12 X 12, 105—one of the most moving passages Bill W. ever wrote), have found comfort in remembering that even the Son of Abba had to suffer, had to ask God, at the nadir of his life, why God had abandoned him (Mt 27:46; see the Third Week in *A 12-Step Approach to the Spiritual Exercises*). And they have found comfort in the fact that the Son's story has nevertheless gone on forever, as we shall recall next Sunday.

We reenact the procession with palms today precisely to remind ourselves of the very different kind of messiah-king that Jesus was. He comes on a donkey, not a warhorse. Instead of goose-stepping storm troopers with gleaming rifles, he is surrounded by a noisy, rag-tag crowd waving palms. *Free* palms—these are poor people. And yet he truly is the Messiah, "therefore": as at every moment of his life, Jesus wins by surrendering to God, by working his 3rd Step. And thus he helps his human sisters and brothers to grasp, once and for all, the kind of self-sacrifice that Love really is.

Note: I haven't included meditations for Holy Thursday or Good Friday. For Holy Thursday, you may want to consult the meditation for Corpus Christi, at the end of this Lent-Easter section, since on that feast Roman Catholics celebrate the gift of the Lord's Supper in a special way.

Easter Vigil

Ex 14:15–15:1; Rom 6:3–11; Mt 28:1–10

The readings for Easter Sunday are fairly similar in each cycle, so this year I would like to study the readings for the Easter Vigil, the great celebration that occurs on Holy Saturday night, or, in some places, as a sunrise service on Easter morning.

> *"'The LORD is my strength and my might, and he has become my salvation'"*
> (Ex 15:2).

Matthew began his Gospel with angels appearing to people, telling them not to be afraid, and giving them news of great joy: Joseph shouldn't be afraid to take Mary as his wife; the Wise Men from the East were filled with great joy. And now, as Matthew's story draws to a close, the atmosphere is similar. The angel tells the women friends of Jesus not to be afraid, even though the guards at the tomb have collapsed in fright. When Jesus himself appears, his first word is "peace" (*shalom* in Hebrew, the everyday greeting of Jesus' contemporaries). Then, because the angel's news leaves them "half-overjoyed, half-fearful," Jesus tells them to keep only the joy, and to carry the message, the good news. What he was born to do—"save his people from their sins," according to the angel who had announced his birth—he has now done.

The first two readings use an ancient image for walking through fear to joy: it's like crossing a deep river or the Red Sea. The First Reading is the song that the children of Israel sing after Moses leads them dry-footed through the Red Sea. In the Second Reading Paul applies this image to Christian baptism, in which each of us individually travels through the waters to safety and freedom.

In John Bunyan's spiritual classic *Pilgrim's Progress*, written in the late seventeenth century, this ancient image recurs at the climax.

The protagonist's last challenge is to walk through the River of Death; the Heavenly City is on the other side. The river is dark and cold, and Christian, Bunyan's hero, dies while crossing it—and yet somehow he also manages to make it to the other side. A follower of Carl Jung, like Joseph Campbell, might see in all this crossing of dark waters a version of the Hero's journey to the underworld and back—or, if you will, through the heart of darkness and out the other side.

For recovering people this journey takes the form of a "searching and fearless moral inventory," a fording of the dark river of our own past, our own souls. We think we won't survive it, and in a sense we don't: as John the Evangelist might put it, once we have brought our deeds to the light, we are reborn. "At once, we commence to outgrow fear"; we begin "to know a new freedom and a new happiness" (BB, 68, 83). May our Easters be "happy, joyous, and free" (BB, 133).

Second Sunday of Easter

Acts 2:42–47; 1 Pt 1: 3–9; Jn 20:19–31

". . . they broke bread at home and ate their food with glad and generous hearts, praising God . . ."
(Acts 2:46–47).

Luke's Gospel tells us that Jesus got his name a week after he was born, on the occasion of his circumcision. In our Gospel today, the risen Jesus acts out his name ("savior") by coming back, a week after Easter, to round up a stray sheep, Thomas. It is just like the risen Jesus to go after a disciple who, like many addicts (including me), gives up all too easily, or needs to experience a miracle before he'll surrender. What exactly is Thomas's problem? Thomas is "discouraged" (BB, 60) by the reports of Jesus' resurrection, just like an alcoholic who has just heard "the good news" (BB, 158; 12 X 12, 83) of the 12 Steps. Thomas's reaction is, "It's 'good news,' all right—too good to be true."

Nor should we look down on Thomas for his doubt, any more than we should look down on people who struggle with the 2nd Step. As St. Gregory the Great noted in the sixth century, "The disbelief of Thomas has done more for our faith than the faith of the other disciples." Because Thomas was so stubborn (like a lot of addicts), he received an invitation to touch the Risen One, to experience a hands-on miracle. And because he held out for his miracle, he is the first to announce the fullest faith of the gospel story: "My Lord and my God!"

Thomas has "come to believe" that Jesus is so completely the presence of Abba in the world, is so totally united with God, that Jesus is Lord ("Messiah," "anointed by God")—and Jesus is God as well. As Jesus puts it in the Gospel of John, during the Last Supper, "Whoever has seen me"—seen the loving way he reaches out to the people nobody wants to go near, no matter what the cost to him—"has seen [Abba]" (Jn 14:8).

What brought Thomas from doubt to faith? Several things: he encountered a miracle he could hear and see and touch and experience. And he met the Risen One in the presence of the community, at a meeting (which he had skipped the week before for some reason). When we are surrounded by people who ought to be dead and yet are alive—recovering alcoholics and addicts—it's much easier to progress from doubt to faith. It's especially at meetings—12-Step meetings or church meetings—that our "new birth . . . unto hope" (1 Pt 1:3) is kept alive.

Third Sunday of Easter

Acts 2:42–47; 1 Pt 1: 3–9; Jn 20:19–31

*"Then they told what had happened on the road, and how
he had been made known to them in the breaking of the bread"*
(Lk 24:35).

This gospel reading, from Luke, has always been important to me. It was the gospel reading at my mother's funeral, and its story of Jesus going after the Easily Discouraged has always spoken to my heart. I will reflect more on this facet of the story when the same Gospel is used on Easter, Year C (see also Meditation 46 in *A 12-Step Approach to the Spiritual Exercises*). For today, let's focus instead on the importance of community in seeing and touching the risen Jesus, a point I made last Sunday. For this Sunday, keep in mind that these runaway disciples couldn't see Jesus, couldn't see that it was Jesus, at first. Like Thomas, it took them a while to come to believe, even though the miracle was right in front of them.

What made these runaways so "slow to believe"? Precisely what had bothered Jesus' closest friends: the notion that God's beloved, the Messiah, would have to suffer. Why on earth, they complained, should God's beloved Son have to accept pain? Like practicing addicts, whose "lives [are] largely devoted to running from pain and problems" (12 X 12, 74), these disciples were fleeing pain, Jesus' and their own. But if we are really going to be disciples, we have to follow Jesus in his pain: there's no other way to "enter into . . . glory." We can see in our pain the necessary condition for "God [to] work[s] through [us]" (Acts). For recovering people, as for Jesus the Messiah, "pain" is "the price of admission into a new life" (12 X 12, 75)—"new life" for us and for those to whom we offer companionship.

The two disciples finally recognized Jesus only when they shared a meal with him. *Companion* comes from two Latin words that mean "[sharing] bread together." So if you want to see Jesus and be his companion, then "create the fellowship you crave" (BB, 164)—break your bread with strangers, and especially those who have a spiritual hunger and thirst (I have gotten this idea from Father Gene LaVerdiere's commentary on Luke).

As Jesus said at the beginning of his Sermon on the Mount, if we are spiritually hungry and thirsty, we finally will be satisfied, we will have enough. "Fleshy" people (see above, Fifth Week of Lent), practicing addicts, can never have enough; their "way of life" is "futile," as 1 Peter points out. Instead, it's people who have offered bread in loving service to the hungry who get their fill, who see Jesus—even when feeding others costs us, as it cost Jesus, dearly.

Fourth Sunday of Easter

Acts 2:14, 36–41; 1 Pt 2:20–25; Jn 10:1–10

"I came that they might have life, and have more than
enough of it"
(Jn 10:10, my own translation).

Each year, the readings on the Fourth Sunday of Easter focus on a favorite image of both the Hebrew and the Christian Scriptures: God (or Christ) is the Shepherd, we are God's sheep. This is partly for the benefit of those just baptized at Easter, those who have just entered the "flock." Like recovering people who have found a meeting that fits them, these new Christians are celebrating the fact that they finally "fits and belong in God's scheme of things" (12 X 12, p. 124). But even old-time members of the "flock" are urged to rejoice this Sunday because they have "recognized [the] voice" of the Good Shepherd.

However, I have to confess that I squirm at being compared to a sheep. This analogy may have made sense in a time and place in which society was a pyramid, with the king-shepherd on top and most people toward the bottom. In fact, the advice in today's reading from 1 Peter is being offered specifically to Christians who were slaves, at the very bottom of the pyramid. But my society is democratic; and nowadays, when we call someone "sheepish," we don't often mean it as a compliment.

Still, it's worth noticing that the sheep in our readings today are not dull, solidly respectable, "normie" (an affectionate A. A. term for non-alcoholic) sheep, but colorful, rebellious, headstrong sheep—addicted sheep, if you will—that have "gone *astray*." This word appears in today's First Reading, from Peter's speech in Acts on the first Pentecost: "Save yourselves from a generation that has gone astray." The Greek word here means "twisted," or even "bent through dryness." The same word occurs in 1 Peter, in the passage just before our Second Reading: slaves should try to get along, not just with good masters, but even with "twisted" ones. A different Greek word, also translated "straying," is used in today's reading from 1 Peter—"At one time you were straying like sheep." This word means "wandering," but it also means "deceived, fooled."

When we were trying simultaneously to have addictions *and* lives (an impossible task), some of us got a little "twisted"; even in recovery we may have periods when we're a little "bent through dryness." And God knows our baffling addictions had us "deceived." So—like it or not—"straying" people like us *do* need a good shepherd, one who will "guard[s] our souls" (1 Peter). Our shepherd will lead us "[b]eside restful waters"; he will "refresh[s] our souls" (Ps 23, today's suggested Responsorial Psalm). No more dryness.

Fifth Sunday of Easter

Acts 6:1–7; 1 Pt 2:4–9; Jn 14:1–12

*"How can you say, 'Show us the Father'? Do you not believe
that I am in the Father and the Father is in me?"*
(Jn 14:9–10).

As I pointed out on Easter, the special greeting of the risen Jesus is
"shalom," "peace." We who call on Jesus' name need not be afraid,
nor should our "hearts be troubled" (Jn, in today's Gospel). Yet Jesus
is not patronizing us with this greeting, for he himself was "troubled" (same Greek word) when he was struggling to deal with the
death of his friend Lazarus. Still, he assures us that he knows the
"way" through death and trouble to new life and peace.

The word for *way* in John literally means "path" or "road" (not
"method"). But, as the hardheaded Thomas asks, How can we know
which path to choose if we don't know where we're going (a question often posed about the 3rd or the 11th steps)? Jesus replies that
he is the path, the path home to Abba. To know Jesus is to know
Abba, because everything Jesus has done (his "works") came
straight out of his relationship with Abba ("the Father is in me"). Do
what he did, and you can be sure you're on the road for home.

But what "works" does he mean? How can we hope to perform
"works . . . greater far than these"? The works are what Jesus has
done from the first ("all this time"): reaching out in compassion to
the unwanted and the unwashed, from the shepherds who announced
his birth, and on. We who come after can do even "greater works,"
because Jesus now gives loving service through the hands of all of
us, and so touches millions he never met during his earthly life. This
is true even if our "works" are as humble as "wait[ing] on tables"
(First Reading) or making coffee or stacking chairs. As Bill W. puts
it, "True ambition [equals 'the truth and the life' in the Gospel of

John] is the deep desire to live usefully and walk [on the 'way'] humbly under the grace of God" (12 X 12, pp. 124–125).

George Herbert, an Anglican priest and poet of the seventeenth century, captures this notion: "Teach me, my God and King, / In all things thee to see, / And what I do in anything / To do it as for Thee. // A servant with this clause [that is, 'for (God's) sake'], / Makes drudgery divine / Who sweeps a room, as for Thy [God's] laws, /Makes that and the action fine." We are "a consecrated nation," and that makes all that we do a "glorious work[s]" (1 Peter).

If we "trudge" down Jesus' "way," the "Road" (BB, 164) of humble service, we will finally get to the "dwelling place," the home that Jesus promised his friends.

Sixth Sunday of Easter

Acts 8:5–8, 14–17; 1 Pt 3:15–18; Jn 14:15–21

*"'. . . [Abba] will give you another Advocate [Paraclete],
to be with you forever. This is the Spirit of truth'"*
(Jn 14:16–17).

We are coming to the end of the Easter season. It will conclude in two weeks with the feast of Pentecost, which celebrates the coming of the Holy Spirit on the followers of Jesus, a coming that formed them, once and for all, into a community, a fellowship. The readings this weekend explain what the relationship between Jesus and the Spirit is, and what the Spirit can mean to us.

In Luke, the Spirit is often synonymous with "power"; the Holy Spirit is, in a way, God as Higher Power. The Gospel of John uses a different term for the Holy Spirit: Advocate or Paraclete. The Greek word here comes from a verb that means "to summon a friend to one's side," and it is often used in a courtroom setting. I once was summoned to small claims court, and I asked a good and fearless friend to go with me because I knew I'd come unglued with all those authority figures present. I asked him to be a paraclete to me (and he was, bless him, but I lost anyway).

In the First Letter of John, Jesus is a paraclete. In today's selection from the Gospel of John, Jesus says that when he "arrives home," where he will dwell with Abba, he will ask Abba to send the Spirit as "another paraclete." What will this second paraclete do? The Spirit will "remind" Jesus' followers of what Jesus said and did.

Elsewhere in the Gospels, Jesus comforts his disciples by telling them that the Spirit will especially be a friend at their side when they are required to tell stories in public, often to an unfriendly crowd, about their *metanoia* (conversion). Recovering people, too, are often called on to tell their stories, or, as the Big Book puts it, to "disclose in a general way what we used to be like, what happened, and what we are like now" (58).

On such occasions, we should keep in mind some suggestions. 1 Peter urges us to "speak gently and respectfully." Bill W. recommends something similar: "We should be sensible, tactful, considerate and humble without being servile or scraping. As God's people we stand on our feet; we don't crawl before anyone" (BB, 83). Christians and recovering people both realize what it is like suddenly to know exactly the right thing to say, even in "situations which used to baffle us" (BB, 84). When that happens, we know the Paraclete-Spirit has come to our side, the Spirit whose gifts include "love, joy, peace, patient endurance, kindness, . . . [and] mildness" (St. Paul to the Galatians, 5:22).

Feast of the Ascension

Acts 1:1–11; Eph 1:17–23; Mt 28:16–20

Note: Many communities celebrate the feast of the Ascension on the Thursday before the seventh Sunday of Easter. If your community does, read this meditation on Thursday and the next meditation on the following Sunday.

"'[Y]ou will receive power when the Holy Spirit has come down upon you . . . ,' [Then] he was lifted up, and a cloud took him out of their sight"
(Acts 1:8, 9).

As I mentioned last Sunday, we are nearing the end of the celebration of the resurrection of Jesus (Easter); next Sunday we will celebrate the sending of the Spirit of Jesus (Pentecost). In between comes the Feast of the Ascension, which answers the question, How did Jesus end his "pitch"? Most people find last words and farewell addresses interesting—for example, Dr. Bob's Last Words to Bill W.: "Keep it [the A. A. program] simple." Christian traditions vary, not just about what Jesus said last, but where and when he said it.

In Acts, Luke tells us that Jesus ended his ministry by ascending outside Jerusalem, forty days after his resurrection. But then Luke's goal in Acts is to show the spread of the New Way, Christianity, outward from Jerusalem. So it makes sense to situate Jesus' farewell there. "Forty" is an important number in Jewish religious thought, since Moses and the children of Israel wandered for forty years in the desert on their way to the Promised Land (compare Jesus' forty-day fast). So perhaps this is the point of Jesus' forty-day post-Easter sojourn in Acts.

The other Evangelists tell different stories to make different points. The Gospel of John, for instance, also places Jesus' ascension in Jerusalem, but John says that Jesus went back to Abba shortly after his resurrection, on the same day, and then returned to meet with his followers that Easter Sunday evening. To John's thinking, Jesus hasn't really left for good.

Matthew, in today's Gospel, cites yet another tradition, in which Jesus met with his loved ones back in Galilee, where Jesus' ministry and their discipleship had all begun. Again, as at the Sermon in Matthew, chapter 5, we are on a mount. There is no need now for Jesus to repeat the program for his ministry that he first announced on a mount; by his death and resurrection, he has acted out that program. Instead of giving a farewell sermon, he sends out his witnesses to carry to others his story, his "message," his "good news" (gospel): "[G]o, therefore, and make disciples of all the nations." And he tells his followers "to practice these principles in all [their] affairs": "Teach them to carry out everything I have commanded you."

The particular message of the Ascension, in all its different versions, is the same: since Jesus has returned to his Father, we can be sure that "[he] will be with [us] always, until the end of the world!" Or, as the Gospel of John puts it, the ascended Jesus will be sure to send us a Paraclete, to provide us with "inspiration, an intuitive thought or decision" (BB, 86). We will "be more and more on the plane of inspiration" (BB, 87), since "inspiring" is what the "Spirit" does best.

Seventh Sunday of Easter

Acts 1:12–14; 1 Pt 4:13–16; Jn 17:1–11

"All these were constantly devoting themselves to prayer,
together with certain women, including Mary the mother of Jesus,
as well as his brothers"
(Acts 1:14).

Blaise Pascal, a seventeenth-century French philosopher well-versed in "spiritual awakening[s]," once observed that all the troubles of the world spring from the fact that people can't sit quietly by themselves in an empty room. Addicts may find such a prospect even more frightening than ordinary people do, since the battle cry of the addict is, "Nothing is going to turn me into a nonentity. If I keep on turning my life and my will over to the care of Something or Somebody else, what will become of *me*? I'll look like the hole in the doughnut" (12 X 12, 36, Bill W.'s italics).

This spiritual fidgetiness, this need to assert one's ego at any cost, can of course take many forms. One form I want to single out this Sunday appears in a very rare word that comes up in our Second Reading, from 1 Peter. One word in Greek, it is translated in the italicized words in this quotation: "See to it that none of you suffers for being a murderer, a thief, a malefactor, or *a destroyer of another's rights.*" However one translates this Greek word, figure that whoever does this must be a real lowlife, if he or she can be classified with murderers, thieves, and evildoers.

Yet the word in question, literally translated, sounds rather mild. It means something like "inspector-of-someone-else's-business." However, if Pascal is right, the inability to mind one's own business is at the root of a great deal of earthly misery. Al-Anon seems to agree: part of the concluding formula read at many Al-Anon meetings cautions against "gossip and criticism" among members. Perhaps compulsive meddling in the lives of others ought to be classed with theft and murder.

A good antidote to this problem is suggested in our First Reading, from Acts. It depicts a period in Christian history when not much is happening; Jesus has returned to Abba, but the Spirit has not yet been sent. So Mary and the disciples are waiting and praying, "quietly," "in a room." But "waiting" doesn't communicate their state very adequately: the italicized words in this quotation— "Together they *devoted* themselves to *constant* prayer"—hint at a special quality in their united waiting. The Greek word is based on the word for "strength." They weren't passive; they were powerfully receptive, they were *really* "together."

In other words, because of their belief in Jesus, they could wait, free of the need to run after various addictions. They were "in fit spiritual condition" (BB, 85). People who regularly work an 11th Step, like them, can be serene when it's time to wait, and brave—as this group will be on Pentecost—when it's time to change things.

Pentecost, Vigil Mass

Gn 11:1-9; Rom 8:22-27; Jn 7:37–39

Note: Since the readings for Pentecost are the same in all three cycles, I have used the readings for the Vigil, in different combinations, for Years A and B. The readings for Pentecost Sunday will be treated in Year C.

"On the last day of the festival, the great day, while Jesus was standing there, he cried out: 'Let anyone who is thirsty come to me, and let the one who believes in me drink'"
(Jn 7:37–38).

Our First Reading for this feast recounts the ancient story of the Tower of Babel. This story attempts to explain the fact that human beings speak different languages, and that somehow this difference seems always to lead to violence. According to the Book of Genesis, our alienation from one another can be traced to the same old human problem, "self-will run riot." Like Adam and Eve before them, the people who built the Tower were "playing God" (BB, 62), with the usual results: "[their] actions make [others] retaliate, snatching all they can get . . . [it ends in] confusion rather than harmony" (BB, 61). This story of the Tower suggests that our "failure to communicate"—as the sadistic head guard immortally phrased it in the movie *Cool Hand Luke*— has been a problem for human societies from the very beginning.

Unhappy families, including alcoholic families, have an analogous problem with communication. Virginia Satir, a seminal thinker in Family Systems Theory, defines a "dysfunctional" person, not as "violent" or "unemployable," but as "one who cannot communicate properly" (in her *Conjoint Family Therapy*, p. 119). "Dysfunctional" individuals in families can't be honest with one another. And, like the baleful results of Babel, this "dysfunction" is passed on in families, generation to generation.

What can be done about this problem, which has for millennia been turning "society" into "warring fragments" (12 X 12, 37)? The Big Book offers the obvious solution: we must acquire "the capacity to be honest" (BB, 58) if we wish to recover, as individuals, as families, or as a species. But what will it take to enable human beings to "communicate properly"? After all, quite a few of us seem "constitutionally incapable of being honest" (BB, 58).

According to the Big Book, our help "must come from a Higher Power" (BB, 43). The feast of Pentecost celebrates the coming of just such a Power, the Spirit of Jesus. Indeed, the story of Pentecost in Acts 2 suggests that Babel has now been reversed. The disciples, full of God's "power" (a frequent term for the Spirit in Luke and Acts), can "communicate properly" with people from many different nations. The Gospel for the Vigil, from John, focuses more on change in the individual: when we "[feel] new power flow in" (BB, 63), our spiritual thirst is finally quenched, and that power flows out from us to other people. We can now "communicate properly" with them, because the Spirit is teaching us "the language of the heart." And this is a language that all people speak.

Trinity

Ex 34:4–6, 8–9; 2 Cor 13:11–13; Jn 3:16–18

Note: Some Christian communities do not celebrate Trinity Sunday because they feel that every time we worship, we honor the God who is somehow Three-in-One (Triune). If your community is one of these, please go to the readings for Sundays in Ordinary Time (2002, Eighth Sunday; 2005, Eighth Sunday; 2008, Seventh Sunday).

"Put things in order, listen to my appeal, agree with one another, live in peace; and the God of love and peace will be with you . . ."
(2 Cor 13:11).

Whenever I talk about the Trinity, I think of a woman I once knew. A Catholic, she and her non-Catholic husband were attending classes on Catholicism. When we got to the Trinity, she suddenly became angry; her complaint was that the idea of the Trinity seemed to her pointless and unintelligible, just another mind-bending dogma imposed on believers. Some of her anger came, I suspected at the time, from a great loss she had once sustained. She may have wondered where this complicated God was for her then.

My point this Sunday is that the Trinity matters. In understanding the Trinity, I have found it helpful to focus on the three words Paul uses in today's Second Reading to say goodbye to his much-loved, wildly dysfunctional community in Corinth. For him, Jesus is about "grace": "The grace of the Lord Jesus Christ . . . be with you all!" Grace is an unexpected favor, a gift, something that surprises you and makes you grateful. People who work a 12-Step program can grasp this easily: "grace" happens when you suddenly have the power to do something—or more often the power to *stop* doing something—that you never had before.

But this power often arrives after—or at the same time as—one becomes conscious of being part of a "we," of not being only "one" after all (the first word of all 12 Steps is "we"). The "we" factor in this profound interior change Paul calls "fellowship"; it is from the Greek word for "common." After all, we feel like we belong when we have something in common with other people. A. A. also speaks of "fellowship." For the purposes of recovery, "fellowship" is crucial, because it is "a sufficient substitute [for drinking]. . . and . . . vastly more than that" (BB, 152). We often use the word *spirit* to describe the common feeling a particular group has, as in "school spirit." So Paul associates the Holy Spirit with community: "[T]he fellowship of the Spirit be with you all!"

Is there any real connection between the center of me and all those "we's" outside me? There is; we call it *love*. Paul associates Abba—or just "God" in general—with this quality: "[T]he love of God . . . be with you all!" The First Letter of John simply says that God *is* love.

In the end, far from being a theological technicality, the Trinity, which we celebrate today, is the most important thing for human beings to know and experience. What God and Jesus are all about is what *we* are about, or try to be about: love—love as an unexpected gift found in fellowship. The gospel story, like any recovery story, is a love story.

Corpus Christi

Dt 3:2-3, 14–16; 1 Cor 10:16–17; Jn 6:51–58

Note: On this Sunday Roman Catholics celebrate the gift to us of the Lord's Supper (Corpus Christi equals Body of Christ). This special feast was created because medieval Christians felt that, with so much going on at the Holy Thursday celebration, the gift of bread and wine, and the fellowship that they symbolize, might get neglected in the larger drama. You may prefer to read this meditation on Holy Thursday, and to read on this Sunday the meditation for the appropriate Sunday in Ordinary Time.

"Because there is one bread, we who are many, are one body, for we all partake of the one bread"
(1 Cor 10:17).

Twelve-Step meetings, for all their emotional richness, have often seemed to me a bit short in one area: for all the wonderful, wise words that are spoken at them, there's a shortage of ritual and gesture. Of course some people dislike ritual. Bill W. and Dr. Bob came from New England, where churches tend to be plain and church services simple. But still I think many recovering people hunger for an object, a gesture that can signify what is happening inside them. Coins commemorating years (or days or months) of sobriety are given out at some meetings, and are treasured by members, and occasionally passed on, sponsor to sponsee.

Sometimes I think this hunger for ceremony is the reason why some meetings begin with a potluck meal, to which individuals in the group bring food to be shared with others. This sharing of food helps to underscore the sharing of wisdom and the sharing of lives that go on at the meeting proper. As St. Paul puts it, sharing in "one loaf," or one tuna casserole, helps to make us, "we who are many, . . . one body."

It's curious that we call such events "potlucks": "luck" may remind us of "grace" (see last Sunday), in the sense of an unexpected gift that makes us want to return thanks. The Greek word for grace is *charis*; *eu* means "well" or, colloquially, "a lot." So too *eucharist* means "to give thanks wholeheartedly for our good fortune." Every Mass, every celebration of Jesus' gift of bread and wine, is a gratitude meeting.

As our First Reading suggests, what we are especially grateful for at every Eucharist is the gift of freedom from slavery. We believe that Jesus linked his gift of a memorial meal to his people's sacred meal, the Passover Seder. The Last Supper was apparently a Passover meal, at which Jesus and his "fellowship" would have commemorated the passage of their ancestors from slavery in Egypt to freedom in the Promised Land. Of course every 12-Step meeting also celebrates a passage from slavery, from obsession and compulsion to freedom and serenity.

Every American knows that Patrick Henry said, "Give me liberty or give me death"; his point was that without freedom it is impossible to have a life. To eat the "bread" of fellowship—the consecrated bread of a Christian service or the garlic bread of a 12-Step potluck—is to taste freedom. As Jesus says in today's Gospel, this bread of freedom is life for us.

✝

Ordinary
Time

Second Sunday in Ordinary Time

Is 49:3, 5–6; 1 Cor 1:1–3; Jn 1:29–34

"To the church of God that is in Corinth,
to those who are sanctified in Christ Jesus, called to be saints . . ."
(1 Cor 1:2).

With this Sunday we begin Ordinary Time. In all three cycles, the pattern for the three readings on Ordinary Sundays is this: we go through a particular Gospel (Matthew in A, Mark in B, Luke in C); the First Reading, usually from the Hebrew Scriptures, gives added depth and perspective to the Gospel; the Second Reading, independent of the other two, is from one of Paul's letters, read a passage at a time.

In all three cycles, the first letter of Paul's that we take up, during the dull, post-holiday, "ordinary" days of January, is the First Letter to the Corinthians. This letter, one of Paul's earliest, was addressed to the funky, cantankerous, exuberant, and quarrelsome Christians of the rowdy Greek port city of Corinth, where a lot of blue-collar people worked the docks. Community did not come easy to this bunch, so Paul had to spend much of the letter straightening out squabbles.

A good analogy for the situation in Corinth would be A. A. during its early years. There was a lot of enthusiasm for this new *Way Out* (the first suggested title for the Big Book), but how were these fervent, opinionated groups to be organized, or at least kept from shattering into fragments? Bill W.'s eventual solution was the 12 Traditions; over the next several Sundays we may want to compare them to the solutions Paul proposes for his budding fellowship.

For this Sunday, note only that Paul begins by calling the rough-and-tumble Corinthians "a holy people." The Greek word for "holy" is *hagios*; in Latin it is *sanctus*, from which we derive the word "saint." When the Corinthians first heard this opening to Paul's letter, they may well have shouted, "We are not saints" (BB, 60). Still, that is what Paul says they are "called" by God to be.

46

So are alcoholics, surprisingly enough. That holiness will appear in our willingness to serve others, as did Jesus, the Servant of God, whom the early church identified with the figure in the four Servant Songs of Isaiah (the First Song is quoted in the First Reading). Alcoholics may not be saints, but "[t]he point is, that we are willing to grow along spiritual lines" (BB, 60). That in itself makes us special, makes us "consecrated," in a world where "people [are] filled with anger and fear," where "society [is] breaking up into warring fragments" (12 X 12, 37). God has given us "grace and peace," as St. Paul reminds his Corinthian friends; these are the "principles" we can "practice in all our affairs" (12th Step).

As people recovering by means of a spiritual experience, we can emulate the Servant by being "a light to the nations." Or, more humbly, we "can be a bright spot" even in local church "congregation[s]" (BB, 132), if we feel drawn to that. But either way, we are, in fact, "called to be a holy people."

Third Sunday in Ordinary Time

Is 8:23–9:3; 1 Cor 1:10–13, 17; Mt 4:12–23

". . . the people who sat in darkness have seen a great light,
and for those who sat in the region and shadow of death,
light has dawned"
(Mt 4:16).

As mentioned earlier, 1 Corinthians is Paul's attempt to resolve some of the conflicts in the young Christian community in Corinth. The first problem he addresses is fundamental: to back up their opinions on things like how a "meeting" ought to be conducted and how the "program" should be practiced, some Corinthians have been dropping names. Names like Apollos: like Paul, he was a Christian circuit speaker with a good reputation for eloquence (Paul was apparently not as good a preacher). Names like Cephas, that is, Simon Peter, nicknamed "Rock," who exercised special leadership in the early church. This Corinthian battle of names, by the way, suggests why anonymity works so well as a "spiritual foundation" (Tradition 12) for a fellowship.

In other words, the Corinth Group # 1 had a problem with some members turning other members into gurus. The guru-worshippers in Corinth were trying to get their way of working the Christian "program" made official, so they would quote their "sponsors" as some kind of "ultimate authority" (contrast Tradition 2). The Apolloids might say things like, "Well, *my* sponsor is Apollos, and *he* says you're not a *real* member unless you become a vegetarian, give up sugar, take cold showers, shave your mustache," and so on. There was an Apollos party and a Peter party and so on. (By the way, Apollos and the others didn't encourage this kind of name-dropping, but members who wanted additional prestige did it anyway.)

Yet another faction, the Christ party, may have said something like "I get *my* opinions straight from Christ—so there." Or perhaps Paul is needling the Corinthians when he mentions a Christ party. Maybe there was no such thing, and Paul's point is precisely that Christ is not supposed to be "divided into parts." Nor is the Body of Christ, which is the community of everyone who calls upon Jesus' name; all Christians should belong to the "Christ party." Calling on Jesus is the "only requirement for membership" (Tradition 3). The "ultimate authority" for Christians, in Corinth and elsewhere, is the "loving God" (Tradition 2) whom Jesus called Abba, not a guru.

In other words, the first point Paul makes to his friends at the Corinth Group resembles the First Tradition, particularly in its Al-Anon form: "Our common welfare should come first; personal progress for the greatest number depends upon unity." Bill concisely paraphrases this Tradition: "the [12-Step] group must survive or the individual will not" (12 X 12, 130). For any spiritual fellowship to serve its purpose, no individual ego, and the name that goes with it, can get too big.

Fourth Sunday in Ordinary Time

Zep 2:3, 3:12–13; 1 Cor 1:26–31; Mt 5:1–12

"God chose what is foolish in the world to shame the wise"
(1 Cor 1:27).

In the 12 X 12, Bill gently chides those who dismiss the Bible because they can't "see the Beatitudes for the 'begats'" (12 X 12, 30). This Sunday we have a chance to "see the Beatitudes," from the beginning of Matthew's Sermon on the Mount (the "begats" are the long, boring genealogies in the Hebrew Scriptures, particularly in Genesis and Chronicles). The Beatitudes are proclaimed at a solemn moment in Matthew's version of the Good News (Gospel) of Jesus. To underscore the importance of the occasion, Matthew places Jesus on a mountainside, like Moses on Mount Sinai. All through the Sermon, Jesus will be comparing the Law given through Moses with his new Law. Jesus' new Law, Jesus' "commandment," as John the Evangelist constantly affirms, is to love one another as Jesus has loved us.

The Beatitudes—from the Latin word for "blessed [by God]"— are a series of statements about whom God likes. Jesus begins by affirming that the God whose love he shows forth is above all fond of the "poor in spirit." Following God's lead, Jesus came among us, as he often noted, to gather especially with this kind of people. These are people who need God's help so badly, whose lives are so unmanageable, that they have stopped trying to cover it up, and have admitted their powerlessness. The prophet Zephaniah puts it this way: "[A] people humble and lowly . . . shall take refuge in the Lord."

In his turn, Paul follows Jesus' lead by trying to remind the Corinthians of God's peculiar preference for those whose lives are too messy to allow them the dubious luxury of self-reliance or snobbery. Some of Paul's Corinthian friends have forgotten where they came from. But, Paul insists, they have no business looking down their noses at each other, since few of them are "wise," "influential" (this word could also be translated "powerful"), or "well-born." Corinth was a "lunch-bucket" town. The Corinthians were nobodies, nothings; but God chose them, God called them, and that was the real source of their uniqueness, their "blestness."

As Bill W. stresses in his commentary on the 7th Step in the 12 X 12, humility—remembering where we came from—is essential, not just at the beginning of recovery, but ever after as well. The first of the Beatitudes is particularly true for alcoholics: if we can gain humility, we can acquire "a priceless gift," "a healer of pain," a source of "newfound peace" (12 X 12, 74, 75)—"none" shall "disturb [us]" (Zep). If we gain humility, "blest" are we.

Note: The date of Easter varies every year. As a result, there is also variation in the number of Ordinary Sundays that occur before Lent begins: some get postponed until after the Easter season, some get dropped altogether in a given year. If, like me, you are the kind of recovering person who gets uneasy when things get shifted around, don't worry: sooner or later we'll get to all the meditations in this section.

Meanwhile, when Ash Wednesday occurs, just go to the Lent-Easter meditations. See you back here after Pentecost.

In 2008, go next week to the First Sunday of Lent. After Corpus Christi, return to the Ninth Sunday in Ordinary Time.

Fifth Sunday in Ordinary Time

Is 58:7–10; 1 Cor 2:1–5; Mt 5:13–16

"'. . . let your light shine before others, so that they may see your good works and give glory to your Father in heaven'"
(Mt 5:16).

This week's Gospel continues with Jesus' Sermon on the Mount, his inaugural address. Last week he told his followers that a Power greater than themselves responds to their cries of powerlessness by blessing them, because "God hears the cry of the poor" (one translation of Ps 34:18). In fact, being able to admit powerlessness is already a blessing. But what are we to do with this gift of God, this "blestness"? Exactly what we are to do with the "spiritual awakening" that is "the result of [the 12] steps": we "carry the message," we "practice these principles in all our affairs" (12th Step). In other words, we let our "light shine before people."

I have often wondered exactly what "principles" the 12th Step is talking about. Are these the "principles" implicit in the previous eleven steps—like honesty about our need for God, willingness to face the wrongs we have done, and openness to being reconciled with those we have harmed? Perhaps, but there are also some excellent "principles" in the First Reading this week, from Isaiah, which we might do well to "practice." Jesus liked these "principles"; he cites some of them as the criteria by which all human beings will finally be judged (see Mt 25:31–46). They include "Share your bread with the hungry, shelter the oppressed and the homeless; clothe the naked when you see them, and do not turn your back on your own" (Is; as we will see on the Seventh Sunday in Ordinary Time, Jesus reinterprets "your own" to mean "everybody").

These "principles" don't fit very well with the "human wisdom" that Paul rejects in the Second Reading. "Human wisdom" would be far more likely to agree with Charles Dickens's Ebenezer Scrooge, whose "principles" were a fair sample of the "political economy" that was the "human wisdom" of nineteenth-century England. According to these beliefs, the homeless ought to be sent to workhouses to remedy their shiftlessness; and if the hungry starve, that will help "to decrease the surplus population" (a notion which Scrooge derives from the "human wisdom" of a well-meaning clergyman, Thomas Malthus).

Of course, Scrooge undergoes a *metanoia,* a "complete psychic change"—that is what *A Christmas Carol* is about. Our readings this Sunday urge us recovering people to get on with our "spiritual awakening." If we do, people will see our "wisdom," our "principles," in our service, given gratefully to others because God has kindly given us (like Scrooge) a second chance. And seeing that, they will "give praise to" Abba.

In 2005, go next Sunday to the First Sunday in Lent. Then return after Corpus Christi to the Tenth Sunday in Ordinary Time.

Sixth Sunday in Ordinary Time

Sir 15:15–20; Cor 2:6–10; Mt 5:17–37

"'Do not think that I have come to abolish the law or the prophets; I have come not to abolish but to fulfill'"
(Mt 5:17).

Each of the four Gospels has a different tone, a different focus, different lights and shadings. The Gospel of Matthew, which we are reading this year, was written for a Jewish-Christian audience—contrast Mark, who often has to explain Jewish religious practices to his Gentile audience, sometimes a little flippantly. For Matthew, Jesus is the new Moses, whose mission is not to destroy the Jewish Law (the Torah), but to bring it to fulfillment by grounding it more firmly in a heartfelt, loving relationship between people and the God Jesus called Abba (affectionate term for "father"; using a nickname for God was apparently unique with Jesus).

This part of Matthew is concerned with Jesus' keynote address, the Sermon on the Mount. In the course of the Sermon, Jesus often contrasts What It Was Like (under the Law) with What It's Like Now, in order to get across this theme of "fulfilling the Law." He uses phrases such as "Our ancestors said . . . but *I* tell you." What he tells us is that love, not the Law, can be the foundation of our choices and our behavior.

Sound good? Well, if you think about it, love is a much sterner taskmaster than duty. With love there are no job descriptions. One example of love entailing more work than the Law does: Jesus points out that a perfect religious sacrifice is meaningless if we are feuding with our brother or sister. Heartfelt reconciliation is a better gift to Abba than ritual exactitude. But from the human point of view, ritual exactitude seems like a much "easier" and "softer way" (BB, 58) to get on God's good side than approaching a relative we can't stand. So Jesus' hearers might well have responded to his New Law of Love with "What an order! I can't go through with it" (BB, 60). But Jesus is not just giving a new, more searching insight into the "will of God." Abba, who is "mighty in power" (Sir), is also giving us "the power to carry it out" (11th Step), the power to choose life lovingly.

Jesus is also telling us in many ways in the Sermon to Keep It Simple (K.I.S.S. equals "Keep It Simple, Seekers"). Between those who love, the best way is to "say yes when you mean yes and no when you mean no." This is Christian wisdom, not the intricacies of philosophy that Paul dismisses ("a wisdom of this age"), but "a mysterious, a hidden wisdom." Like many mysteries, however, the "hidden wisdom" is hidden in plain sight: it turns out to be love. Love is what St. Paul calls "the deep things of God" (and later theologians call "the Trinity"). To receive and to pass on that love is to be a citizen of the kingdom of God.

Seventh Sunday in Ordinary Time

Lv 19:1–2, 17–18; 1 Cor 3:16–23; Mt 5:38–48

Note: These readings aren't used between 2001 and 2010; but I include meditations on them for communities that follow a different plan for Sunday Scriptures.

"... *you shall love your neighbor as yourself: I am the* LORD"
(Lv 19:18).

The word *holy* occurs in our first two readings this Sunday. In Leviticus God tells God's people to be holy; and Paul tells the quarrelsome Corinthians to recall that the other members of their community with whom they're bickering are holy. Each member is a "temple of God." As I noted on the Second Sunday of Ordinary Time, recovering people may well wince at the thought of having to become "holy." "Many [might] exclaim[s], 'What an order!' . . . We are not saints" (BB, 60). And it only gets worse if we note the last line of the Gospel, where Matthew seems to ratchet our task up a notch by telling us to be "perfect," as perfect as God. Are we going to have to be perfect in addition to being holy?

As Bill W. might say, "Happily for everyone, this conclusion is erroneous" (BB, 569). The reading from Leviticus omits many verses in which examples of "holiness" are given; most of them have to do with compassionate treatment of our neighbor. For example, "holy" persons won't harvest their wheat or pick their grapes too carefully: poor people will come after them and pick up what the "holy" have thoughtfully left behind for them. And the Corinthians will honor each other's "holiness" if they stop sniping at one another. If this is holiness, it should be hard, but not impossible, for members of 12-Step groups to be holy.

In addition, one should be aware that, in Luke's version of this passage from Matthew's Sermon, the word is not *perfect*, but *compassionate*, or *empathetic*. Both statements, in fact, mean the same thing. The word that gets translated *perfected* here literally means "achieving one's end," "doing or being whatever you were created to do or be." The end for human beings is to become empathetic, to feel what others are feeling. *That* is, in fact, what God does, what makes God who God is: God feels for us. This quality of empathy is what makes God, and us, "holy." What we spiritual pilgrims claim is progress, not perfection, is empathy.

If we want to be like God, then, we have to go beyond empathizing only with people who are like us. Nearly anyone can empathize with a friend. If we are going to be children of Abba, we will have to go further. "The question of how to approach the man we hated will arise. .... It is harder to go to an enemy than to a friend, but we find it much more beneficial to us" (BB, 77).

Eighth Sunday in Ordinary Time

Is 49:14–15; 1 Cor 4:1–5; Mt 6:24–34

Note: These readings aren't used between 2001 and 2010, but I include meditations on them for communities that follow a different plan for Sunday Scriptures.

"'[D]o not worry about your life, what you will eat or what you will drink, or about your body, what you will wear. Is not life more than food, and the body more than clothing?'"
(Mt 6:25).

"Fear of people and of economic insecurity will leave us"
(BB, 84).

As an introvert, I would never put a bumper sticker on my car. But if I were in the market for a 12-Step bumper sticker, it would read: "One Day at a Time." This might not sound all that brilliant to someone else, but it was a great help to me in early sobriety. Somewhere I had gotten the gloomy notion that a bad today invariably foretells a dismal tomorrow. A friend who thought I needed to change that thinking once gave me a self-help coffee mug with the affirmation "I Never Worry" on it. Finally, when I got a little hope from the 2nd Step, I found I could live more and worry less, one day at a time.

Jesus is giving his version of "One Day at a Time" in this Sunday's reading from the Sermon on the Mount: "Enough, then, of worrying about tomorrow. Let tomorrow take care of itself." This section of the Sermon seems to be especially directed at worriers: *worry* appears six times in nine verses—it keeps coming back, just as worrisome thoughts do. "[D]o not *worry* about your livelihood": fear of economic insecurity. "Which of you by *worrying* can add a moment to your life span?": the Big One—fear of death. "As for clothes, why be concerned?": fear of looking silly, a surprisingly large fear, for ordinary people and alcoholics alike. "Enough, then, of worrying about tomorrow": this sounds a little like the vague, general fear we call "anxiety," with which many 12 Steppers have some acquaintance. And so on.

Why shouldn't we worry? Two reasons: first, "Your heavenly Father knows all that you need." Or, as the beautiful passage from Isaiah puts it, even if a mother could forget her own child, God will never forget us. If we believe this, we're ready to take the 3rd Step.

But we also shouldn't worry, second, because worry is a "defect of character which stands in the way of [our] usefulness to [God] and [our] fellows" (BB, 76, 7th Step Prayer). The way Jesus puts this is, "Seek first [God's] kingship over you"—that is, work with others—"and all these things will be given you besides." If we help the kingdom to come, we will "bec[o]me less and less interested in ourselves, our little plans and designs. . . . [W]e [will] beg[i]n to lose our fear of today, tomorrow, or the hereafter" (BB, 63).

Ninth Sunday in Ordinary Time

Dt 11:18, 26–28; Rom 3:21–25, 28; Mt 7:21–27

"'Everyone then who hears these words of mine and acts on them will be like a wise man who built his house on rock. The rain fell, the floods came, and the winds blew and beat on that house, but it did not fall, because it had been founded on rock'"
(Mt 7:24–25).

The New Testament Letter of James was a great favorite of Doctor Bob's wife, Anne, during the early days of A. A.—long before this group of recovering alcoholics was even called "A. A.," in fact. The

Smiths and Bill W. would read the letter when they gathered for prayer around the Smiths' kitchen table in Akron, Ohio.

It's not surprising, then, that the Letter of James is quoted in the Big Book: "But this [prayer and meditation] is not all. There is action and more action. 'Faith without works is dead'" (BB, 88—from Jas, 2:17; see also BB, 14, 76). The 12th Step itself, a description of which immediately follows this quotation, makes pretty much the same point: if we have "had a spiritual awakening," it will presumably show itself in the way we "practice these principles in all our affairs."

I don't know whether Bill W. and the Smiths knew it, but these apparently simple ideas have been the center of religious controversy for hundreds of years, controversy based in large part on Paul's Letter to the Romans, parts of which will be the Second Reading for the next several weeks. Like the creators of A. A., I have no desire to enter into religious controversies; like them, I am trying to "deal[s] only with general principles common to most denominations" (BB, 94). However, the Gospel today urges us to consider fundamentals, no matter how "controversial" (BB, 19) they may be: Jesus tells a story about two approaches to foundations of buildings, and before that, he insists that the only practical foundation is to carry out "the will of my Father in heaven."

Fundamentally, then, just saying nice things to or about Jesus, is insufficient. "To be vital, faith must be accompanied by self-sacrifice and unselfish, constructive action" (BB, 93). Matthew's entire Gospel is built around this idea. It is the climax of Jesus' inaugural address, the Sermon on the Mount: "None of those who cry out 'Lord, Lord,' will enter the kingdom of God . . ." And it will be the conclusion of his farewell address, in Mt 25:31–46: "[A]s often as you [took care of] one of my least brothers or sisters, you [took care of] me" (Mt 25:40). Those who serve others, who work their 12th Step as if their lives depended on it—which is "appallingly true" for recovering people (BB, 14)—are "blest," as in the Beatitudes, and enter the kingdom of God. These people have chosen a "blessing" rather than a "curse" (Dt).

Tenth Sunday in Ordinary Time

Hos 6:3–6; Rom 4:18–25; Mt 9:9–13

"'Those who are well have no need of a physician, but those who are sick. . . .I have come to call not the righteous but sinners'" (Mt 9:12, 13).

Most people think of tax collectors as necessary evils, I suppose—maybe a little bureaucratic and unfeeling, but people doing a job that someone has to do. Even recovering people don't bear grudges against them as a class. But at the time of Jesus, "tax collector" was a vile occupation; frequently in the Christian Scriptures "tax collectors and prostitutes" are linked as members of the two worst professions for men or for women.

This hatred of "tax collectors" had several causes. First, tax collectors were collaborators with the occupation forces, the Romans. The Jewish people, because of their own experience of trying to maintain their identity during exile, had a strong sense of separateness from the *goyim,* the Gentiles—and the Romans were conquering Gentiles. Thus only disloyal Jews would cooperate with them. Second, tax collectors were practically by nature extortionists or gangsters. They were given a particular quota of money or goods to raise; but anything they could squeeze out of taxpayers beyond that was theirs to keep as their profit, no questions asked. Roman soldiers helped tax collectors beat profits out of the taxed.

All of this underscores the point of this Sunday's Gospel, in which a tax collector is called by Jesus to be his follower. That Jesus would call such a lowlife is already an eyebrow-raiser. Even more surprising, the tax collector experiences a *metanoia,* a religious experience, of a very dramatic kind: he drops his truncheon and his thumb screws and follows Jesus at once. And not only that: the Gospel in which this story occurs is traditionally understood to have been written years later by the converted tax collector.

Challenged about his taste in friends, Jesus quietly points out the moral: it's awful people, like tax collectors and prostitutes, who need God's help, not people who have worked themselves up to respectability. In 12-Step language, you have to hit bottom, take a 1st Step, and acknowledge that you simply won't make it without God, for God to restore you to sanity.

How do you show that you have had a genuine change of attitude, that you have come to your senses? Like this tax collector, you give a dinner for your fellow thugs and molls; you show your gratitude by service. "For it is love that I desire, not sacrifice," says our God (Hos 6:6). Why did Matthew invite disreputable people to his banquet? Because one of the A. A. Promises was being realized for him: despite "how far down the scale [he had] gone" socially and religiously, he saw "how [his] experience [could] benefit others" (BB, 84). And, finally, he had grasped that these were the kind of people Jesus, his guest of honor, liked to spend time with. Good news for recovering people.

Eleventh Sunday in Ordinary Time

Ex 19:2–6; Rom 5:6–11; Mt 9:36–10:8

"[Y]ou shall be my treasured possession out of all the peoples.
Indeed, the whole earth is mine"
(Ex 19:5).

In the Second Reading this Sunday, Paul says that Christ laid down his life for us when we were "powerless" and "godless." In the Gospel Jesus himself says that he is sending the Twelve on a 12th-Step call to help people "lying prostrate from exhaustion"; his followers are to "cure the sick." The word for "sick" here comes from the same root as the word *powerless* in Romans; both mean "without strength." "[T]he heart of Jesus is moved with pity" this Sunday for people who are sick and tired and powerless.

In other words, the people Jesus feels for look a lot like people who need recovery, who are in the active phase of addiction, of "attachment." Back when we were in this fix, we may have thought that we ought to have the strength to change our destructive behavior, to stop making ourselves and the people we love miserable. But instead, all our efforts only served to bring us closer to our 1st Step, the step in which we admit we are "without strength," "powerless" over our addiction(s). And no wonder we were also "godless" in those dark days and nights. This word literally means "people who don't worship." Why would we worship anybody, when our experience was that "If there is a God, he certainly hasn't done anything for me" (BB, 56)? Paradoxically, as the Big Book remarks, we *were* in a sense worshippers, of "people, sentiment, money, and ourselves"—not to mention alcohol (BB, 54). Anything but God.

Some people, including some future Al-Anons, find the spectacle of an addict "lying prostrate" disgusting. For that matter, addicts are often disgusted with themselves under these circumstances, although they rarely admit it. Jesus, on the other hand, is deeply "moved" by our "prostration." The Greek word for *moved* is strong, and literally means "his guts ached" for the "prostrate" crowd (Jesus' contemporaries believed that they felt with their guts, not their hearts, which is actually not a bad guess). "Moved" usually occurs in the Christian Scriptures when Jesus sees someone who badly needs help; when he's "moved," he usually heals.

In the 1st Step we cry out—or maybe we just lie there, pitiably "prostrate." The 2nd Step describes the aftermath—somebody hears us, somebody sees us, somebody is "moved" by our plight, and suddenly the power to heal us is there. It feels a little like being "[borne] up on eagle wings" (Ex). " . . . God is doing for us what we could not do for ourselves" (BB, 84).

Twelfth Sunday in Ordinary Time

Jer 20:10–13; Rom 5:12–15; Mt 10:26–33

"'And even then the hairs of your head are all counted.
So do not be afraid'"
(Mt 10:30–31).

Our readings this Sunday are pretty grim, but it's worth keeping in mind that the passage from Matthew is part of a blunt speech Jesus gives to his disciples as they are setting out on their first 12th-Step call. Bill W. paints an equally candid picture in the chapter "Working with Others" in the Big Book: even though would-be 12th Steppers, like the disciples, may be profoundly convinced that "there is a solution," a lot of drunks won't be ready to hear it. So Bill urges his fellows not to be discouraged, just as, several times in this passage, Jesus tells his message-carriers not to be afraid of the opposition they'll encounter.

In the following passage in Matthew, not quoted here perhaps *because* it is so bleak, Jesus notes that the message carried by his disciples will actually cause division, not healing, in some families. The same is often true when only one member of a family recovers, while everyone else tries to continue with business as usual. As Family Systems therapists note, families are linked together like a mobile (to use family counselor John Bradshaw's metaphor). When one member changes radically, *even for the better*, the whole system is jangled, and many other members may well try to bring the system back to the Way Things Have Always Been.

The prophet Jeremiah, famous for his "capacity to be honest" (BB, 58) about painful matters affecting his nation, the kingdom of Judah, grimly describes the reaction that whistle-blowers—in families or in nations—often evoke: "Yes, I hear the whisperings of many: 'Terror on every side! Denounce! Let us denounce him!' All those who were my friends are on the watch for any misstep of mine. . . ."

Anyone who thinks Jeremiah is paranoid here should try saying some candid things about family drinking patterns at the next Thanksgiving feast.

Nothing new about any of this—it's as old as Original Sin (an early version of this theological concept occurs in today's reading from Romans). Family pain often seems to be handed down from generation to generation, in large part because people can't bring themselves to talk honestly about what's going on. It takes a lot of courage, then, to stick to the path of recovery, which must begin with "rigorous honesty" (BB, 58). We may be breaking down family patterns of dishonesty that seem to go back to Adam and Eve. No wonder Jesus (in Mark and Luke) sends his disciples out in pairs: we need companions to help us stay brave. But with the help of a fellowship, we can reach the point where we are "not . . . afraid of anything" (Mt).

Note: In 2008, Roman Catholics will celebrate the feast of Sts. Peter and Paul (June 29th) on the following Sunday. See the meditation in Special Feasts.

Thirteenth Sunday in Ordinary Time

2 Kgs 4:8–11, 14–16; Rom 6:3–4, 8–11; Mt 10:37–42

"'Those who find their life will lose it,
and those who lose their life for my sake will find it'"
(Mt 10:39).

If you ask most people to define "prophet," they will probably say "someone who can correctly tell the future," someone like the late Jeane Dixon, at least in her own view. But as Bible students have noted, this is not exactly the case: *prophet* in Greek literally means "one who speaks out"; prophets are most often speaking about the present, not the future. The reason people think prophets are forecasters is that someone who "speaks out" the *truth* about the present is often going to be right about the future as well, since such a person is not in denial, like the rest of us.

Jeremiah, for example, was a great prophet because, as I hinted last week, he told his contemporaries that they were going to *lose* their war with Babylon and should plan accordingly. He stuck to his grim perceptions at a time when all the other "prophets" were assuring the nation of Judah that God was on their side. Naturally his people threw Jeremiah into jail for being so "gloomy" and unpatriotic. I suppose today he would be treated for depression and forced to watch motivational videotapes full of well-dressed young men with very white teeth.

What makes someone a prophet, or a "holy" person, then, is what makes someone a recovering person: "the capacity to be honest" (BB, 58). Only the truth, as Jesus said, can set us free (Jn 8:32), can bring us to life; Jesus said that he himself was both truth and life, and the Way, the Road, as well (Jn 14:6).

The First Reading this Sunday begins a story about Elisha, who was a prophet long before Jeremiah's time. In the part of the story we hear today, he promises a woman who has "welcomed" a prophet that she will be given a child as her "reward." But that isn't the end of her story; in the sequel (not cited this Sunday), Elisha later raises her child from the dead. Once again, there is a connection between truth and life. If you tell the truth like a prophet, you're in touch with life. "Death has no power over" such truth-tellers, as it had no power over "Christ Jesus" (Rom).

It's by no means always easy to tell the truth, especially in unhealthy families or groups (including some religious groups; including some 12-Step groups), as Jeremiah's experience demonstrates. But even if we sometimes are too scared to be truth-speakers ourselves, remember that we can still get a reward even for "receiving" or "welcoming" prophets—instead of booing them like everyone else.

Fourteenth Sunday in Ordinary Time

Zec 9:9–10; Rom 8:9, 11–13; Mt 11:25–31

"'Take my yoke upon you, and learn from me;
for I am gentle and humble in heart'"
(Mt 11:29).

In *Varieties of Religious Experience*, William James gives a wonderfully concise and accurate description of what the Gospels call *metanoia* and what 12 Steppers call the 2nd Step. When Jesus began his preaching by telling people to "repent" (*metanoete*, roughly translatable as "change your attitude"), he was referring to an "experience" that, according to James, feels something like this: "The transition from tenseness, self-responsibility, and worry, to equanimity, receptivity, and peace"—that is, the transition from attachment to serenity—"is the most wonderful of all those shiftings of inner equilibrium, those changes of the personal centre of energy, which I have analyzed so often." Jung was trying to describe the same experience when he spoke of "huge emotional displacements and rearrangements" (BB, 27) as an effective therapy for alcoholism.

James continues, in language that echoes today's passage from Matthew: "[T]he chief wonder of it is that it [the 'transition'—the part of an A. A. story that tells 'what happened' (BB, 58)] so often comes about, not by doing, but by simply relaxing and throwing the burden down" (p. 233).

As addicts, or as people who care about addicts, we have spent years trying hard to "do" it, to handle it, to control it, to throw willpower at it. But "it"—whatever our obsession/compulsion is, a drug or a drug-user—just keeps, weighing us down, as a yoke does oxen pulling a plow. As a result, we "are weary and find life burdensome." Nevertheless we grimly continue to insist that we humans ought to be more powerful than alcohol, no matter how "cunning, baffling, and powerful" alcohol may be (BB, 58–59). Paul would comment that, unless and until we "relax[s] and throw[s] our burden down," we are acting in a "fleshy" way (see the Fifth Week of Lent for more on "fleshiness").

We finally enter recovery when we simply stop trying—the words for "refresh" and "rest" in Matthew both come from a root that means "cease, stop." Bill W. describes this moment of surrender: "And we have ceased fighting anything or anyone—even alcohol. . . . [O]ur new attitude to liquor . . . just comes! That is the miracle of it. We are not fighting [alcohol], neither are we avoiding temptation. . . . Instead, the problem has been removed" (BB, 84–85).

The First Reading today, which is also used on Palm Sunday, reminds us that Jesus, as a Messiah who is "gentle and humble of heart," rides a donkey, not a foaming warhorse. This Messiah would agree with William James: conversion is a matter of surrender, of taking a 1st Step, of letting our burden drop. As he notes in today's Gospel, his burden is "light"—as light as love.

Fifteenth Sunday in Ordinary Time

Is 55:10–11; Rom 8:18–23; Mt 13:1–23

"[M]y word . . . shall not return to me empty,
but it shall accomplish that which I purpose,
and succeed in the thing for which I sent it"
(Is 55:11).

For the next several Sundays, the gospel readings will contain some of Jesus' parables (for more on these parables, see Meditation 31 in *A 12-Step Approach to the Spiritual Exercises*). Like nearly all of the great spiritual teachers, Jesus used stories to carry his message. Stories have two advantages: they are portable, easy to carry from place to place; and they are rich, as poetry is rich, compacting a lot of wisdom in a small space.

I believe that it is our stories that make us human. When we come to recovery, we don't have stories—we have messes, a fistful of pointless, incoherent events. Twelve-Step meetings are, among other things, storytelling schools: we hear people tell about "what we used to be like, what happened, and what we are like now" (BB, 58), which is the basic structure of a life story. If we stay, eventually the scattered fragments of our lives will fall into place, and we will see that we, too, have a story. And not only does our story restore us to the human family but it also reunites us to God. As Elie Wiesel, the Holocaust survivor, has said, God made human beings because God loves stories. (I found this quotation in Kurtz's *The Spirituality of Imperfection*—p. 246, n. 8. Kurtz stresses the crucial importance of stories in recovery, in part by relaying some wonderful spiritual tales.)

And then, having been renewed ourselves, we carry the message to others. If we are wise, we carry it in the shape of our stories, because people (and especially alcoholics) are always more likely to listen to a story than a lecture: "[W]e ourselves [that is, wives of alcoholics] don't always care for people who lecture us" (from chapter 8, "To Wives," in the Big Book, p. 121). When it first dawned on me that all I needed to do to recover was hear and tell stories, I couldn't believe my luck; I have always loved stories.

Isaiah and Matthew both compare seeds to God's word, to stories, in today's readings. When we broadcast our recovery stories, like someone flinging seed, we are sending out a word of God. However, much as we might like to, it's not up to us to decide which seed will grow. We browbeat a hard-drinking loved one, who ignores us, while some eavesdropping stranger gets the message and runs with it. We need to remember that our stories are God's gifts to us. So it's up to God to decide how they can best "achiev[e] the end for which I [God] sent [them]" (Is).

Sixteenth Sunday in Ordinary Time

Wis 12:13, 16–19; Rom 8:26–27; Mt 13:24–43

". . . you have taught your people that the righteous must be kind"
(Wis 12:19).

An Al-Anon friend of mine called me on the Sunday when these readings came around. At her church, the deacon who preached had said that the point of this gospel passage, about weeds mixed in with wheat, was that there were some very bad people in the world, even in the Church, who needed to be ferreted out, rounded up, and burned. Then he proceeded to describe these offensive people in considerable detail, so that the congregation could recognize the enemy and start ferreting without losing time. My friend was puzzled, because she thought Jesus was making exactly the opposite point.

She was right, of course. This week's story asserts that weeds and wheat are so close together that it doesn't make sense to try to sort them out. Such matters are best left to the Lord of the harvest, and in the Lord's good time. A "loving God" (Tradition 2) will surely make a better job of this than human beings, who are in many cases "filled with anger and fear" (12 X 12, 37).

There are two 12-Step slogans that are relevant here: "Live and Let Live" and "Let Go and Let God." It is God "who searches hearts" (Rom); human beings tend, as 12 Steppers often say, unfairly to compare other people's outsides to their insides. As a result, we sometimes conclude that our insides are morally greatly superior to other people's outsides. By contrast, Jesus, who as God's beloved Son presumably really knew other people's insides—John says Jesus "knew what was in everyone" (2:25)—made a point of spending time with people who had the least lovely outsides: prostitutes, lepers, tax collectors, and adulterers.

Oddly enough, the most merciless people on this score (including some "ex-problem drinkers") are often those who have in the past most needed mercy (as another parable of Jesus' makes clear—see the Twenty-Fourth Sunday in Ordinary Time). Because we forget so easily where we came from, "what we used to be like" (BB, 58), we are really too impaired to be deciding who in this world is a weed and who is wheat. Anyway, there is too much hunger in the world for us to risk wasting good wheat by trying to hack down what we believe to be weeds. Some people might go spiritually hungry if we make the wrong call.

Seventeenth Sunday in Ordinary Time

1 Kgs 3, 5, 7–12; Rom 8:28–30; Mt 13:44–52

"'Because you have asked . . . for yourself understanding
to discern what is right,
I now do according to your word'"
(1 Kgs 3:11–12).

The story of the dragnet at the end of today's Gospel makes the same point as the parable of the weeds and the wheat last week: the reign of God, like a dragnet, collects "all sorts of things." Those of us with control issues may wish we could tidy those things up *now*; but Jesus reserves that task for angels, who don't need meetings, and even they don't get to straighten things out until "the end of the world." As with the weeds and wheat, the task is too important to leave to human beings, who might throw away a pearl.

The first two parables talk about finding such a treasure, a "pearl of great price" as older translations put it. Bill W. might well have liked these parables: he was fond of using mercantile imagery like "inventory" and "capitalize" to describe spiritual practices—no wonder, since he was a failed stockbroker. In fact, he uses an image somewhat like Jesus to describe the "really valuable pearl" of recovery: "Like a gaunt prospector, belt drawn in over the last ounce of food, our pick struck gold. . . . For a time [we] may try to hug the new treasure to [ourselves]. [We] may not see at once that [we have] barely scratched a limitless lode which will pay dividends only if [we] mine[d] it for the rest of [our lives] and insist[ed] on giving away the entire product" (BB 128–9, in "The Family Afterwards").

What exactly is the treasure, the pearl that Jesus speaks of? As our First Reading shows, it's what we pray for every time we get to the climax of the Serenity Prayer: the pearl is wisdom. Bill W. reaches the same conclusion about his "gold." When he describes "the permanent and legitimate satisfactions of right living," like Solomon, he doesn't mention "long life" or "riches" or lots of dead "enemies." Instead, he says, quoting the prophet Micah, "True ambition is the deep desire to live usefully and walk humbly under the grace of God" (12 X 12, 124–5). Surely the key to such a humble, useful life is wisdom. The gold is wisdom.

Even pain, sorrow, and loss can become a kind of treasure, as Paul suggests in Romans: ". . . God makes all things work together for the good of those who have been called." Bill W. agreed with this, too; a few pages after the image of the lucky prospector, he talks like a stockbroker again: "Avoid then, the deliberate manufacture of misery, but if trouble comes, cheerfully capitalize it as an opportunity to demonstrate [God's] omnipotence" (133). The key to this spiritual alchemy, this transmuting suffering into gold, is wisdom.

Eighteenth Sunday in Ordinary Time

Is 55:1–3; Rom 8:35, 37–39; Mt 14:13–21

"Taking the five loaves and the two fish, he looked up to heaven,
and blessed and broke the loaves . . .
And all ate and were filled"
(Mt 14:19–20).

(For further reflections on this and next Sunday's Gospels, see *A 12-Step Approach to the Spiritual Exercises,* Meditations 33 and 34.)

I have often remarked how much difficulty we addicted people have with the word and the concept *enough*. I don't think I ever took a drink, from the first to the last, without worrying about whether I could get another. I was never satisfied (*satis* is Latin for "enough"). And the same can be said about other people and other powerful "substances," like money, power, and sex. Bill W. succinctly sums up the essence of addiction: "Never was there enough of what we thought we wanted" (12 X 12, 71).

Isaiah has a word this Sunday for all such "attached" people, and especially for those who have difficulties with chemicals, food, or money. The prophet urges his listeners to stop wasting money on things that leave them feeling empty, that "fail to satisfy." Strangely enough, what truly satisfies turns out to be free of charge.

Jesus acts out Isaiah's words when he breaks the bread in today's Gospel and satisfies the crowd. "[H]is heart [is] moved with pity" (as in the Gospel for the Eleventh Sunday in Ordinary Time), and when his heart is touched, miracles happen. Not only do the people get fed on bread and fish, but there is more than enough. The word for "ate their fill" could be crudely translated "were stuffed"; it's related to the word for "grass," suggesting contented grazing. And still there was bread left over—a basket apiece for each of Jesus' disciples, so they could keep on giving if need be.

We might wonder why Jesus works a bread miracle at this point in his ministry, when he had refused to work one at the beginning, at the Tempter's suggestion. Of course, Jesus may simply have considered the source of that early suggestion. But the critical difference may be that, if Jesus had worked this wonder right after his own fast, he would have fed only himself. By working it now, though, he feeds many others. Like Bill W.'s prospector, Jesus is able to make the bread stretch precisely because he "insists on giving away the entire product" (BB, 129).

Paul makes a similar point in today's reading from Romans, but negatively: nothing bad, including "hunger," can come between us and the love Christ has for us (the word actually means "famine," group hunger, not just individual hunger). Christ's feeding of the five thousand demonstrates positively that, if we let God feed us, we will in our turn be able to feed, not just ourselves, but all the hungry people. Enough, already.

Nineteenth Sunday in Ordinary Time

1 Kgs 19:9, 11–13; Rom 9:1–5; Mt 14:22–23

"[T]he LORD *was not in the wind. . . . the earthquake . . . the fire, and after the fire a sound of sheer silence"*
(1 Kgs 19:11–12).

People in early recovery will readily identify with Peter in today's Gospel, yelling for help. How did he get into this mess? He took literally Jesus' challenge to stop fearing and show some courage. But then he looked down—and he lost his nerve.

Something similar happened to me when I was in an alcoholism treatment program. I had gone there expecting some kind of sophisticated medical intervention, something concrete and reassuring, like a really big bottle of pills. When I was informed that I was expected to forego all mind-altering chemicals, and to do this simply by trusting in God, I was as scared as Peter. Worse: I felt like I had already tried the way of trust, over many years in a seminary and as a member of a Catholic religious order. But all I had gotten for my trust was a bad case of alcoholism.

Eventually the treatment staff pushed me out of the boat. Or, more precisely, they asked me to climb a sheer rock face, since a weekend of Outward Bound was the conclusion of that treatment program. As the oppressively healthy Outward Bound staff explained rock climbing to the other patients and me, we stood huddled in shivering clumps at the bottom of a cliff in the Colorado Rockies, too stunned at what they expected of us to grasp the instructions. I'm afraid of heights, but—so—I asked to be one of the first to try the climb, largely because I thought that I'd lose what little nerve I had if I waited very long.

I began climbing, but, like Peter, I made the mistake of looking down. Like him I yelled at what I saw, yelled for help. And like him, I was saved because a "hand" was "stretched out." In my case it wasn't actually hands, it was voices: I asked my fellow patients down on the ground to cheer me on—and up—this was perhaps the first time in my life that I had so nakedly asked anyone for help. The waves of their voices lifted me to the top.

Since then, I have discovered again and again that Bill W. is right about trust in God. God reaches out a hand to us, as Jesus did to Peter, through lots of human hands. Bill puts it like this: "What seemed at first a flimsy reed has proved to be the loving and powerful hand of God. A new life has been given us" (BB, 28). And the real miracle of it is that God reaches down, not noisily or showily, with fire and earthquake, but gently, with the "tiny whispering" breeze we call the Spirit. Even a "little faith" is enough to save us.

Twentieth Sunday in Ordinary Time

Is 56:1, 6–7; Rom 11:13–15, 29–32; Mt 15:21–28

"[M]y house shall be called a house of prayer for all peoples"
(Is 56:7).

Teresa of Avila, the great Spanish mystic, was traveling once by coach. A violent storm came up, the horses balked, the coach got stuck in the mud, and its passengers fell out. Dirty and bedraggled, Teresa was overheard to say, "Lord, if this is the way you treat your friends, no wonder you have so few of them."

The woman in today's Gospel is very much a sister of Teresa's when it comes to speaking her mind to the Lord. Her "conscious contact" is *full* contact. To grasp the story, it's essential to note that she is a Canaanite, and that her repartee with Jesus takes place in "the district of Tyre and Sidon." That is, Jesus is in Gentile territory, and the woman is a *shiksa* (non-Jewish). In fact, the Canaanites were age-old enemies of the Jews; the Israelites under Joshua, Moses' lieutenant, had squatted on Canaanite land, and hadn't been gentle about it. So we know that the woman has swallowed any national pride when she asks a Jew for help.

Why does Jesus seem to humiliate her even more by giving her a very traditional answer, in essence, "I have been sent only to God's people, not to you Gentiles"? Maybe the notion of including the Gentiles in the New People of God only dawned gradually on Jesus (or dawned later, on his followers, with the help of Jesus' Spirit). Or perhaps he is needling the disciples by quoting the conventional thinking—theirs—on this point. Or maybe he said this with a twinkle in his eye, daring her to contradict him and break through to a new, more honest communication between former enemies.

What matters most, however, is not that he speaks this way to her, but that she wittily comes right back at Jesus. Like many Jews, Jesus seems to love verbal fencing, even when the other person wins, as this woman seems to—he does what she asks. And thus he also acts out Isaiah's prophecy about Gentiles with faith becoming part of God's people. God's kingdom, like recovery, is not for those who need it; it is for those who want it, Jew or Gentile. And want it enough not to take no for an answer.

"Conscious contact" (11th Step) with God means, I think, that we get to feel anything we feel and say anything we need to say to God. With God, as with people, a "functional" relationship depends on "the capacity to be honest" (BB, 58). Of course, if we are frank with God, we have to expect that God will be just as frank with us. But, like the Canaanite woman, or the woman whose story appears toward the end of the Big Book (BB, 553), we can still expect that in the end we will get exactly what we need.

Twenty-First Sunday in Ordinary Time

Is 22:15, 19–23; Rom 11:33–36; Mt 16:13–20

"For from him and through him and to him are all things.
To him be the glory forever. Amen"
(Rom 11:36).

Our Gospel this Sunday tells the story of Jesus entrusting "the keys of the kingdom of heaven" to Peter (this Gospel is also studied on the Feast of Sts. Peter and Paul, in Special Feasts). The Christian churches disagree about the implications of this statement for their own community structures, their different "traditions." So rather than focus on things that divide us, I would like to take a different tack, and ponder the "keys" in the First Reading and the Gospel from a 12-Step point of view.

Recovering people have invoked the "keys of the kingdom" in a different context than church structure, as a metaphor for something else that is crucial for us. An A. A. "pioneer," a "worldly lady [who] helped to develop A. A. in Chicago," calls her story in the Big Book "The Keys of the Kingdom." The conclusion of her story explains her title: "There is no more 'aloneness,' with that awful ache, so deep in the heart of every alcoholic that nothing, before, could ever reach it. That ache is gone and never need return again.

"Now there is a sense of belonging, of being wanted and needed and loved. In return for a bottle and a hangover, we have been given the Keys of the Kingdom" (BB, 312).

Another alcoholic might describe the "ache" to which this woman refers as a sense of having "lost all and [been] locked up" (BB, 62). "Keys" unlock doors; for recovering people, what is on the other side of that door is "a sense of belonging." Most addicted people, and many others who care about addicts, have a nagging feeling that they don't belong, that they have been locked out somehow, so no treasure could be more precious than the one the "worldly lady"—and so many others—have found in the community of recovering people. We can therefore readily make our own the words of Paul's hymn of gratitude to the Higher Power in the First Reading, from Romans. Paul stresses how much bigger—and how much more generous—God is than we humans: "How deep are the riches and the wisdom and the knowledge of God! . . . Who has given God anything so as to deserve return?" Paul also notes that God's "ways" are "unsearchable." The word translated "unsearchable" comes from the word for "steps," and literally means something like "[God] takes such big steps that they can't be followed." But in God's generosity, human-sized Steps are available, Steps that form a path that can lead us to the "kingdom."

Twenty-Second Sunday in Ordinary Time

Jer 20:7–9; Rom 12:1–2; Mt 16:21–27

"[P]resent your bodies as a living sacrifice,
holy and acceptable to God,
which is your spiritual worship"
(Rom 12:1).

In our First Reading today we have a powerful passage from what has been called "The Confessions of Jeremiah." The prophet is complaining bitterly to God: the message God has entrusted to him is so terrible that it makes everybody hate and scorn him. Yet he can't keep it in; that feels even worse.

Anyone who believes you should say only nice, polite things to God would do well to study this reading. Jeremiah bluntly blames God for the mess he's in: "You duped me, O Lord, and I let myself be duped; you were too strong for me, and you triumphed." The word translated "duped" is strong, and has sexual overtones; a nice synonym for it would be "seduced," and we've all heard more pungent synonyms for it at 12-Step meetings and in R-rated movies. But whatever the word, it describes fairly accurately the feeling that people who are on a spiritual path get from time to time. We get "knowledge of God's will for us," as the 11th Step puts it, but it seems far from "good, pleasing and perfect" (Rom). Instead of asking for "the power to carry it out," our first reaction may be, "What an order! I cannot endure it" (BB, 60 and Jeremiah).

Bill W. writes movingly about miserable times like these in the 12 X 12. He comforts those who "feel themselves cut off from God's help and direction," and notes that "[a]ll of us, without exception, pass through times when we can pray only with the greatest exertion of will. Occasionally we . . . are seized with a rebellion so sickening that we simply won't pray." His advice is sound: "When these things happen we should not think too ill of ourselves. We should simply resume prayer as soon as we can, doing what we know to be good for us" (105). Take Jeremiah, for example: miserable as he is, he's still talking to God, still praying, still in "contact."

Today's Gospel depicts just such a "sickening" moment in Peter's life. Last week he correctly guessed that his friend Jesus is the Messiah: naturally Peter had gone on to imagine a bright future for his friend (and for himself). This week, by harsh contrast, Jesus has immediately proceeded to tell his friends that the kind of Messiah *he* is will end up dying a disgusting slave's death. Peter tries to pray this away ("May you be spared!"), but Jesus only tells him to shut up.

Peter may well feel "duped." Like him, it may take us a while to realize that we too need not an unbeatable warrior but a Lord who knows suffering—suffering like ours. Unbeatable warriors tend to leave fields full of corpses in their wake. Better to follow the steps of the gentle Messiah, who, the night before his death, could "pray only with the greatest exertion of will."

Twenty-Third Sunday in Ordinary Time

Ez 33:7–9; Rom 13:8–10; Mt 18:15–20

"Owe no one anything,
except to love one another"
(Rom 13:8).

Matthew likes to organize his Gospel around big speeches that Jesus gives at key moments in his ministry. This week's selection is from Matthew 18, which Scripture scholars call "the community discourse." The aim of this discourse is the same as the aim of the 12 Traditions: to give some hints about how the groups that have formed around Jesus' message, around his vision of God's kingdom, can best be organized. Scripture scholars believe that the specific problems of Matthew's church, many years after Jesus' lifetime, have helped to shape what is said here.

This explains what might otherwise puzzle us: Jesus tells the disciples to treat a wrongheaded member of the community, as a last resort, "as you would a Gentile or a tax collector." And yet in the Gospels, Jesus treats "Gentiles and tax collectors" rather well; he even made a tax collector one of the Twelve, and tradition has it that that very tax collector was the author of this Gospel. Where has this harsh exclusiveness come from?

At the time when the Gospel of Matthew was composed, some of the Jewish-Christian members of Matthew's community may have been expelled from the synagogue, being told they were no longer in good standing as Jews. As Bill W. notes, nothing is more common in human affairs than the "wish to retaliate" (BB, 61), especially when people have hurt us by excluding us. Perhaps these members of Matthew's community, stung by their exclusion, decided it was time to tighten up on the entrance requirements for the *Christian* assembly.

The impulse to protect the group from "the wrong kind of people" also affected the early members of A. A. Bill W. relates that the groups of that time had "long [lists] of 'protective' regulations," reflecting the early members' "anxiety and fear" (12 X 12, 140). Nevertheless, A. A. eventually got over this "anxiety and fear," and produced the 3rd Tradition: "The only requirement for A. A. membership is a desire to stop drinking."

As Christians we might do well to follow A. A.'s lead on this point. And we would, I think, also be following Jesus as well. Another passage in today's Gospel sounds more like the Jesus we usually meet: "Where two or three are gathered together in my name, there am I in the midst of them." This sounds a lot like the Long Form of Tradition 3, which includes these sentences: ". . . A. A. membership [ought never] depend upon money or conformity. Any two or three alcoholics gathered together for sobriety may call themselves an A. A. group . . ." (12 X 12, 189).

To sum up: as Christians and/or as recovering people, we should always bear in mind the principle Paul enunciates this week in Romans: "Love never do no evil to the neighbor; hence, love is the fulfillment of the law."

Note: In 2008, Roman Catholics will celebrate the Feast of the Holy Cross (September 14) on the following Sunday. See the meditation in Special Feasts.

Twenty-Fourth Sunday in Ordinary Time

Sir 27:30–28:7; Rom 14:7–9; Mt 18:21–35

*"Does anyone harbor anger against another
and expect healing from the Lord?"*
(Sir 28:3).

This Sunday's Gospel sounds more like Jesus than parts of last week's Gospel. Instead of the "three strikes and you're out" approach to forgiveness that Matthew's Christian fellowship later fell into, we have "seventy-seven times." This of course does not mean "Forgive them 490 times and *then* lower the boom," but "Forgive them no matter how many times they ask for forgiveness." In the same way, the "huge amount"—literally, "10,000 talents"—that the Mean Servant owes in the parable is best translated non-literally, as they do in *Godspell:* "a million, bazillion smackers." The point is really that God is willing to forgive us no matter how much we owe.

The point of the story of the Unforgiving Servant—and of our other readings this week—is painfully clear: "If you want forgiveness, forgive." The parable acts out what we ask for every time we say Jesus' prayer: "Forgive us our trespasses as we forgive those who trespass against us."

This may remind us of a stroke of genius in the way the 12 Steps are constructed. Travelers on the 12-Step Way are urged to "list people, institutions or principles" that they resent for harming them (BB, 64, on Steps 4 and 5). Then they are to ask God for healing of their own character flaws (Steps 6 and 7). And then they list the people they have harmed (Step 8; in Step 9 they ask these people for their forgiveness).

The genius of this lies in the shift of focus from those who harm to those who have been harmed. As today's Gospel makes clear, there is nothing like needing someone's forgiveness to make one a forgiving person—at least in theory. In fact, my first 8th-Step list was a long list of people who, I thought, had harmed me. Of course this wasn't a real 8th-Step list, but at least I was getting warm. Flannery O'Connor wrote a marvelous story that makes this point. An old man from the backwoods of the South, lost in the big city with his only companion in life, his grandson, is so frightened when the grandson accidentally runs into and knocks down a rich matron that the grandfather denies knowing the boy—his own flesh and blood. And for a while—until a miracle reconciles them—the old man gets a taste of what his life would be like without the boy's forgiveness. The moral, of O'Connor's story and of today's Gospel, is: "We're people who've been given a big break; let's remember to give breaks in our turn."

Twenty-Fifth Sunday in Ordinary Time

Is 55:6–9; Phil 1:20–24, 27; Mt 20:1–16

"For my thoughts are not your thoughts,
nor are your ways my ways, says the LORD"
(Is 55:8).

Bill W. made no secret of the fact that he first got sober in part because of his contact in New York City with the Oxford Groups. The Oxford Groups consisted of Protestant laypeople who gathered in homes to share how Jesus had transformed their lives and solved their problems. Bill later borrowed some features of this movement for A. A. Dr. Bob, the co-founder of A. A., was a member of an Oxford Group in Akron. However, within a year or two of Bill's getting sober and helping to start what later became A. A., he found it necessary to pull his bunch of drunks, as yet unnamed, out of the parent group. He did this in part because some members of the New York Oxford Groups felt Bill shouldn't be focusing his efforts so exclusively on people as sordid as alcoholics. A trait of the Oxford Groups that Bill chose *not* to copy was their spiritual snobbery: they preferred to meet in really nice homes for spiritual weekends, not in mildewed church basements like A. A did.

The attitude to religious "'last-gaspers'" (12 X 12, 22) of some nice Christians is rather like the attitude of the workers in this week's Gospel "who have worked a full day in the scorching heat." The problem of the respectable folks is not dishonesty; they really *have* worked longer than the "eleventh hour" types, the chronically disorganized folks who only get around to *metanoia* at the very last minute. Rather, the mistake of the all-day workers is thinking that the spiritual life, or one's relationship with the Higher Power, is about all the notable things one has achieved, by which God really ought to be impressed. The truth is, if God really is as big and as good as we believe, God is not going to be easily bowled over by human accomplishments. The relationship between God and us works a lot better if it's based instead on humble gratitude for favors received. Even the great Paul doesn't blow his horn about what an Important Christian he is because he's in jail and may be sentenced to death. Instead, he sticks to the 11th Step and asks only what God's will for him is, since "I do not know which to prefer"—death, or life and more service (Phil). If, as he thinks more likely, God decides to send him back to "productive toil" in the hot sun, admittedly less glamorous than martyrdom, that's fine with him. Service work is not a bill that we eventually present to God. Rather, the chance to do *sober* service is God's gift to us—like everything else.

Twenty-Sixth Sunday in Ordinary Time

Ez 18:25–28; Phil 2:1–11; Mt 21:28–32

". . . [Jesus] did not regard equality with God as something
to be exploited, but emptied himself,
taking the form of a slave"
(Phil 2:6–7).

The parable in this Sunday's Gospel has always been a favorite of mine. The second son in this story sounds like an alcoholic; in fact, I think he sounds like me. When the father orders him to go to the vineyard, this son says, "What an order! I can't go through with it" (BB, 60). He blows up and stomps off, and broods a while, and then eventually (probably after he has decided it's really *his* idea to go), he goes. The other brother, much like the Elder Brother in the parable of the Prodigal Son, is a bright-eyed and bushy-tailed Eddie Haskell type, so of course he says yes right away. Unlike the "alcoholic brother," he doesn't tie himself into knots of guilt and defiance brooding over the father's command. Why should he? He's the respectable son. And since he doesn't think twice about his father's command, it slips his mind.

In other words, we have in this week's Gospel a story much like the one from last week: both involve working in vineyards. And in both cases, the point of the story is that Abba loves people who throw tantrums and procrastinate when first notified of their responsibilities, but eventually come around, quite as much as Abba loves the good souls who quietly shoulder their burden from the very first.

This Sunday's story is slightly different, though: instead of starting to work right away and then complaining later, like the all-day workers, about his shiftless brother's laziness, the Other Brother does no work at all. So another moral could be "Easy Does It—But Do It." Anyway, in the end, the real point is not so much the behavior of the brothers; it's God's incredible patience.

Jesus was most like God in his willingness to share fellowship even with the most ornery of humanity—even with those who tell God off and only later come sheepishly back. Jesus could do this because he had a wonderfully humble "attitude"—"[n]ever [did he] act out of rivalry or conceit" (Phil 2:3). As St. Paul urges, we should try to "change our attitude" (*metanoia*) to "Christ's." And this is why we take the 7th Step: "The Seventh Step is where we make the change in our attitude which permits us, with humility"—for Christians, the humility of Jesus giving up his life—"as our guide, to move out from ourselves toward others and toward God" (12 X 12, 76).

Twenty-Seventh Sunday in Ordinary Time

Is 5:1–7; Phil 4:6–9; Mt 21:33–43

". . . whatever is true, whatever is honorable, whatever is just,
whatever is pure, whatever is pleasing, whatever is commendable,
if there is any excellence and if there is anything worthy of praise,
think about these things"
(Phil 4:8).

In this section of the Gospel of Matthew, Jesus has entered Jerusalem and is just a few days away from his death. He is debating for the last time with the people whom he loved most, most wanted to set free, and was most frustrated by: the Pharisees, devout Jewish laymen. They were so close to "getting it"; and yet they couldn't get past, among other things, how disreputable some of Jesus' followers were.

In this Sunday's gospel parable, we are back in a vineyard, for the third Sunday in a row. Vineyards are an ancient symbol for the people of Israel, as in today's reading from Isaiah. This week's parable doesn't contrast a Pharisee-like character (the Nice Brother last week, the all-day workers the week before) with a disreputable seeker of the kingdom (the Stubborn Brother, the Workers Come Lately). Instead, they are nothing but good solid grape-growers. They are the Pharisees, who are certain that they are respectable people. But Jesus is reminding them that respectable people have always killed prophets, because prophets dress oddly and say horrible, discouraging things. Even worse, what prophets say is true, and many respectable people hate to hear ugly truths, in public or in private life.

At the literal level, the parable doesn't really work: Why would the "tenants" get the vineyard if they killed the son-and-heir? But at the allegorical level, the point is that Jesus, as Son of Abba, is trying to open up the vineyard—to open up membership in God's people— so that even the disreputable can belong. And that's what the respectable can't stand. So they'd rather die—or, better yet, have

someone else die—than let just anybody in. They seem to have forgotten that they're just "tenants"; they're acting as if they own the
vineyard already.

Note: those of us who used to be disreputable need to bear in
mind that it helps to stay grateful. Otherwise, now that—sheerly by
God's grace—we look sort of respectable, we may want to shut the
vineyard gate on the *really* disreputable people who are trying to get
in. We need to recall that it's not really our vineyard; we're just passing it on, as it was passed on to us. That's the point of "lay[ing] aside
. . . very human aspirations"—like owning a vineyard with our name
on the gate—and seeking instead the "humility" that is "expressed
by anonymity" (12 X 12, 187).

Twenty-Eighth Sunday in Ordinary Time

Is 25:6–10; Phil 4:12–14, 19–20; Mt 22:1–14

*" . . . [T]he LORD of hosts will make for all peoples a feast of rich food,
a feast of well-matured wines . . .
Then the LORD GOD will wipe away the tears from all faces"*
(Is 25:6, 8).

This Sunday Jesus moves on from the metaphor of the vineyard
to the metaphor of a banquet (a natural chain of associations:
vineyard-grapes-wine-banquet). Just as Isaiah used the vineyard as
an image of God's people Israel in the here and now, so the prophet
used the banquet as an image of God's hopes and dreams for his
chosen people hereafter. Today's passage from Isaiah looks forward
to a joyful time when "[t]he Lord God will destroy death forever.
The Lord God will wipe away the tears from every face." "On that
day"—or better, "Day," since Isaiah and the other prophets believed
that there was a New Day coming, God's Day—"the Lord of hosts
will provide for all peoples . . . juicy, rich food and pure, choice

wines." Matthew embellishes on Isaiah by making the banquet a wedding reception: Abba's Son is marrying Abba's people.

But even though we have a different symbol, the point is still the same as in the vineyard parables: Jesus is making a last-ditch effort to get through to his much-loved enemies, the Pharisees. His point this week is that the respectable people refused to come to Abba's wedding banquet. So the servants had to go out and "round up everyone they met, bad as well as good." Even those people that decent folk were certain were "bad," those people who were like weeds in wheat, were "rounded up . . . from the byroads"—what we call "the streets" these days. Some of the servants probably found some "wedding guests" in "the most sordid spot on earth," or at least at "plain ordinary whoopee parties" (BB, 101–2). But no matter where these guests were found, or what shape they were in—probably none too good in some cases—they were still God's welcome guests—and they got the places that had originally been reserved for Nice People.

Jesus and his friends liked to think that Abba's Big Party had already broken out with Jesus' "advent" among them. Whenever Jesus "broke the bread" in his special way, they all felt that the feast of the Messiah in the "hereafter" was somehow beginning here and now: the Day is today. So much was this Jesus' trademark that two disciples in Luke's Gospel recognize Jesus only when he "[breaks] the bread" (Lk 24:30–31). Bread-breaking was his characteristic gesture, like Carol Burnett tugging on her ear. And this is why we remember him when we break bread together, and why we believe that we will ultimately break bread with him in the kingdom that he came to proclaim. At that everlasting banquet, be prepared to hobnob, as at any 12-Step meeting, with some very interesting and unusual guests.

Twenty-Ninth Sunday in Ordinary Time

Is 45:1, 4–6; 1 Thes 1:1–5; Mt 22:15–21

". . . because our message of the gospel came to you not in word only,
but also in power"
(1 Thes 1:5).

In this Sunday's Gospel, Jesus' antagonists have set a trap for him.
If Jesus says, "Yes, pay your taxes," they can dismiss him as a pal of
the hated Roman occupation forces, no better than a "tax collector."
If he says, "No, don't pay them," then they can turn him in to the
Romans as a rabble-rouser. Jesus' answer "take[s them] aback,"
since apparently it steers between the two horns of the dilemma they
had set up for him. Unfortunately, it has also "taken aback" interpreters ever since: what exactly does the Lord mean?

One interpretation is that Jesus is simply refusing to take any position in this matter. From the point of view of Jesus' "primary purpose"
(see A. A's Tradition 5), Caesar just isn't that important. Jesus' "primary purpose" is to "carry [the] message" of the kingdom of God, a
reality much greater than Caesar's kingdom. After all, God, as the First
Reading from Isaiah points out, has used earthly kings like the mighty
Cyrus of Persia as mere errand boys, even when, like the Gentile
Cyrus, they had no idea that God was using them.

A. A. takes a similar position on political and other questions.
These issues need to be weighed against A. A's "primary purpose,"
which is "to carry its message to the alcoholic who still suffers." In the
light of this "purpose," many questions, important in themselves, are
irrelevant. Tradition 10 phrases it like this: "Alcoholics Anonymous
has no opinion on outside issues; hence the A. A. name ought never
be drawn into public controversy."

This does not mean, I think, that individual members of A. A.
should have no opinions on "outside issues" when these members
are outside A. A., functioning as public citizens, with their full

names. Indeed, one reason for drafting this 10th Tradition was that A. A. members are so very full of opinions. When members gather for spiritual purposes, however, the emphasis needs to be on what unites them—a common disease and a common solution—rather than on the hundreds of issues on which they disagree.

To drive the point home, consider this week's selection from Paul. We are beginning a series of readings from 1 Thessalonians, a letter of Paul's that was the first Christian Scripture; and the first words of it, after the address (which is, so to speak, on the outside of the envelope), are "Grace and peace." "Peace" was the first greeting of the risen Jesus; "peace" should characterize the groups that claim to follow him. If Christians and recovering people stick to their "primary purpose," with a little "grace" we can remain at "peace."

Thirtieth Sunday in Ordinary Time

Ex 22:20–26; 1 Thes 1:5–10; Mt 22:34–40

"If your neighbor cries out to me,
I will listen, for I am compassionate'"
(Ex 22:27).

In today's Gospel, Jesus summarizes the entire Law of Moses: we are to love God, and love our neighbors as ourselves. This second point also summarizes a concept around which a lot of the recent Sunday readings have circled: one way to love our neighbors as ourselves is to forgive them as we have been forgiven. If we believe in God, who "*is* compassion and love" (Ps 103, 8), and in Jesus, "[whom] God raised from the dead" (1 Thes) because of the compassion Jesus had displayed, we in turn ought to have compassion for our neighbor.

But who is our neighbor, as the "lawyer" asks in Luke's version of this incident (Lk 10:29; the lawyer is of course hoping to find a loophole)? As the First Reading, from the Holiness Code in Exodus makes clear, our neighbors are especially those whose rights are in the most jeopardy in a tribal society like ancient Israel: widows, orphans, and "aliens." Our neighbor is the person who is in no position to repay our kindness.

However, as we saw in the parable of the Unforgiving Servant a few weeks ago, the unfortunate human fact is that none are more likely to treat an "alien" badly than those who were themselves aliens just a little while ago. Whatever the reason for this human shortcoming, "it cannot be that way with you [followers of mine]," as Jesus said on another occasion (at the Last Supper, in Lk 22:26). As his followers, we ought to remember the ancient creed of our Jewish forebears, in Deuteronomy, which begins, "A wandering Aramean was my ancestor; he went down into Egypt and lived there as an alien . . ." (26:5).

I will never forget an A. A. member from South Africa who spoke at the 1990 world convention in Seattle. At the beginning of her talk, she said simply that in her country the 3rd Tradition ("The only requirement for membership is a desire to stop drinking") was upheld. The audience cheered, because she was hinting that, for A. A. members in her country, sobriety outweighed even apartheid. White ex-problem drinkers in South Africa remembered what not belonging felt like, and welcomed aliens, welcomed newcomers, as their "neighbors," whatever their color.

Later at that same convention, a noted singer performed "Amazing Grace." Members were reminded that they once were lost, but now were found, by God's grace. So, in the spirit of the 3rd Tradition, recovering people need to keep the door open as wide as they can for the wanderers who are constantly arriving. That is how they "will learn the full meaning of 'Love thy neighbor as thyself'" (BB, 153).

Note: In 2008, Roman Catholics will celebrate the Feast of All Souls (November 2) on the following Sunday. See the meditation in Special Feasts.

Thirty-First Sunday in Ordinary Time

Mal 1:14–2:2, 8–10; 1 Thes 2:7–9, 13; Mt 23:1–12

"'The greatest among you will be your servant'"
(Mt 23:11).

Over the next several Sundays we reflect on the end of this year in the Church's life and the beginning (traditionally associated with the Advent season) of another year. The end of a cycle is often an occasion for reflection, for inventory; we may as a group be especially conscious at such times of our unhealed, unreconciled relationships.

And so this Sunday we have a harsh gospel reading, growing out of a failure to communicate that still needs healing. This reading probably does not reflect the situation during Jesus' lifetime. Rather, this denunciation of the Pharisees reflects the bitter feud between Christians and Jews that had grown up by the time of Matthew's Gospel, and especially in Matthew's Jewish-Christian community (see the Twenty-Fourth Sunday in Ordinary Time). This violent attack—which occupies an entire chapter in Matthew, not just the passage in today's Gospel—should not be an occasion for those of us who have found a Way Out to look down our noses at those who, we believe, have *not* found it, at those we may consider the "Pharisees" of our day. Remember: *St. Paul* was a Pharisee, and proud of it. Many Pharisees were good people. Jesus particularly loved them, loved them enough to struggle with them and for them.

The real problem, as "How It Works" (BB, chap. 5) makes clear, is not that someone is a Pharisee (or a Christian, for that matter); the problem is an inability to be honest. M. Scott Peck says human evil can most easily be discerned in "the people of the lie": these are people who cannot admit they are flawed, broken, and powerless, that they have failed, that they need help. They cannot take the 1st Step. They cannot ask for God's help, or anyone else's. They can't do any of these things because they believe they can't afford to: their God, they think, would abandon them if they admitted their imperfection.

We used to be people like that, before grace ended our "alien" days. Let us remember those days, now that we have been given the gift of "the capacity to be honest" (BB, 58). This might be a good week to repeat the 4th Step Prayer: "When a person offend[s] we [say] to ourselves, 'This is a sick man [or woman]. How can I be helpful to [them]? God save me from being angry. Thy will be done'" (BB, 67).

Note: In 2008, Roman Catholics will celebrate the Feast of the Dedication of the Church of St. John Lateran (November 9) on the following Sunday. See the meditation in Special Feasts.

Thirty-Second Sunday in Ordinary Time

Wis 6:12–16; 1 Thes 4:13–18; Mt 25:1–13

"Keep awake therefore,
for you know neither the day nor the hour"
(Mt 25:13).

During these Sundays when we are ruminating on the end of all things, it's natural to think about the return of Jesus at the end of time. To grasp Paul's point this Sunday in 1 Thessalonians, and often in his other letters, we need to recall that Paul and his generation of Christians (around the mid-50s A.D.) firmly believed that Jesus was going to come back very soon. In fact, they wanted him to, because he had been such a marvelous, compassionate person, and they wanted to see him and touch him as his first disciples had. Only gradually, and with some regret, did Christians come to acknowledge that the Return of Jesus was apparently not imminent. This change can be traced through the Gospels: in Mark, the earliest, there is a lively sense that Jesus is coming back soon. In Matthew and Luke, which are middling (say, the 80s) there is more of a sense that there's plenty of time to form a fellowship before Jesus' return. In John, probably the latest, there is a greater emphasis on meeting Jesus in our everyday lives.

Once Christians accepted the notion that it was going to be a long haul, there was a natural tendency "to let up on the spiritual program of action and rest on [their] laurels" (BB, 85). Matthew directs this Sunday's parable at them, to remind them that "[e]very day is a day when we must carry the vision of God's will into all of our activities" (BB, 85).

We do not know the day of Jesus' Big Return; indeed, just before today's gospel passage Jesus says that even the Son doesn't know it—only Abba does. And that's a good thing; since we don't know about the Big Return, we can focus on the millions of Little Returns, when Jesus asks for our help, Jesus in the form of the poor, the sick, and the imprisoned. Matthew's Gospel, in which, early on, the Sermon on the Mount stated the theme, is building to a climax. That climax will come on the last Sunday of this church year, when the Roman Catholic Church celebrates the Feast of Christ the King. The gospel reading from Matthew on that feast will be Jesus' closing statement, in which the final Beatitude is proclaimed: Blessed are those who can see Jesus *now*, in all who "still suffer" (Tradition 5). As Bill W. reminds us, "Near you, alcoholics are dying helplessly like people in a sinking ship. If you live in a large place, there are hundreds" (BB, 152). May God "keep our eyes open," "ready" to see them.

Thirty-Third Sunday in Ordinary Time

Prv 31:10–13, 19–20, 30–31; 1 Thes 5:1–6; Mt 25:14–30

"So then let us not fall asleep as others do,
but let us keep awake
and be sober"
(1 Thes 5:6).

The parable in today's Gospel is one of my favorites. The One-Talent Man always reminds me of the male characters in the fiction of the great American novelist Henry James (his brother, the philosopher-psychologist William James, is one of the "godfathers" of A. A.—see BB, 28). Take John Marcher in Henry James's story "The Beast in the Jungle," for instance: he spends his whole life telling a close woman friend that he believes he has been marked out for a special fate, so special that he can make no commitments in the meantime. He thinks of it as a "beast in the jungle," ready to pounce on him at any moment.

The woman guesses the truth about his fate, but refuses to tell him what it is. After she dies, he finally "gets it" one day when he is visiting her grave and notices another man at another tombstone. The other man, a widower, is distraught with grief for his wife. Marcher now realizes his own special fate: to be a person without a life, because he never took the chance of reaching out to the woman who loved him. Because he had "never wanted to deal with the fact of suffering" (12 X 12, 74), he has never experienced any other emotion, either. The 50-ish bachelor Lambert Strether, in James's novel *The Ambassadors*, comes to a similar realization: he tells a group of young people at a garden party that they should have their lives—because, if they don't, what *will* they have?

Marcher and Strether are soul brothers of the One-Talent Man, who is so afraid of the Master who bestows talents that he doesn't use his "talent" for anything; he just buries it. But to whine that one's gift is too small to be of much use to anybody is a huge failure of gratitude to God, the source of "every generous act of giving, with every perfect gift" (Jas 1:17). Nor does the Master/God have to heap punishments on the ungrateful: knowing that you have thrown your life away is punishment enough.

This story fits with last week's and next week's Gospel. The moral of all three is that we need at any moment to be ready to use the gifts God has given us, because Jesus is returning all the time. Our greatest gift as recovering people is, I think, our story; our story is our message. And if we do not "carry" that "message" to others, if we do not work our 12th Step, we bury our talent. The last words that the great Broadway lyricist Oscar Hammerstein wrote go in part, "A song's not a song till you sing it / A bell's not a bell till you ring it." And a story's not a story till you tell it.

Feast of Christ the King

Ez 34:11–12, 15–17; 1 Cor 15:20–26, 28; Mt 25:31–46

"I myself will be the shepherd of my sheep,
and I will make them lie down, says the LORD GOD.
I will seek the lost, and I will bring back the strayed,
and I will bind up the injured,
and I will strengthen the weak,
but the fat and the strong I will destroy.
I will feed them with justice"
(Ez 34:15–16).

The last Sunday in the church year is called the Feast of Christ the King in the Roman Catholic community. This feast was established by Pope Pius XI in 1931, in part because he wanted to remind his contemporaries that the kingdom which Jesus announced can never be identified with a particular nation or form of government. This was especially important in a decade that saw the rise of fascism in Italy and Germany, but it's a point we need to keep in mind today, too. All people have a place in the kingdom that is coming, not just the ones we believe are on our side because they dress or talk or think like we do.

The parable in Matthew today is Jesus' final statement before his passion and death. He is, once and for all, announcing the membership requirement for the kingdom of Abba. When Jesus first told this story, it may have carried a comparatively narrow moral, something like this: if you support missionaries and preachers, those who carry the message, you will receive a reward like theirs (a point made in the Missionary Discourse in Mt 10).

But given the position of the parable of the Sheep and the Goats in Matthew, just before Jesus lays down his life for "all the nations," it makes sense to broaden its application, as Christians have done from early on. In this interpretation, it's not just about bedraggled missionaries, but about all who need help, the "widows," "orphans," and "aliens" of the Hebrew Scriptures, the sick and naked and hungry of this passage. Christians have understood it this way in every age, believing that in touching the needy in Jesus' name, they touched Jesus.

In 12-Step terms, this point can be expressed by citing two phrases from the 12th Step: if we have "had a spiritual awakening," we do more than "carry the message to alcoholics," we also "practice these principles in *all* our affairs" (my emphasis). As Jesus pointed out a few weeks ago, the great principle is to love God wholeheartedly and our neighbor as ourselves. Who is my neighbor? "The alcoholic who still suffers" (Tradition 5), of course: "it happens that because of your own drinking experience you can be uniquely useful to other alcoholics" (BB, 89). But love tends to spread, or, as the great theologian Thomas Aquinas put it, *Bonum est diffusivum sibi* ("The Good pours itself out"—see Meditations 49 and 50 in *A 12-Step Approach to the Spiritual Exercises*). And so compassion will come to characterize "all our affairs," our relationships with addicts, and co-addicts, and "normies" as well.

CYCLE B

December 2002–2003
December 2005–2006
December 2008–2009

✛

Advent
and Christmas

First Sunday of Advent

Is 63:16–17, 19; 64:2–7; 1 Cor 1:3–9; Mk 13:33–37

"God is faithful; by him you were called
into the fellowship of his Son, Jesus Christ our Lord"
(1 Cor 1:9).

This quotation from St. Paul was ornately inscribed over the door of the main classroom in my novitiate (first stage of Jesuit formation, as well as the building in which it takes place). Since this was thirty-five years ago, the quotation was in Latin, then the official language of the Roman Catholic Church. In Latin the word for "fellowship" is *societas,* as in the official Latin name of the Jesuits, which is *Societas Jesu*—"the fellowship of Jesus" (hence the S.J. initials). As someone from a long line of alcoholics, on both sides of the family, I felt a fierce need to belong, so I took great comfort in these words. I interpreted this bit of Scripture over the classroom door to mean that I really belonged in this particular Jesuit "fellowship," on the word of no less than God, who had "called" me, despite my cheesy heritage.

For many years after that I resisted the gradually dawning notion that I also possessed the qualifications to belong to a different fellowship, the one to which so many of the males on both the German and the Irish sides of my heritage had belonged. This was the fellowship of those who are consoled by alcohol, however briefly, for the fact that life never seems grand or safe enough. I could never have believed during those drinking years that God had anything to do with my being "called" to this "fellowship." Indeed, I had probably sought membership in the Jesuit "fellowship" with a largely unacknowledged desire to bury deeply these grubby roots of mine. But in time, those roots produced—predictably, in retrospect—blooming alcoholism.

And still God is faithful. When I finally sought help for my alcoholism, I learned that I was called to yet another fellowship, a fellowship of the spirit that links recovering women and men. And I have since learned that my belonging to this society has made me an infinitely better member of the Society of Jesus, and of the largest fellowship of all—the fellowship of struggling human beings.

As we begin another Advent, I give thanks again that I have been spiritually awakened, like the servants of the homecoming traveler in today's Gospel. My awakening was quiet; God did not "rend the heavens and come down, with the mountains quaking," as Isaiah prayed. But since I woke up, God, who is the "potter" to our "clay" (Is), has done deeds of faithfulness for me that I never would have imagined back in my novitiate.

Second Sunday of Advent

Is 40:1–5, 9–11; 2 Pt 3:8–14; Mk 1:1–8

"A voice cries out: 'In the wilderness prepare the way [i.e., road] of the LORD, make straight in the desert a highway for our God'"
(Is 40:3).

This year we will be reading from the Gospel of Mark most Sundays. A few words about Mark. Since it was the first Gospel written, its style is a bit down-home compared to Matthew's or Luke's, but that also makes Mark more vivid, like country-and-western songs. Matthew's theme, as I noted last year, was that Jesus is the New Moses, fulfilling the Law. Mark's theme is announced in the first line of his work: this is "the gospel [good news] of Jesus Christ, the Son of God." Mark will shape his work to show how this truth was only gradually perceived by the people about Jesus. Some of them didn't get it at all; Mark attributes this to Jesus' keeping it a secret until the right time—the time of the crucifixion and resurrection.

Matthew and Luke, writing twenty or thirty years after Mark, often base their Gospels on Mark's, with additions from other materials, and with changes that Luke and Matthew make in the light of their themes and their audiences. So today's Gospel should sound familiar, since we read Matthew's later version of it on the Second Sunday of Advent last year. John the Baptist is in the wilderness, preaching *metanoia* ("change your attitude, get a new story/life"). This theme of *metanoia* turns up constantly all through the Christian Scriptures, from a document as early as Mark's Gospel, to 2 Peter, the last piece of the Christian Scriptures to be written: God "wants none to perish but all to come to *metanoia*."

Mark sees John the Baptist, the central figure of the Second and Third Sundays of Advent each year, as the fulfillment of a prophecy of Isaiah. This part of Isaiah was written for the Jews who had been taken to Babylon after the fall of Jerusalem in 587 B.C.E. Isaiah "comfort[s]" the exiles by depicting a herald, "a voice," who announces the road in the desert on which the exiles will be returning home to the Promised Land. For recovering people, this desert can remind us of the days before recovery—days of thirst, days of wandering, days of wishing we could go home, but with no idea of how to get back on the road. Lucky for us there were people who showed us how to get a *metanoia*, and so put us, on the "highway" (Is) of "Happy Destiny" (BB, 164).

Third Sunday of Advent

Is 61:1–2, 10–11; 1 Thes 5:16–24; Jn 1:6–8, 19–28

"[God]has sent me . . . to comfort all who mourn; . . . to give
them . . . the oil of gladness instead of mourning, the mantle
of praise instead of a faint spirit"
(Is 61:1, 2, 3).

This Sunday we have a passage, not from the first Gospel (Mark), but from the last written, John. John's Gospel benefits from many more years of thought and prayer about the story of Jesus, so it's useful to get John's reflections on the significance of John the Baptist.

When I think of John the Baptist, I remember a man I'll call Calvin. A fiercely committed member of A. A., he had a lot of hair, including a shaggy beard, and a prophet's fiery zeal about recovery. He denounced any other approaches to sobriety (psychiatry, medicine, and so on), because they had failed to help him. He announced one evening that the topic of a particular meeting would be "How alcoholism treatment centers are an invention of the devil." Some newcomers to A. A. he helped; others he terrified. He died a prophet's death, as I think he would have wanted: having heard that recovering people in Los Angeles weren't "doing it right," he was driving there to straighten out the ex-drunks. He had a heart attack in the mountains above L.A., standing next to his pick-up truck loaded with Big Books, looking down on and gloating over the wicked city on which he was about to descend. Kaddish, Calvin.

John the Evangelist makes very clear that John the Baptist is "a witness to testify to the light," but is "not the light." Like Calvin, the Baptist was certainly sincere, but he was pretty ferocious, like the prophets before him in the Hebrew Scriptures. He would have made a frightening Messiah (for more thoughts on John, see his birthday, June 24th, in Special Feasts). Lucky for us, then, that the "real light" was Jesus. Jesus, by contrast with John, adopted the gentle words of Isaiah, in the First Reading today, as his charter at the beginning of his ministry: God "has sent me to bring glad tidings to the lowly, to heal the brokenhearted, to proclaim liberty to captives" (see Luke 4).

That Jesus is this kind of Messiah should be "glad tidings" (Is), "good news" (which is what *gospel* means), for "the alcoholic who has lost all and is locked up" (BB, 62), or for anyone else who feels imprisoned, either by personal compulsion or by social injustice. Those who have experienced the "real light" (Jn) have come to know "a new freedom and a new happiness" (BB, 83); they are no longer "brokenhearted" or "captives." Such people will find it easy to comply with "God's will for you," which is to "[r]ejoice always, never cease praying, render constant thanks" (1 Thes). Or, as Bill W. phrases it, "We are sure God wants us to be happy, joyous, and free" (BB, 133).

Fourth Sunday of Advent

2 Sm 7:1–5, 8–11, 16; Rom 16:25–27; Lk 1:26–38

*"Now to God who is able to strengthen you according
to my gospel, . . . to the only wise God, through Jesus Christ,
to whom be the glory forever! Amen"*
(Rom 16:25, 27).

The Gospel of Mark, since it was the first, doesn't bring up Jesus'
birth or childhood; interest in those events came later. By the time of
Luke's Gospel, for example, there was a great deal of interest in
Jesus' origins. Since the Fourth Sunday of Advent always focuses on
Mary, the mother of Jesus, we turn this week from Mark's Gospel to
Luke's, and specifically to Luke's description of the moment when
it was announced to Mary that she would give birth to a "great," a
"holy" child.

Two important words in Luke's story of Mary's "spiritual awakening" are *grace* (translated "favor" here) and *power.* The word for
"grace" (*charis*) can mean several things—a stroke of luck, or the
gratitude one feels for that luck (cf. *eucharist*, which means "giving
thanks"). *Charis* can also mean "joy." And finally, it is a greeting (as
Australians now say "g'day," in Jesus' time people said "Rejoice").
So the angel greets Mary thus: "Rejoice, you who have plenty of reason to rejoice."

Yet it may not have seemed to this young girl—probably thirteen
or fourteen, the usual age for marriage when women were often old
at thirty—that she had much reason to be grateful. As she points
out to the angel, she is not yet married, while the message is that
she is nevertheless to become pregnant. If she accepts God's will for
her, she'll be, as Bill W. might put it, "in an awful jam." Should she
turn her will and her life over to a God whose plans for her are this
frightening?

The answer lies in God's power, "the power of the Most High." When the angel reminds Mary that "nothing is impossible with God," the word for "impossible" echoes the word for "power." "Lack of power" is her "dilemma" (see BB, 45); but when the angel assures her that God has power, and then some, she takes her 3rd Step. As Paul notes in his prayer to God this week, God is the One who "is able" (from the same word for "power"). God "is able to strengthen" the powerless: so it is wise to "trust infinite God rather than our finite selves" (BB, 68), as Mary does, thus reversing Eve's bad primordial decision (a point often made about Mary, with the added fillip that "Ave," the angel's greeting in Latin to Mary, is "Eva" [Eve] backward).

Just after today's Gospel, a female relative of Mary will pronounce this beatitude on her: "And blessed is she who believed that there would be a fulfillment of what was spoken to her by the Lord" (Lk 1:45). Blessed too are we who have trusted that a Power greater than ourselves could do "great things for" us (Step 2 and Mary's song in Lk 1:49). God's power has made us "happy, joyous, and free" (BB, 133).

Christmas, Mass at Dawn

Is 62:11–12; Ti 3:4–7; Lk 2:15–20

"The shepherds returned, glorifying and praising God
for all they had heard and seen,
as it had been told them"
(Lk 2:20).

Last year we studied the readings for the Christmas Mass at midnight. That gospel reading, from Luke, told about the confusion surrounding Jesus' birth in Bethlehem, and about the announcement of the good news to some "shepherds in that region, living in the fields." This year we focus on the Mass at dawn, the Gospel which

picks up where last year's left off. The shepherds follow up on the
angels' message by "go[ing] over . . . in haste" to Bethlehem.

To get in the mood to contemplate the scene of the shepherds'
visit to Jesus and his parents, you might want, if you're a music
lover, to listen to the Pastorale from Handel's *Messiah*; Bach and
Corelli also wrote pieces depicting the shepherds' visit, which has
been a favorite subject for composers and painters. Music that characterizes the shepherds tends to be homely and simple, which under-
lines the point I made last year: the good news of Jesus' birth is
brought first to ordinary people, of no great importance in the world.
The Hebrew Scriptures called such people the *anawim*, the lowly; in
Matthew's Beatitudes, Jesus follows those Scriptures in proclaiming
the lowly to be specially loved and blessed by God.

In reflecting on the further adventures of the shepherds, I'd like
to emphasize a favorite word of Luke's, used often in the first two
chapters of his Gospel, chapters portraying the birth of Jesus. The
word is *rhema*, and it means "word," "announcement," "something
said." Luke used it in a key sentence in last Sunday's Gospel of the
announcement to Mary: when Gabriel assured Mary that God's
power was sufficient to manage events, the angel's reassuring words,
translated "nothing is impossible with God," literally mean "everything said (*rhema*) is possible with God." In our Gospel this Christmas morning, *rhema* shows up three times: the shepherds decide to
go to Bethlehem and check out "this *rhema* that has happened"; once
they see the baby, they understand "the *rhema* about the little one";
and Mary, who has by now had acquaintance with more than one
rhema, "treasures" and "reflects" on them all.

In other words, we're not just talking about a baby here; we're
also talking about a message, a *rhema*, which needs to be carried,
as in the 12th Step. The shepherds "carry the message": "All who
heard [the *rhema*] were astonished at the report given them by the
shepherds." The content of this message is that God "through
Jesus Christ" is a Savior, full of "kindness and love" for human
beings (Ti). Or, as the angels sang to the shepherds, ". . . and on
earth peace among those whom he favors!" (Lk 2:14). The *rhema* of

recovery is similarly gentle yet powerful: "What seemed at first a flimsy reed, has proved to be the loving and powerful hand of God" (BB, 28; Bill W. is alluding to Is 42:3, on God's gentle Servant).

Holy Family

Sir 3:2–6, 12–14; Col 3:12–21; Lk 2:22–40

"'Master, now you are dismissing your servant in peace, according to your word [rhema—see Christmas, above]'" (Lk 2:29).

Note: In 2006, since Christmas and New Year's fall on Sunday, this Feast of the Holy Family is not celebrated on the weekend. Today's Gospel is also used on the Feast of the Presentation, February 2: see Special Feasts.

In reflecting on this feast last year, I mentioned that, for a lot of recovering people, families, current or remembered, are a large part of what makes holidays painful. So it may be a bit risky this year to spotlight today's reading from Paul, especially since the last few lines reflect the very patriarchal family values of Paul's time, not of ours. Nevertheless, Paul urges us to "practice" some excellent "principles" here. These principles can help to create peaceful families, not just during the holidays, but all year round.

Morally speaking, Paul advocates dressing in layers. One of the virtues on a lower layer is "heartfelt mercy." These words could be more literally translated "deep-down willingness to say 'Oy!' along with someone else"—a very Jewish form of empathy (see Cycle C, Seventh Sunday in Ordinary Time). A second virtue that Paul cites is "humility," literally "low-mindedness." For most Greek speakers, this was, in fact, a negative quality; but Jews like Paul thought humility was "dressier," partly because of their tradition of the *anawim* (see Christmas, above; Simeon and Anna in today's Gospel are *anawim*).

"Low-mindedness" also has a high rating in recovering circles, where it is considered "the nourishing ingredient which can give us serenity" by "transform[ing] . . . failure and misery . . . into priceless assets" (12 X 12, 74, 75). "Meekness" echoes Matthew's Sermon on the Mount, as well as the First Tradition: we need "meekness" in order to place "our common welfare . . . first." And then there's "patience," which literally means "large-heartedness." Finally, in the spirit of the Lord's Prayer, and of the 9th Step, Paul tells us to give one another a break, as the Lord has given us a break: "Forgive as the Lord has forgiven you."

The top layer of clothing, of course, is love. Paul switches metaphors here: in addition to being a kind of moral overcoat, love is also a sort of belt or sash that "binds the rest together and makes them perfect." Love is the finishing touch. If we "wear" an ensemble like this, the natural results will be serenity ("peace") and gratitude ("thankfulness").

These qualities may or may not characterize the biological families from which we came. But with practice of the 12-Step programs, there's a good chance that they can characterize the spiritual "families" we have chosen and created. And these "families" are also a part of God's design for us: "as members of the one body you have been called to that peace. . . . Give thanks . . ."

January 1, New Year's Day

Nm 6: 22-27; Gal 4: 4-7; Lk 2: 16-21

"The LORD bless you and keep you;
the LORD make his face shine upon you,
and be gracious to you;
the LORD lift up his countenance upon you"
(Nm 6:24–26).

Last year we reflected on the Gospel for today, about the circumcision and the naming of Jesus. This year let's consider the fact that this is the first day of the New Year (at least in some cultures), and focus on the First Reading. This reading contains the blessing that "Aaron and his sons," the priestly clan, were supposed to recite over the people. It asks that God would smile on us, that God would be "gracious" and "kind" to us, and thus give us "peace" and prosperity, especially as a new year on the "Road of Happy Destiny" begins.

A good blessing and one Bill W. liked enough to include at the end of the first part of the Big Book: on p. 164 he says, "Still you [a prospective A. A. member] may say: 'But I will not have the benefit of contact with you who write this book.' We cannot be sure. God will determine that . . . Give freely of what you find and join us. We shall be with you in the Fellowship of the Spirit, and you will surely meet some of us as you trudge the Road of Happy Destiny.

"May God bless you and keep you—until then."

This blessing of Aaron was given to Moses by God, who remarks, "This is how [the priests are to] invoke my *name* upon the Israelites." The power of the blessing comes from the use of God's name. We considered last year the name of Jesus, bestowed at his circumcision, and what his being called Savior implied for those of us who have experienced the narrow confines of powerlessness and unmanageability. And during our study of Matthew last year we noted that Jesus' name for God was Abba. But what was the name by which Moses knew God ("my name")?

Moses asks God for God's name at the scene of the Burning Bush in Exodus 3. God is sending Moses to "carry [God's] message" to Moses' people, so Moses believes that, to do this task, he needs the power that comes from knowing God's own name. The sounds with which God replies to Moses are so sacred that no devout Jew will utter them, and their meaning is not perfectly clear. However, experts believe it may mean something like "the One who simply is." As we enter into all the changes this new year will bring, let us once again "turn our will and our lives over" (3rd Step) to the powerful One who is always there, and who blesses us day after day.

Epiphany

Is 60:1–6; Eph 3:2–3, 5–6; Mt 2:1–12

"Nations shall come to your light,
and kings to the brightness of your dawn"
(Is 60:3).

Last year my theme on this feast was the meaning of the word *epiphany*, the "shining out of light" on the world. This year I'd like to underscore that what has been "revealed by the Spirit" (Eph) is for the *whole* world.

The author of the Third Part of Isaiah (Is 56–66) looks forward to a day when "Nations shall walk by [the] light of" Jerusalem, city of God's people, and when "the wealth of nations shall be brought to you." That is, even Gentiles, *goyim*, will come to Jerusalem to worship "the One who simply is." Ephesians announces that this prophecy has come true in Jesus: "the *goyim* are now co-heirs with the Jews."

Ephesians (probably written in the spirit of Paul by a disciple of his) calls this inclusion even of the Gentiles a "secret plan," a *mysterion*. The word *mystery* comes from this Greek word, which does not mean "something inscrutable," but rather "something clear to those in the know," like people who read the last page of a mystery story first.

If we read Ephesians, of course, we will be in the know. But, as with any good mystery, there had been plenty of hints along the way, for instance, from people like Isaiah. However, most people didn't catch these hints, because an optimistic vision like Isaiah's, in which Gentiles and Jews become one, often seemed like an impossible dream, given the events of Jewish history. In fact, during the centuries after Isaiah, many Jews became very bitter about their persecution by some *goyim*, like the Syrian king Antiochus Epiphanes (circa 165 B.C.E.), or like the Romans during the time of Jesus and

Paul. The last thing these Jews would have wanted was sharing faith and worship with the *goyim*.

Paul, in his early life just such an exclusivist, nevertheless celebrated in his writings the fact that the old dream had finally come true. Today's Gospel depicts the moment when it came true: the astrologers come "from the east," and may well be *goyim*. And, like the Jewish shepherds, they come to worship. The astrologers make a well-matched set with Luke's shepherds as early followers of Jesus. His mission was to just such "lost sheep," the poor, the outcast, the un-belonging—even the *goyim*. If the God of Jesus is our Higher Power, let's celebrate on this feast "the well-understood fact that in God's sight all human beings are important" (12 X 12, 124).

Baptism of the Lord

Is 42:1–4, 6–7; Acts 10:34–38; Mk 1:7–11

Note: In 2006, this feast of the Baptism of the Lord is not celebrated on a Sunday; go straight from Epiphany to the Second Sunday in Ordinary Time.

"I have called you in righteousness . . . to open the eyes
that are blind, to bring out the prisoners from the dungeon,
from the prison those who sit in darkness"
(Is 42:6–7).

As in every church year, the Christmas season (focused largely on Jesus' childhood) ends with a remembrance of Jesus' baptism by John (the gateway to Jesus' adulthood). All four Gospels, each in its different way, describe the baptism, because the early Christian church saw this as a defining moment for Jesus, his coming of age, his realization of his identity and of his mission from God. Today's reading from Acts underscores this: how did Jesus' story begin? The apostle Peter says that it began (as it literally does in the Gospels of

Mark and John) "in Galilee with the baptism John preached." It began when Jesus was anointed by God "with the Holy Spirit and power."

What's special about Mark, the first Gospel, which we are reading this year, is that he depicts Jesus' "anointing" as almost a private event, a personal insight, of Jesus'. In the other Gospels there's mention of the crowd, or at least of John the Baptist, being witnesses of Abba's endorsement of Jesus, but not in Mark. According to Mark, "Immediately on coming up out of the water [Jesus] saw the sky rent in two and the Spirit descending on him [that is, Jesus] like a dove. Then a voice came from the heavens: 'You [not 'He' as in other versions of the baptism] are my beloved Son. On you my favor rests.'"

Mark's Jesus, after years of 11th-Step work, has a spiritual awakening, and realizes at some deep level that he is Abba's Son. He "intuitively know[s]" (BB, 84) what he should do about this new insight: he should go about spreading the good news of Abba's kingdom. Nor was this a spiritual experience of the "educational variety" (BB, 569); Jesus "suddenly realize[d]" (BB, 84) that Abba would do for him what he could not do for himself. "Suddenly" is one of Mark's favorite words (translated "immediately" in this passage); he uses it forty times, so that his Gospel is full of gasps of surprise and insight.

However we understand God, and whether we came to this understanding "suddenly" or gradually, all of us who have felt the Promises come true in our lives feel like we belong here and have a purpose. In the light of the Steps of the program, we have also come to a clear and healthy sense of who we are before God, and what God's purpose is for us. We believe that we are ex-prisoners who have been freed from "confinement" (Is). So, like Jesus, we try to carry this message to others.

✦

Lent
and Easter

First Week of Lent

Gn 9:8–15; 1 Pt 3:18–22; Mk 1:12–15

*"Now after John was arrested, Jesus came to Galilee,
proclaiming the good news of God, and saying,
'The time is fulfilled, and the kingdom of God has come near;
repent, and believe in the good news!'"*
(Mk 1:14–15).

Jesus goes out into the desert after his baptism by John. Mark puts it more forcefully: the Spirit *drove* him out. The Spirit had just helped Jesus to realize that he was God's beloved; now Jesus has to wrestle with what kind of beloved he will be. So he spends forty days in the desert, reminding us of the forty years his people spent there; it will be a liberating experience for him, as it had been for them. What he needs to be freed from is clear enough in Mark, even though he doesn't spell it out the way Matthew and Luke do.

Instead, Mark tersely observes that "Satan" tested Jesus, and mentions "wild beasts" and "angels." Even this brief note gives some sense of what's at stake in this "test." Will Jesus behave in a "merely human" way, by acting out of the "fleshy" kinship all human beings share with "wild beasts"? Or will he take the high road, in fidelity to Someone greater than himself, greater even than angels?

Matthew and Luke more specifically state that Jesus was tempted to cash in on his special relationship with God, to be a fast-food Messiah. But the fact that his first move after his baptismal encounter with God is to pray, in Mark's Gospel as in the others, rather than to spread the word "at the level of press, radio, and films" (Tradition 11), tells us that he's already on the right track. So does the message with which he returns from "the wasteland": "Reform your lives [*metanoete*—Greek for 'Our whole attitude and outlook upon life will change,' BB, 84] and believe in the gospel!" He does *not* say, "I'm full of power—trust me and send money."

112

Deserts have always been a place where people go to "improve [their] conscious contact with God" (11th Step). God let the children of Israel wander in the desert to see if they could keep going, rather than turn back to their old addictions (the proverbial "fleshpots of Egypt"). Jesus' desert experience served a similar purpose. And this Lenten season, of about forty days, gives us too our annual chance to see if "out of [this] season" we can learn "new lessons for living" (12 X 12, 105), can come "to know a new freedom and a new happiness" (BB, 83). The best place to share any of these "lessons" is "a fellowship" of men and women. And specifically men and women who—to switch metaphors from desert to ocean—resemble "the passengers of a great liner the moment after rescue," or the survivors aboard Noah's Ark, saved from "the world tide of alcoholism" (BB, 17, 153; see today's baptism-flavored reading from 1 Peter).

Second Week of Lent

Gn 22:1–2, 9, 10–13, 15–18; Rom 8:31–34; Mk 9:2–10

"He who did not withhold his own Son, but gave him up
for all of us, will he not with him also give us everything else?"
(Rom 8:32).

The story of Abraham and Isaac has shocked and fascinated people for centuries, including, for example, St. Paul and the Danish spiritual writer Kierkegaard. Wilfred Owen, the doomed English poet who fought in World War I, also retold the story, but gave it a different ending. In Owen's version, Abraham refuses to substitute "the ram of pride"; instead, he kills "his son." And, with a nod to the Elder Statesmen who insisted on waging World War I, the "war to end all wars," Abraham also kills "half the seed of Europe, one by one." Owen's scathing revision of this ancient story only serves to underscore the questions it raises: What kind of parents even consider sacrificing their own child? What kind of God asks a parent to do this?

Whatever the story may have meant at the time of Abraham, our Gospel today suggests that we consider it in the context of Jesus' own suffering. But this only makes it harder to answer the question, Why would God want a son killed? Even though Jesus is being transfigured in glory, with the approving words of God echoed from his baptism, Mark also flashes forward to Jesus' agony in Gethsemane. The words "Jesus took Peter, James and John off by themselves" in today's glorious Gospel will be repeated when Jesus enters the Garden of his great suffering. In Gethsemane Jesus will call God Abba, the only time in the Gospels when he uses this Aramaic word for Father. All of this makes even more acute our question today: If Jesus is God's beloved and radiant Son, why does he have to die so horribly? Even Abraham's beloved son didn't have to die; Isaac got a bad scare, but at the last moment a ram was substituted.

Mark's way of answering this question is that Jesus' willingness to suffer is precisely his way of being the "beloved Son," of being the "Messiah." He is neither a brutal commander-in-chief nor a flashy charlatan—the Temptations settled that. Mark especially is trying by his Gospel to make clear the gentle kind of Messiah Jesus is trying to be, at great cost to Jesus. Why must Jesus die? Because only by this act of unconditional love can Jesus be a good Son to God by showing who God really is.

If you study the whole story of Jesus, the beginning, this transfiguring moment in the middle, and the ending, "[t]hen you will know what it means to give of yourself that others may survive and rediscover life" (BB, 153). Then you will know how to "carry the message," to provide "[s]ervice, gladly rendered" (12th Step; 12 X 12, 124).

Third Week of Lent

Ex 20:1–17; 1 Cor 1:22–25; Jn 2:13–25

". . . [W]e proclaim Christ crucified . . . to those who are the called,
both Jews and Greeks, Christ the power of God
and the wisdom of God"
(1 Cor 1:23, 24).

In both the selection from Paul and in the Gospel today, people ask for "signs," "signs" that will prove that Jesus is who he claims to be. Paul feels that asking for signs is characteristic of his fellow Jews. Given their history, it's easy to see why they would: Moses' God had showed the Israelites a sign first, by having Moses lead them from slavery to freedom, before God asked them to return the favor by adopting God's commandments. Their descendants, Jesus' contemporaries, naturally wanted Jesus in his turn to show some credentials to justify a "powerful" act like driving the money changers out of the Temple. Like these challengers of Jesus, alcoholics tend to be skeptical, to want some kind of proof, before they'll risk having faith in someone.

Paul says that the Greeks, for their part, being *goyim* and so unfamiliar with God's powerful acts of liberation on behalf of God's people, Israel, ask for "wisdom" rather than "signs." *Wisdom* in this context suggests one of the philosophical systems, like Plato's or Aristotle's, that are Greek specialties. But whatever the merits of these systems for "normal men [and women]" (BB, 66), alcoholics mostly find that they need something stronger: "If a mere code of morals or a better philosophy of life were sufficient to overcome alcoholism, many of us would have recovered long ago . . . Many of us had moral and philosophical convictions galore, but we could not live up to them even though we would have liked to. . . . [T]he needed power wasn't there" (BB, 45, 62).

Paul's response to Greeks and Jews—and alcoholics—is that Jesus offers a paradoxical wisdom in which power flows out of weakness. In fact, one of Paul's favorite notions is that God's "weakness [is] more powerful than [human beings]." If so, a human being is wise to follow "Christ crucified" (1 Cor) by acknowledging weakness, as 12 Steppers do in the 1st Step, so that "new power [can] flow in" (BB, 63). This "new power" is the solution to our "dilemma," which is "lack of power" (BB, 45). This "new power" is also the sign—so quiet, so "educational" that you might miss it—that alcoholics are looking for.

Both the "sign" and the "wisdom" that Jesus offers are paradoxical. At first blush, they don't seem like "signs" and "wisdom" at all, especially to alcoholics, who tend to be "worldly indeed" (BB, 50). But if like Jesus we can become "aware of" changes "in the human heart" (Jn), and especially in our own, we may "come to believe" that we have found a "folly" that is "wiser" than wisdom, and a power in weakness that is "more powerful" than power.

Fourth Week of Lent

2 Chr 36:14–17, 19–23; Eph 2:4–10; Jn 3:14–21

"For we are what he had made us, created in Christ Jesus for good works, which God prepared beforehand to be our way of life"
(Eph 2:10).

At the end of A. A. meetings, after the closing prayer, people frequently recite this tag: "Keep coming back; it works if you work it." This always gives me the theological shivers, for reasons that are hinted at in today's reading from Ephesians. I worry that people will hear this tag as, "It [the 12-Step program] works *only because* I work it," or worse, "It works *only to the extent* that I work it." The problem here is that this leaves little room for God to do something. But presumably the results someone gets from the program come more from the Higher Power than they do from the person working the program. How about this version, proposed by a friend: "It works if you let it"?

Even a text as ancient as Ephesians had to caution spiritual seekers about "good deeds" because this it-works-because-I'm-so-industrious business is a very old heresy. It's always been around, and it's been making people more compulsive, instead of more free, for centuries. Ephesians is blunt about it: "[S]alvation . . . is not your own doing, it is God's gift; neither is it a reward for anything you have accomplished, so let none pride themselves on it" (2:8–9). As our readings last week stressed, God's power is shown to best advantage in the midst of human weakness, not in the midst of human arrogance, where God tends to fade into the background.

Of course there's an old loophole on the other side: "If what I do doesn't matter, Las Vegas here I come!" To which Ephesians rejoins that we were created in Christ "to lead [a] life of *good* deeds."

John comes at this from a slightly different angle. As the "John 3:16" signs at football games remind us, the point of Jesus' story is that "God so loved the world that God gave us his only Son." But as a result of God's love—always there ahead of us—we now have the power to "practice . . . principles," to do "good deeds" that we don't have to be afraid to bring to the light. To put it very briefly, we do "good deeds," not to impress God or to earn God's love, but out of gratitude, because we wouldn't have made it this far without God's love. Lent is a time for us to be reminded that, when it comes to "spiritual progress," we don't need to work harder, we need to work more thankfully.

Fifth Week of Lent

Jer 31:31–34; Heb 5:7–9; Jn 12:20–33

"No longer shall they teach one another, or say to each other,
*'Know the L*ORD*,' for they shall all know me,*
*from the least of them to the greatest, says the L*ORD *. . ."*
(Jer 31:34).

Father Martin, a much-loved speaker on recovery topics, has voiced the touching thought that every unfortunate who dies drunk buys sobriety for someone else. This week's readings touch on this theme of redemption: What does it mean to say that Christ died for us?

The readings from Hebrews and John make very clear that Jesus was human in the face of death—that he prayed and wept. The Letter to the Hebrews says that the human ("in the flesh") Christ "offered prayers and supplications with loud cries and tears to God, who was able to save him from death" (5:7); the author may have in mind the scene in Gethsemane, after the Last Supper. The gospel passage from John may be another version of the Gethsemane moment, in which Jesus' "soul is troubled" by his deep wish that God would "save me from this hour."

God's will for him seemed so awful that he clung to the hope that God, even at the last minute, would listen to him and "save him from death." Nevertheless, in the end, he anticipated Bill W.'s suggestion about prayer: "when making specific requests, it will be well to add to each one of them this qualification: ' . . . if it be Thy will'"(12 X 12, 102).

Above all, Jesus hoped, even at the painful "hour" in today's Gospel, that his nonviolent acceptance of death—if that was God's will—would give glory to God by showing once and for all how God feels about people: God's love for us is not limited, as our love is, by human fear and rage. A voice from above confirms his hopes, just as a voice from above had supported his mission at his baptism and at the Transfiguration: "I have glorified [my name], and will glorify it again." God's name is God's self; and John often says that God's self is love. God's name—"love"—will shine out, be "glorified," when Jesus gives his life, since "No one has greater love than this, to lay down one's life for one's friends" (Jn 15:13).

In other words, Jesus' death will fulfill Jeremiah's prophecy: people will no longer need to teach one another about who God is, about what God's name is, because the crucifixion will make clear to everyone that God's name is love. God *will* answer Jesus' prayer, will "save [Jesus] from death" (Heb)—not by keeping him from dying, but by making his death an everlasting source of new life. This is how Jesus redeems us. And we "pass it on" when we "[c]ling to the thought that, in God's hands, the dark past is the greatest possession you have—the key to life and happiness for others" (BB, 124). "[I]f [the grain of wheat] dies, it produces much fruit" (Jn 12:24).

Palm Sunday, Procession

Mk 11:1–10; Mass: Is 50:4–7; Phil 2:6–11;
St. Mark Passion, Mk 14:1–15:47

"He said, 'Abba, Father, for you all things are possible;
remove this cup from me; yet, not what I want,
but what you want'"
(Mk 14:36)

Many years ago, a movie version of Jesus' life came out. Jesus was blonde and had shaved armpits, and looked more like a surfer than an itinerant Jewish preacher whose family thought he was crazy. But a note of realism intruded even so: poor old John Wayne, looking very much like someone who had gone a few rounds with John Barleycorn, had a cameo as the centurion. At the climax of the crucifixion scene, he turned and faced the camera and drawled, "Trooly this ma-hun was the sunnuv Gahd."

This statement is the climax of Mark's Gospel, just as it was the theme announced at the very beginning of it (see the Second Sunday of Advent, Cycle B). Up to now it was a hidden theme, because Jesus in this Gospel has insisted so strongly that no one goes public with the fact that he is Abba's beloved Son. But now it can be told, because the way he is dying makes clear *how* he is the Messiah, how he is the Son of God.

From Jesus' Temptations onward, his point has been that he is neither a commando nor a con man. Whatever the crowds may have thought when he entered Jerusalem—which we re-enact on Palm

Sunday—his choice of a donkey rather than a warhorse proclaims that he comes in peace. Of course, this was a hard point for Jesus' Jewish contemporaries, people like his disciples, to grasp, because commandos and con men are often quite effective at "wrest[ing] satisfaction and happiness out of this world [by] manag[ing] well" (BB, 61). Only the centurion, who is a *goy*, catches on and blurts out Mark's "secret." Maybe the centurion, like John Wayne, knew something about hitting bottom.

What does this imply for recovering people? Exactly what it implies for all people who hear the story of Jesus, and particularly this climax of it: "As God's people" (BB, 83), we should follow Paul's suggestion, and let our "attitude . . . be Christ's" (Phil). Even at the worst moment of his life, Jesus still called God "Abba," still believed in "a loving God" (Tradition 2). If we can change our "attitudes and actions" (12 X 12, 24; equals *metanoia*), into Christ's, we can drink from the "cup" of God's will for us. Alcoholics who have undergone this kind of transformation can do amazing things: for instance, they can "meet and transcend their other pains and trials [in addition to alcoholism]." They can "calmly accept impossible situations, seeking neither to run nor to recriminate" (12 X 12, 31). When these are our "attitudes and actions," we show that we are children of a loving God, following in Jesus' footsteps.

Note: I haven't included meditations for Holy Thursday or Good Friday. For Holy Thursday you may want to consult the meditation for Corpus Christi, at the end of this Lent-Easter section, since on that feast Roman Catholics celebrate the gift of the Lord's Supper in a special way.

Easter, Mass at Dawn

Acts 10:34, 37–43; Col 3:1–4; Jn 20:1–9

". . . your life is hidden with Christ in God.
When Christ who is your life is revealed,
then you also will be revealed with him in glory"
(Col 3:3–4).

Paul is fond of adding the Greek prefix *syn* ("with") to verbs to express the fact that, whatever Jesus did and experienced, his followers do and experience with him, and vice versa. In today's reading from Colossians, for example, we are told that we "have been raised up in company with [*syn*] Christ." Easter is not just about the resurrection of Jesus—we rise and shine, too.

Peter says something similar in his speech from Acts: those who can testify to the resurrection of Jesus are the ones who "ate and drank with [*syn*] him after he rose from the dead." Even though our lives may look ordinary, a mere matter of eating or drinking, there are times, even now, when, because we share Christ's "attitude," we "testify to the resurrection," and as a result we "appear with [*syn*] him in glory" (Col).

In other words, Christianity, like the 12-Step program, is a "we" program. This is especially good news for addicts, because addicted people seem especially to suffer from a sense of isolation. "Almost without exception, alcoholics are tortured by loneliness. Even before our drinking got bad and people began to cut us off, nearly all of us suffered the feeling that we didn't quite belong. . . . There was always that mysterious barrier we could neither surmount nor understand. . . . That's one reason we loved alcohol too well. It did let us act extemporaneously" (12 X 12, 57).

Belonging to a "we" or a "with" fellowship can effectively disperse "the chilling vapor that is loneliness" (BB, 151). If we eat together and drink together with other people who are on a spiritual path, we come to believe that we need never be alone, that we share a common spirit that keeps us going. Having someone to share our belief makes it easier to believe. In addition, if we share a common spirit, that spirit will shine out ("glory") from time to time, and attract people who still suffer from loneliness.

It's significant that *two* disciples run together to the empty tomb in today's Gospel, and that Jesus appears to *two* disciples traveling together to Emmaus in Luke's Gospel. Of course, the beloved disciple got to the tomb first, where he "saw and believed" in Jesus' resurrection. But he wasn't alone long; Peter got there, and the first disciple's belief in Jesus' new life got a lot stronger when Peter arrived. Together—"with" each other and "with" Jesus—they "commence[d] to outgrow fear." "[A]s [they] became conscious of His presence, [they] began to lose [their] fear of today, tomorrow, or the hereafter" (BB, 68, 63).

Second Sunday of Easter

Acts 4:32–35; 1 Jn 5:1–6; Jn 20:19–31

"With great power
the apostles gave their testimony
to the resurrection of the Lord Jesus, and great grace
was upon them all"
(Acts 4:33).

A word that links our three readings this Sunday is *testify*. The reading from Acts talks about the apostles bearing witness (testifying) "with power" to Jesus' resurrection. The reading from 1 John says that our faith in Jesus is grounded in the testimony (essentially the same word in Greek as "bore witness") of the Spirit.

The Greek word for "testify" is the root of our word *martyr*; people who give up their lives for the truths that they believe have given ultimate testimony to that belief. "Testify" has also been frequently used in a more ordinary context, to describe what goes on in spiritual fellowships. Giving testimony at meetings was one practice that A. A. took over from its parent fellowship, the overtly Christian Oxford Groups. The Oxford Groups in turn borrowed it from several older Christian denominations; especially in the evangelical tradition, people at "revivals" who have undergone a "spiritual awakening" are expected to "testify" about God's working in their lives.

In 12-Step groups "testifying" constitutes a large part of the 12th Step: we carry our message to others by "testifying" to what a Power not ourselves has done in our lives. Recovering people "testify" about "what we used to be like, what happened"—a spiritual awakening of some kind—"and what we are like now" (BB, 58). And our "testimony" is validated (or not) by the way we practice (or fail to practice) "these principles in all our affairs." That is, we have to walk our talk, a point that 1 John makes over and over: "Little children, let us love, not in word or speech, but in truth and action. And by [love in action] we will know that we are from the truth and will reassure our hearts before him [God]" (3:18–19).

In today's Gospel—which is used every year on the Sunday after Easter—Thomas comes to believe, and testifies that Jesus is God's Son, because he has seen Jesus. Jesus notes that most other people will come to believe, not because they have seen him, as Thomas has, but because they will see believers "practice these principles." It's often said at A. A. meetings that a member may be the only Big Book—a living Big Book—that someone encounters. By the same token, a follower of Christ may be the only New Testament someone ever "reads." The best way to "carry the message," to "testify," is to "practice these principles in all our affairs" (12th Step).

Third Sunday of Easter

Acts 3:13–15, 17–19; 1 Jn 2:1–5; Lk 24:35–48

*". . . 'and that repentance and forgiveness of sins
is to be proclaimed in his name to all nations,
beginning from Jerusalem'"*
(Lk 24:47).

In today's Gospel, the risen Jesus tells his friends to go out and preach "penance for the remission of sins" (literally, "*metanoia* and the letting go of sins") in his name "to all nations." In the reading from Acts, Peter does just that early in Christian history. He preaches to a crowd, brought together by news of his miraculous cure of a crippled man, that they are to "reform your lives [*metanoesate*]! Turn to God, that your sins may be wiped away!"

The word for "turn" here refers originally to a physical turning around, just as does the Latin word from which we get *conversion*. *Conversion* and *metanoia* are more or less interchangeable terms. When we undergo *metanoia*, "our attitude and outlook upon life" changes (BB, 84); we turn our heads and our lives around.

This is a tall order, of course, and requires a power we may at first feel that we lack. What we need then, according to 1 John, is "an intercessor"—Jesus, in fact. *Intercessor* translates the word *Paraclete*, a word used in the Gospel of John for the Spirit. But whether the Paraclete is Jesus or the Spirit of Jesus, the term derives from a legal setting, as we noted last year (Sixth Sunday of Easter, Cycle A): a paraclete (or advocate) is someone who goes to court with you to be on your side.

There are times in our lives when we need someone on our side more than anything else—especially times when we are our own worst enemies. Perhaps we need a paraclete most when we are about to do a 4th Step—and this is why Steps 2 and 3 come where they do. I suspect that one reason why so few alcoholics recovered before A. A. was that drunks back then tried to go directly from admission of defeat (which later became Step 1) to self-scrutiny (which later became Step 4). In other words, problem drinkers, already full of shame, plunged, by themselves or accompanied by the "constructive" criticisms of resentful loved ones, into their own murky depths. Predictably, they only found reasons there for fresh shame, and soon sought numbness in more drinking.

The genius of the 12 Steps lies in large measure in the placement of Steps 2 and 3, where addicted people acquire a "paraclete" to support them in the painful and necessary effort of self-scrutiny. And better a paraclete like the risen Jesus, who has "suffer[ed]" (Lk) and knows how difficult life can be. With a good paraclete, and a sympathetic listener, we can approach Steps 4 and 5 with confidence, and so experience "the beginning of true kinship with man and God" (12 X 12, 57). We can turn around better if there's someone directing us, filling in our blind spots.

Fourth Sunday of Easter

Acts 4:8–12; 1 Jn 3:1–2; Jn 10:11–18

"'For this reason the Father loves me, because I lay down my life
in order to take it up again. No one takes it from me,
but I lay it down of my own accord. I have power to lay it down,
and I have power to take it up again'"
(Jn 10:17–18).

The First Reading this Sunday, like last Sunday's, is from one of Peter's speeches in Acts. These speeches are important because they give us some sense of exactly how the early Christians carried the message of Jesus' life, death, and resurrection, as well as how the fellowship was organized—their Steps and their Traditions, so to speak. This week Peter is addressing the Sanhedrin, the ruling body of Judaism. The key word in his "sermon" is *name*: Peter has healed a crippled man in Jesus' *name*, and he tells the "leaders" of his people that Jesus' is the only *name* by which people can be saved. This exuberant statement has always raised questions, especially when we try to reconcile it with other beliefs in the Christian Scriptures, like the one in today's Gospel asserting inclusively that "other sheep that do not belong to this fold . . . shall hear my voice." What about all those people who have never heard the message, the "voice," of Jesus in a way that touched them? Or, even worse, what about those who, having mainly heard the name of Jesus from a viciously abusive adult, naturally balked? Are they "saved" somehow?

The great Jesuit theologian Karl Rahner made a gallant attempt to solve this riddle: he suggested that people of goodwill, people who "practice . . . principles in all [their] affairs" are "anonymous Christians." Twelve-Step people may like the "anonymous" part of this, but a devout Jew or Muslim might well squirm at the idea of being declared Christian without even knowing about it. For that matter, why not call Christians "anonymous Muslims"?

1 John can perhaps help us with this problem. This letter repeatedly makes the point that we know that people are children of God because they keep God's commandments, and primarily Jesus' "new commandment": ". . . that we should love one another" (3:11). Or, as Jesus puts it in the Sermon on the Mount, getting into the reign of God depends, not on calling him "Lord," not on knowing or using his "name," but on carrying out God's will as generously as he did. Whatever the "name" we call God, we must be ready to "lay down" our lives for one another in service. This is what makes us look "like [God]," the "loving God" of the Second Tradition. ". . . that we have passed from death to life"—that we have been "saved"—"because we love one another" (3:14).

Fifth Sunday of Easter

Acts 9:26–31; 1 Jn 3:18–24; Jn 15:1–8

"'If you abide in me, and my words abide in you,
ask for whatever you wish,
and it will be done for you'"
(Jn 15:7).

This week's readings from Acts and 1 John have an interesting word in common: *parrhesia*. It is translated one way at one point in the story of Saul-Paul, newly converted to Christianity: ". . . Saul had been *speaking out fearlessly* in the name of Jesus at Damascus" (emphasis mine). Right after that, the same word recurs, with a slightly different translation: "Saul stayed on with them, moving freely about Jerusalem and *expressing himself quite openly* in the name of the Lord" (emphasis mine). It also appears in today's passage from 1 John: *"[W]e can be sure* that God is with us and we will receive at [God's] hands whatever we ask" (emphasis mine). The common idea behind these different translations is that, if you truly believe something, you can speak out about it with confidence and freedom.

What 12 Steppers mostly speak out about is their "personal adventures before and after" (BB, 60). "Before and after" what? A "spiritual awakening," according to Step 12. Can we have enough confidence in our spiritual awakening, in this message we are supposed to carry, to speak out bravely and freely? How?

Some grounds for confidence are given today in both the reading from 1 John and from John's Gospel. A key word in these texts is a favorite of John's: *remain* (*menein*; see below, Second Sunday in Ordinary Time, Year B). John uses it twice in the passage from 1 John, seven times in today's Gospel. His point: we can tell our spiritual story fearlessly if we believe God makes a home in us. Or, as the Big Book puts it, if "[w]e [find] the Great Reality deep down within us" (BB, 55).

To express this inner connection, this way that God feels right at home with us, John adapts a favorite image of the prophets, who talked about the people of Israel as God's vineyard (compare Matthew's vineyard parables). John reshapes this ancient image by saying that Jesus is the vine, as we are the branches. Jesus is as intimately the source of each individual Christian's life as a grapevine is of its branches'. Jesus—and thus the God of Jesus—has moved into us: root, stem, and branch.

But can we be *sure* that God has made a home in us? After all, "our consciences" may tell us that God must have better taste than to take up residence in such a dingy abode. John, whose mind circles ideas like the eagle that is his symbol, comes back to the same old grounds for confidence: if we are keeping the commandment of love, we can be sure that God is quite comfortable in us, our "defects of character" (Step 6) notwithstanding. So if you walk your talk, then talk boldly, tell your story, carry the message—and expect to bear fruit abundantly.

Sixth Sunday of Easter

Acts 10:25–26, 34–35, 44–48; 1 Jn 4:7–10; Jn 15:9–17

"'This is my commandment, that you love one another
as I have loved you. No one has greater love than this,
to lay down one's life for one's friends'"
(Jn 15:12–13).

Our readings from the First Letter of John and the Gospel of John this Sunday clearly focus on love: love as verb and noun appears ten times in the passage from 1 John, nine times in the gospel selection. So what is love? Many people misuse the word, and active alcoholics and co-dependents have abused it so badly that the word makes them pretty nervous, even after they enter recovery. Thank heaven Bill W. dropped the Four Absolutes of the Oxford Groups—one of them was

Absolute Love, an ideal that would have scared off many prospective A. A.'s.

Still, progressing love—not Absolute, not perfect love—is an important part of a recovery program. Even people who have been in recovery a long time need occasionally to be reminded that "love and tolerance of others is our code" (BB, 84), especially when we are criticizing groups of which we "rightly" disapprove. So our "love" should include tolerance; but what else is true about love?

Our readings from John today contain a real shocker: what matters most is not how we love God or other people; what matters most is that God loves us. This may well make an alcoholic or a co-dependent *very* nervous. If it's an issue of our loving—well, clumsily as we do it, confused as we are about what love really is—we'll give it another try. But to be told that love is out of our control, that someone else already loves us, and loves us beautifully . . .

Many alcoholics would agree with Martha, the hard-drinking shrew in Edward Albee's *Who's Afraid of Virginia Woolf?*: having someone love you can seem like an unforgivable insult if you are deeply convinced you are unlovable. Nevertheless, this is what God asks us to accept, that we have always been loved. In fact, as addictions expert Earnie Larsen notes, we can never win God's love—because we already have it (p. 68).

The only sensible response to this is to finally and forever abandon the idea that no one can or should love us. Jesus died to prove us wrong; his resurrection insists that love has the final word. All we can do is "[g]ive freely of what [we have found]" (BB, 164). Even if we should find ourselves laying down our lives for our friends—suddenly, or one day at a time—we will have "joy," another favorite word of John's, because we will be giving back, not giving up.

Feast of the Ascension

Acts 1:1–11; Eph 1:17–23; Mk 16:15–20

Note: Many communities celebrate the Feast of the Ascension on the Thursday before the Seventh Sunday of Easter. If you are one of these, read this meditation on Thursday and the next meditation on the following Sunday.

"And they went out and proclaimed the good news everywhere,
while the Lord worked with them
and confirmed the message by the signs that accompanied it"
(Mk 16:20).

As I mentioned last year on this feast, the idea that Jesus spent forty days with his friends after his resurrection and then went home to Abba is based solely on the account Luke gives in today's reading from the Acts of the Apostles. The other Evangelists provide different endings for the story of Jesus. Last year on this feast we had Matthew's Mission on the Mountain. Next year we will have the version in Luke's Gospel, which like John's Gospel seems to say that Jesus ascended on Easter Sunday.

This year we have the ending of Mark's Gospel. But it's an ending added later by someone else, an ending partly reminiscent of other Gospel endings, which suggests that it was written after, and modeled on, the earlier Gospels. In fact, there are several alternative endings to Mark. Why do they all exist?

One theory is that Mark originally ended his Gospel with the women at the empty tomb of Jesus (Mk 16:1–8). The angel of the resurrection tells them to remind the other disciples to go meet the risen Jesus in Galilee (as in Matthew), but the women are too frightened to "carry the message." However, while the silence of the women rounds out Mark's theme of keeping secret the "Messiahship" of Jesus, it's rather lame as an ending. It's as if Elliot came home from school to find a note from E.T. saying he had had a swell time on Earth, but had gone home. Perhaps that's why someone else decided to play script doctor to Mark.

In any event, the ending of Mark that we mostly use now talks about Jesus' friends, after his departure, going out and carrying "the message," "the good news," the gospel. It makes sense that, having had a spiritual awakening, they would tell others about it. And as they trudged the Road of Happy Destiny, they found that some very sick people "recovered." All the disciples had to do was imitate their Master; like him "they la[id] their hands" on people who had previously believed they were untouchable, and "the sick . . . recover[ed]."

Twelve-Step people should "Go and do likewise" (Lk 10:37): "You should not hesitate to visit the most sordid spot on earth on such an errand [to be helpful to others]. Keep on the firing line of life with these motives and God will keep you unharmed" (BB, 102, near the end of chapter 7, "Working with Others"). This 12th-Step "work" will "confirm the message" (Mk). However, for 12-Step purposes we might want to take the business of "handl[ing] serpents" to refer to "serpents as you understand them."

Seventh Sunday of Easter

Acts 1:15–17, 20–26; 1 Jn 4:11–16; Jn 17:11–19

". . . God lives [menei] *in us,*
and his love is perfected in us"
(1 Jn 4:12).

During this Easter season, which is almost over, our Second Reading has been from the First Letter of John. As I have mentioned before, John characteristically thinks in circles, or better, spirals: he keeps coming back to the same few spiritual truths, each time adding a little more. One of these truths, which we have touched on before, is John's notion that Jesus and the God of Jesus "make a home in" those who follow Jesus (*menein*). Forms of *menein* occur five times in today's reading from 1 John, most notably in the well-known concluding sentence: "God is love, and those who *make a home* in love *make a home* in God, and God *makes a home* in them" (emphasis mine).

The 12 Steps speak of "God *as we understood [God]*" (italics in original). And there are of course many ways to understand God, inside and outside of 12-Step programs. Tradition 2 understands God in an appealing way, as "a loving God." This brings us spiraling back to John.

The theologian Michael Himes has made the interesting point that, when we say "God is love" with John, or invoke "a loving God" with this Tradition, we do not mean that there is a Higher Power who engages in several activities, some of them perhaps a bit scary but one of which is love, luckily for us. No; Himes says a more accurate translation of John's phrase is "God is loving." And vice versa. Who God is is what God does, and that is loving.

The Gospel for this Sunday is from Jesus' Prayer of Consecration, the end of his Farewell Address at the Last Supper. Since this is in John's Gospel, it spirals among all of John's favorite ideas. So when Jesus asks God in today's passage to "consecrate" his followers, he means "make them holy," which is the same as "make a home in them," which is the same as "make them people who give themselves in love, as I do." In a sense, the Big Book is wrong when it says that recovering people "are not saints" (BB, 60). Since we are people who have come to believe "that love freely given surely brings a full return" (12 X 12, 124), we are, in John's sense of the word, "holy" people.

If your reaction to this is "What an order! I can't go through with it," "[d]o not be discouraged" (BB, 60). "It will seldom matter how haltingly we walk. . . . The only urgent thing is that we make a beginning, and keep trying" (12 X 12, 68). It takes a lifetime to learn to love well.

Pentecost, Vigil Mass

Ez 37:1–14, Rom 8:22–27; 1 Jn 7:37–39

Note: Since the readings for Pentecost are the same in all three cycles, I have used the readings for the Vigil, in different combinations, for Years A and B. The readings for Pentecost Sunday will be treated in Year C.

> *"Thus says the Lord GOD to these bones:*
> *I will cause breath to enter you, and you shall live"*
> (Ez 37:5).

This year, the readings I choose to study from the Vigil, the service for the evening before the feast, are from Ezekiel 37 (quoted above), from Romans 8, and from the Gospel of John. Pentecost celebrates the sending of the Spirit, and each of these readings offers a different metaphor for this "Higher Power." One of these, perhaps the metaphor most commonly used, is breath ("spirit"), with which God brings the dry bones back to life in Ezekiel (for more on this, see Baptism of the Lord, Year C). A second metaphor is a favorite of Paul's: the Spirit is "first fruits," the early promise of a later rich harvest. John, who loves metaphors, gives a third: "If any thirst, let them come to me [Jesus]; . . . 'From within them rivers of living water shall flow.' (Here he was referring to the Spirit, whom those that came to believe in him were to receive)."

This third metaphor is especially inviting for alcoholics. The word John uses—"If anyone *thirst*"—is the source of our word *dipsomaniac*, a fancy word for "alcoholic" that literally means "crazy with thirst." Not a bad description of the practicing alcoholic, but it's worth noting, as Carl Jung did in his 1961 letter to Bill W., that the alcoholic's thirst is also, and ultimately, a spiritual one. No wonder that thirst is never satisfied by alcohol, which dries people up physically, emotionally, and spiritually.

But why does John go on to say, "There was, of course, no Spirit as yet"? Hasn't God always been God, including God the Spirit? The point here is that the Spirit is not some generic, wispy part of God, with fuzzier outlines than Jesus and his Abba. The Spirit is specifically the Spirit *of Jesus*. No one can receive *that* Spirit until Jesus is "glorified." And Jesus is "glorified" in John only when Jesus lays down his life for his friends. At the moment of Jesus' death in John's Gospel, the Evangelist uses words that can mean "he expired"; but they more literally mean "he handed over the Spirit."

Our readings all during the Easter season have circled this point: the power, the Spirit, that we receive from Jesus' death and resurrection is the power to give our lives in loving service as he gave his. Like an early member of A. A., let us stand "in the Presence of Infinite Power and Love," pouring "over and through [us] with the certainty and majesty of a great tide at flood" (BB, 56). The spirit that flows through us will then flow out to many people whose spiritual thirst has never yet been satisfied.

Trinity

Dt 4:32–34, 39–40; Rom 8:14–17; Mt 28:16–20

Note: Some Christian communities do not celebrate Trinity Sunday, because they feel that every time we worship, we honor the God who is somehow Three-in-One (Triune). If your community is one of these, please go to the readings for Sundays in Ordinary Time (2003, Eleventh; 2006, Tenth; 2009, Tenth).

"For all who are led by the Spirit of God are children of God . . .
and if children, then heirs, heirs of God and joint heirs
with Christ—if, in fact, we suffer with him so that we may
also be glorified with him"
(Rom 8:14, 17).

The Trinity is a central belief of Christianity because it sums up so much of our experience of the God of Jesus Christ. And so the readings on this feast weave together many of the themes on which we have reflected during this Easter season. For instance, in today's reading from Romans, we have some of Paul's favorite *syn* ("together with"—see Easter this year) words: "The Spirit . . . gives witness *with* our spirit that we are children of God. But if we are children, we are heirs as well: heirs of God, heirs *with* Christ, if only we suffer *with* him so as to be glorified *with* him" (my emphasis).

To get across what Paul communicates by *syn*, John uses *menein* ("make a home in"—see Fifth Sunday of Easter). John says that we are meant to share in everything that goes on between Jesus and Abba. They live in us, they make themselves at home in us. We do the kinds of things that they do, since we "breathe" their Spirit (*spirit* is from the word for "breath" or "wind"—see Pentecost).

What kinds of things? Bill W. might quote here one of his favorite prayers, by a saint full of the Spirit of Jesus, Francis of Assisi: "Lord, make me a channel [more usually translated "an instrument"] of thy peace—that where there is hatred, I may bring love . . . grant that I may seek rather to comfort than to be comforted—to understand, than to be understood—to love, than to be loved" (12 X 12, 99). To call God a "Trinity" is to say God is a relationship, specifically a love-relationship. The Second Tradition suggests something similar when it speaks of "a loving God." So then, if this God is at home in us, is "with" us, we will act in a loving way that tends to break down barriers between people.

Paul repeats this Sunday the point that John made last week: the Holy Spirit is specifically the Spirit of Jesus, and above all the Spirit of Jesus who called God "Abba" during the Agony in the Garden. Even—especially—at that most human moment, the love for us and the trust in God that Jesus was demonstrating gave God "glory," as John likes to say. Giving God "glory" means shining light on exactly who God is, on what God's Spirit is. When we in our turn have this Spirit, our actions show forth who God is at God's deepest level. Our "spirit," our "inheritance," is "[l]ove and tolerance of others" (BB, 84).

Corpus Christi

Ex 24:3–8; Heb 9:11–15; Mk 14:12–16, 22–26

Note: On this Sunday Roman Catholics celebrate the gift to us of the Lord's Supper (Corpus Christi equals Body of Christ). This special feast was created because medieval Christians felt that, with so much going on at the Holy Thursday celebration, the gift of bread and wine, and the fellowship that they symbolize, might get neglected in the larger drama. You may prefer to read this meditation on Holy Thursday, and to read on this Sunday the meditation for the appropriate Sunday in Ordinary Time.

"Then he took a cup, and after giving thanks he gave it to them . . .
He said to them, 'This is my blood of the covenant,
which is poured out for many'"
(Mk 14:23, 24).

As I mentioned in Cycle A, Corpus Christi is the feast on which Roman Catholics thank God for the Eucharist, the everlasting Gratitude Meeting. Last year we reflected on the Eucharist as a meal; this year we focus on another rich theme: the Eucharist as a sacrifice sealing a covenant.

The Greek word for "covenant" has at least two meanings, both cited in this Sunday's reading from Hebrews. *Covenant* can mean "will," an instrument through which a woman or man bequeaths gifts to loved ones after her or his death. It can also mean "treaty," an agreement by which two parties agree to be allies, with certain commitments on both sides. The writer of Hebrews is using both meanings in order to explain the graces concealed in the violent death Jesus underwent.

In terms of the first sense, covenant-as-will, Jesus bequeathed us many gifts. Bill W.—before his conversion, at any rate—could go no further than seeing Christ as a "great man" whose "moral teaching" was "most excellent" (BB, 11). But Christians also believe that Jesus, by his self-sacrificial death, released into the world a new "power to carry [God's will] out" (11th Step). In particular, Jesus left us the strength to give openhearted service. Some early members of A. A. demonstrated this kind of strength when they decided to admit a "stigmatized" newcomer to their fellowship after asking the question, "What would the Master do?" (12 X 12, 142)

Early Christians, like the writer of Hebrews, also saw Jesus' death as sealing a new covenant-as-treaty. In this view the first covenant was the one described in today's First Reading, from Exodus: "brokered" by Moses, it binds God to the people of Israel. The people's side of the deal is keeping certain commandments (including, but far from restricted to, the Ten Commandments). Under the new covenant-as-treaty, made "official" by Jesus' gift of his life, people are bound only to the New Commandment, to love one another as Jesus loved us. On the other side of this new treaty, God agrees always to give us the power we need to keep this commandment.

Recovering people don't readily use words like *covenant*, in either sense; we usually have a bad track record when it comes to promises and commitments. "Lack of power, that was our dilemma" (BB, 45). So, as Christians and as recovering people, we need to tap into "a source of power much greater than [ourselves]" (BB, 163). That power is available at meetings of the fellowship: 12-Step meetings and Christian Eucharists. After all, as Paul liked to stress, "Body of Christ" (Corpus Christi) refers not just to the bread and wine but also to the fellowship of people who share the bread and wine. And as Tom Weston, S.J., says, go where you're fed—go where the power is.

✣

Ordinary
Time

Second Sunday in Ordinary Time

1 Sm 3:3–10, 19; 1 Cor 6:13–15, 17–20; Jn 1:35–42

"They came and saw where he was staying,
and they remained with him that day"
(Jn 1:39).

As in the other cycles of readings, we begin post-holiday Ordinary Time—*very* Ordinary Time for most of us, especially in January—by reading from 1 Corinthians. Recall that the Corinthian Christian community was a lot like a big inner-city A. A. group—loud and quarrelsome, with all kinds of gurus and their supporters proclaiming wildly divergent interpretations of the good news.

In this Sunday's reading, the problem referred to by Paul is one that he had to deal with repeatedly in his letters. His message was always that Jesus had set us free from the Law of Moses. Therefore, Gentiles need not become Jews first, and then later Christians. Some Corinthians (and some early Christians elsewhere) thought like addicts, and so immediately spotted the loophole here: "If Jesus has set me free from the Law, including the Law's moral prescriptions, I can do anything I want, right?"

Naturally one of the first areas such "thinkers" turned to was sex. And so among the Corinthians, some took the "straight pepper diet" approach to sex (BB, 69). Paul's response to such "freethinkers," time and again, is that Jesus has not only set us free *from*, but also set us free *for*, and specifically for loving deeds. Being set free by Jesus links us to him in an intimate way—"whoever is joined [literally "glued"] to the Lord becomes one spirit with him" (1 Cor). But if you share Jesus' spirit, you will walk Jesus' walk.

Today's passage from John's Gospel makes a similar point. Jesus asks these two disciples of John the Baptist, "What are you looking for?" And they answer, using one of John's favorite words (thirty-six times in his Gospel), "Rabbi, . . . where do you stay?" The

140

word in question—*menein*, here translated "stay"—means "remain," "dwell in," "make a home in." It's John's way of describing the same union with God that Paul calls "becoming one spirit with the Lord." In other words, what they're "looking for" is the opportunity to find out where Jesus feels at home morally, what spiritual center he lives from. His answer: "Come and see." That is, "Come and see if I walk my talk, and draw your own conclusion about 'staying' with me."

As we begin Ordinary Time, let's try to "improve our conscious contact with God as we underst[and God]" (Step 11). We may want to follow Paul by adding more glue to our bond, or follow John by getting to feel more at home with our Higher Power.

Third Sunday in Ordinary Time

Jon 3:1–5, 10; 1 Cor 7:29–31; Mk 1:14–20

"The time is fulfilled, and the kingdom of God has come near; repent, and believe in the good news'"
(Mk 1:15; this passage overlaps with the passage
for the First Sunday in Lent this year).

Jonah is one of my favorite books of the Bible. It looks like a prophetic book, but it is really a gentle and very funny satire on religious narrow-mindedness. You could think of Jonah as a forerunner of many Jewish comedians, a Rodney Dangerfield who never quite catches on to the fact that God is a whole lot smarter and stronger—and a whole lot more compassionate—than he is.

Consider the passage in this week's reading: Jonah has arrived in Nineveh, the capital of the Assyrians. A flashback: when Jonah had first received God's command to prophesy, back in the first chapter of the Book of Jonah, he had run like hell in the opposite direction. With good reason: the Assyrians—extinct for centuries when the Book of Jonah was written—were fearsome warriors, and Jonah would have wanted to go to Nineveh as much as an accountant would want to go to a bikers' party. So Jonah tried to escape God by a taking ship. God, who does not take "no" for an answer, sent a storm. This led to the famous episode in which some pious Gentile sailors, praying fervently all the while—sailors have always been famous for their devoutness—reluctantly and gently threw Jonah overboard to send him on the right way. The next leg of his journey occurred in a fish.

Now delivered to Nineveh, Jonah has grudgingly decided to comply with God's original command. Halfheartedly he starts muttering to the Assyrians that God is going to destroy their city; as a matter of fact, he very much hopes God will. Unfortunately (to Jonah), even his slovenly attempt at prophecy works, and the Assyrians instantly experience *metanoia*, and repent. This is bad enough, but what finally puts Jonah into a colossal snit is that God *accepts* their repentance. God changes God's mind, which makes Jonah look pretty stupid. In chapter 4, after today's reading, God will gently interrupt Jonah's huge complaining and suggest that a little compassion might be nice.

Jesus cited the Book of Jonah on a couple of occasions. This suggests that Jesus may have had a Jewish sense of humor, with a lively sense of the incongruous distance between God's will and silly human cunning. In any case, the message of the Book of Jonah is rather like Jesus' in the parables: lighten up, because God may love Gentiles—even Assyrians—and other "sleazy" people quite as much as God loves respectable folk. Or, as A. A.'s memorable "Rule 62" puts it: "Don't take yourself too damn seriously" (12 X 12, 149).

Fourth Sunday in Ordinary Time

Dt 18:15–20; 1 Cor 7:32–35; Mk 1:21–28

Note: In 2003, Roman Catholics will celebrate the Feast of the Presentation of the Lord (February 2nd) on the following Sunday. See the meditation in Special Feasts.

> *"They were astounded at his teaching, for he taught them as one having authority . . . 'He commands even the unclean spirits, and they obey him'"*
> (Mk 1:22, 27).

The healing stories we have considered up to now, mostly from Matthew and John, have depicted Jesus giving sight to the blind or enabling the lame to walk. With this week's Gospel, we need to come to terms with a kind of healing that Jesus frequently brought about, a healing which at first glimpse may seem completely alien to us: expulsion of a devil. We find these healings especially in Mark, the first Gospel to be written.

Actually, this kind of healing may make perfect sense to someone who has been set free by a spiritual experience from a compulsion or an addiction (for more on this, see Meditation 10 in *A 12-Step Approach to the Spiritual Exercises*). I have often said that one of the worst features of alcoholism is that, before it destroys you, it replaces you. Many alcoholics have experiences like mine: during my drinking, I often felt that I had been invaded by an alien being, someone not me. Somehow this primitive creature—all id, to use Freudian lingo—was using my face and my voice to hurt people I really cared about, including myself, as in one of those *Twilight Zone* episodes about a double who takes over your life. Sometimes I wished I could somehow signal over the top of my double's head, telling people, "It's not really me who's doing these destructive—and self-destructive—things; I'm being held prisoner inside this bloated shell."

Jesus' contemporaries used the language of devils and possession to speak of similar kinds of self-alienation. So Mark uses the language of exorcism to describe how the healing touch of Jesus often helped even these distraught people to "come to their senses," as Luke says of the Prodigal Son at the moment of his *metanoia*.

One need not believe in devils to acknowledge that there are diseases, like addiction, that seem to take over every fiber of a person's life, that "take possession" of them. If healing of these diseases is to occur, that healing must go to the sick person's core. And in fact 12 Steppers believe that "[t]he power of God goes deep!" (BB, 114). Step 2 anticipates just this kind of "exorcism": We "[c]ame to believe that a power greater than ourselves could restore us to sanity." It's precisely Jesus' "greater power" ("authority") that excites the crowd in this week's Gospel, a power mighty enough, yet gentle enough, to reach even the most imprisoned heart.

Fifth Sunday in Ordinary Time

Jb 7:1–4, 6–7; 1 Cor 9:16–19, 22–23; Mk 1:29–39

> *"'Let us go on to the neighboring towns,*
> *so that I may proclaim the message there also;*
> *for that is what I came out to do'"*
> (Mk 1:38).

In today's selection from St. Paul, he is defending himself to his Corinthians friends against a rather odd charge. Paul had never asked them to pay him for delivering the message of new freedom in Christ that he had brought them. Now this has led some to claim that Paul's message must be worthless: consider the price!

Paul responds to this strange charge: ". . . I am under compulsion [to preach the gospel] and have no choice. I am ruined if I do not preach it! If I do it willingly, I have my *recompense*; if unwillingly, I am nonetheless *entrusted with a charge*." He can't charge for something he spiritually has to do. Speaking of charging, note that Paul uses the same kind of accountant's language that Bill W., the ex-stockbroker, favored (I've italicized some of the more mercantile words).

Bill W. talks about the 12th Step—the A. A. version of "preaching the gospel"—in similar terms. First, like Paul, the recovered person should "carry the message" free of charge. Recovery is "a limitless lode which will pay *dividends* only if he *mines* it for the rest of his life and insists on giving away the entire *product*" (BB, 129). Second, recovering people are "under compulsion" to "carry the message"; they, too, will be "ruined" if they "do not [carry] it!" Bill puts it like this: "Practical experience shows that nothing will so much insure immunity from drinking as intensive work with other alcoholics. It works when other activities fail" (BB, 89).

Finally, 12 Steppers also have their "recompense" for carrying out the "charge" with which they have been "entrusted." Dr. Bob, the other founder of A. A., sums up, in even simpler prose, the positive side of "passing on what I learned to others who want and need it badly": "I do it for four reasons:

1. Sense of duty.
2. It is a pleasure.
3. Because in so doing I am paying my debt to the man who took time to pass it on to me.
4. Because every time I do it I take out a little more insurance for myself against a possible slip" (BB, 181).

Especially in its Eighth Tradition, A. A. follows the example of the early church's approach to ministry. A. A. puts it this way: "Give freely of what you find and join us" (BB, 164). The Gospel of Matthew says much the same thing: "You received without payment; give without payment" (10:8, from the Missionary Discourse). Jesus walked his talk: in the Gospel today he "move[s] on to the neighboring villages" rather than stay in Capernaum and cash in on his early success there.

Sixth Sunday in Ordinary Time

Lv 13:1–2, 44–46; 1 Cor 10:31–11:1; Mk 1:40–45

"So, whether you eat or drink, or whatever you do,
do everything for the glory of God"
(1 Cor 10:31).

Jesus usually deals gently with the hurt, confused people whom he meets. But there is also, at times, an undercurrent of vehemence in his contacts with those he heals. In today's Gospel, for example, the words translated "Jesus gave him a stern warning and sent him on his way" could be more literally translated "Jesus was angry [literally 'snorted'] at him and immediately threw him out." Last week, when he healed Simon Peter's mother-in-law, he "grasped her hand and helped her up"; the word for "grasped" literally means "laid hands on roughly."

Is Jesus indulging in anger, the "dubious luxury of normal [people]" (BB, 66), and, if so, why with a poor outcast leper or Peter's sick mother-in-law? Various solutions have been proposed, for instance that Jesus is really angry with the social arrangements that make lepers (and a lot of other people) outcasts, or that the anger comes from his fury at the "devils" that beset people.

But perhaps the best explanation is that the anger is meant to underscore Mark's "Messianic secret." Recall that in Mark, Jesus doesn't want those he has helped to "proclaim the whole matter freely," as the ex-leper later does. Why? Because, as Jesus, after his baptism by John, learned in the "desert places"—the place of the Temptations—he is a Messiah with a difference. He will not resort to political violence, nor will he turn his gift for healing into a bid for fame. The God of Jesus is neither violent nor manipulative, and Jesus wants his words and actions to show forth that God. But this is so far from what people expect—even his disciples, who in last week's Gospel were trying to talk Jesus into setting up a "practice" in Capernaum, where "Everybody is looking for you!"—that Jesus doesn't want the word *messiah* loosely thrown around. He wants to remain anonymous, until he is surrendering his life on the cross, when the true meaning of *Messiah* will finally begin to dawn on people. As recovering people, we might bear this in mind when we work our 12th Step. Our job is not to bully people into sobriety or dazzle them with marvels. Unlike the well-intentioned but misguided ex-leper, we are not to "proclaim [this translates the usual word for 'preach' in the Christian Scriptures] the whole matter" at the public level (see Tradition 11). On a 12th-Step call, keep your story simple; and "[s]ee your man [or woman] alone, if possible" (BB, 91). It's well said that the 12-Step program works because fundamentally it's "one drunk talking to another."

Seventh Sunday in Ordinary Time

Is 43:18–19, 21–22, 24–25; 2 Cor 1:18–22; Mk 2:1–12

"Jesus Christ . . . was not alternately 'Yes and No';
but in him it is always 'Yes'"
(2 Cor 1:19).

My friend Tom Weston, S.J., likes to cite the Exodus story—you know, the one with Charlton Heston leading ten thousand extras through the Mojave Desert while the Cinemascope cameras roll—as a parallel to the experience of recovery. Like the children of Israel, recovering people can say, "Once we were slaves, now we're free, and Someone More Powerful Than Us did it." In this Sunday's reading from Isaiah 43, God tells the Jews, exiled in Gentile lands a millennium after Moses, that they need not remember the first Exodus, because God is about to top it with a second, greater Exodus—"something new." And this will happen, not because of anything they have done, but "for my [God's] own sake": freeing people and leading them home is God's job.

In today's Gospel Jesus, too, is doing something liberating. Not only does he free the paralytic from physical bondage, but he also does "something new": he forgives his sins. Some people criticize the 12 Steps for their emphasis on moral renewal, but I believe that the Steps wisely consider a point underscored by Jesus' forgiving the sins of the paralytic: human wholeness is not just a matter of physical improvement, even of dramatic healing; for human beings to be really whole, what most concerns them—their values, their moral choices—must also be mended.

As a matter of fact, one of the things about my drinking that I disliked the most was the destructive effect my "behavior" had, not just "on the dining-room furniture," but on my "moral fiber" (12 X 12, 33). I had always prided myself on my honesty, and now I had to lie about a lot of things, like how I spent my evenings. I had always wanted to be reliable, but drinking threw up for grabs whether I would be where I said I'd be, or do what I said I'd do, or how coherent I would be even if I did show up.

So one of the biggest gifts of recovery for me has been my re-found ability to say "yes" to people and mean it, to be a reliably moral person. I can do this because "God is the one who firmly establishes [me] along with you [everyone in recovery]." And I believe, with Paul, that this change in me has happened "in Christ"—one of Paul's favorite expressions—because Christ was and is a thoroughly consistent person: was "not alternately 'Yes and No'; . . . but in him it was always 'Yes'"(2 Cor).

In 2009, go next week to the First Sunday in Lent. After Corpus Christi, return to the Twelfth Sunday in Ordinary Time.

Eighth Sunday in Ordinary Time

Hos 2:16–17, 21–22; 2 Cor 3:1–6; Mk 2:18–22

"Not that we are competent of ourselves to claim anything
as coming from us; our competence is from God . . . "
(2 Cor 3:5).

Recovering alcoholics distinguish between "dry" and "sober." A "dry" person is not currently drinking, but "inwardly . . . would give anything to take half a dozen drinks and get away with them" (BB, 152). "Dry" people are characteristically "restless, irritable, and discontented," to cite the classic formulation of Dr. William Silkworth, an early supporter of A. A. (see "The Doctor's Opinion," BB, xxvi). "Dry" people know all about Thoreau's "quiet desperation," because they "cannot picture life without alcohol. Some day [they] will be unable to imagine life either with alcohol or without it. Then [they] will know loneliness such as few do" (BB, 152).

A "sober" person isn't drinking either, but this woman or man doesn't "sit with a long face in places where there is drinking, sighing about the good old days" (BB, 102). Indeed, some people might even be "shocked at . . . [the] seeming worldliness and levity" (BB, 16) of the Sober. But the point is that they are very different from the "dry"; the "dry" are in fact Puritans, who were well-defined by H. L. Mencken as people seething with disapproval because "somebody somewhere is having a good time."

In today's Gospel, Jesus twits his critics with just such a Puritan attitude. These people claim they prefer the austere John the Baptist to Jesus and his friends, who seem, to the critics, to know too much about "plain ordinary whoopee parties" (BB, 101). In fact it's true, according to the Evangelist John, that Jesus once even provided additional wine at a wedding feast when supplies ran low. Jesus' response to these "Puritans" is that something worth celebrating is going on: the reign of God is near. So gloom would be a stupid, pompous response.

In the Hebrew Scriptures, for instance in the Book of Hosea, God often speaks in the role of a groom who is marrying a bride, the people of Israel. Christians believe that, in Jesus, God has made good on God's promise to "espouse" us ordinary people "in right and in justice," "in love and in mercy," "in fidelity." Nobody but a killjoy sighs "about the good old days" at a wedding. Instead, as the old Quaker hymn puts it, "How can I"—how can we Sober Folks—"keep from singing?" After all, we "have recovered from a seemingly hopeless state of mind and body" (BB, xiii). That's reason to celebrate; and this persistent feeling of gratitude is what mainly distinguishes the "sober" from the "dry." So pass the carbonated apple juice, please.

In 2003, go next week to the First Week of Lent. After Corpus Christi, return to the Thirteenth Sunday in Ordinary Time. In 2006, go next week to the First Week of Lent. After Corpus Christi, return to the Twelfth Sunday in Ordinary Time.

Ninth Sunday in Ordinary Time

Dt 5:12–15; 2 Cor 4:6–11; Mk 2:23–3:6

"But we have this treasure in clay jars,
so that it may be made clear that this extraordinary power
belongs to God and does not come from us"
(2 Cor 4:7).

It's common in spiritual writing to describe conversion or enlightenment—what the Christian Scriptures call *metanoia* and the 12 Steps call "a spiritual awakening"—as a treasure. Jesus told parables about "a treasure hidden in a field" and "of fine pearls" (Mt 13:44, 46); Bill W. compares recovery to a "new treasure . . . something better than gold" (BB, 129). In today's reading from 2 Corinthians, Paul uses the same image of a "treasure": his "treasure" is his ministry, his message, his story. It is a story of the "surpassing power [that] comes from God"; and it is a story about light shining in darkness, as at the dawn of creation (Paul quotes the Book of Genesis). As he says a bit later in this letter, "[I]n Christ . . . [we are] a new creation" (5:17). Someone who has had a "spiritual awakening" gets to start over: if we "turn . . . to the Father of Light[,]" "we [feel] new power flow in, . . . we enjoy peace of mind . . . We [are] reborn" (BB, 14, 63).

As Paul also notes, however, we carry this light, this "glory," this message of power, "in earthen vessels." These vessels are our bodies, but they are also our whole "fleshy" lives, those aspects of our lives where we may encounter the darker human experiences, like being "afflicted in every way possible," "full of doubts," "persecuted," "struck down." Still, the light shines out even from—especially from—the fragile vessels that we are. "Almost any experienced A. A. will . . . report that out of every season of grief or suffering, when the hand of God seemed heavy or even unjust, new lessons for living were learned, new resources of courage were uncovered, and that finally, inescapably, the conviction came that God *does* 'move in a mysterious way [God's] wonders to perform'" (12 X 12, 105; italics Bill W.'s).

People will see that, because of our "spiritual awakening," we can "match calamity with serenity" (BB, 68). We ask for this when we take the 3rd Step: "Take away my difficulties [not for my sake, but so] that victory over them may bear witness to those I would help of Thy power, Thy Love, and Thy Way of Life" (BB, 63). Paul agrees; somehow, even when contained in "clay jars," the "surpassing power" of God insures that "we are not crushed . . . we never despair . . . we . . . are never destroyed." Instead, "the life of Jesus [is] revealed in our mortal flesh." In this we truly follow Jesus; for it was in his "mortal flesh" that the "loving God" (Tradition 2) that he called "Abba" was fully "revealed."

Tenth Sunday in Ordinary Time

Gn 3:9–15; 2 Cor 4:13–5: 1; Mk 3:20–35

Note: These readings aren't used between 2001 and 2010; but I include meditations on them for communities that follow a different plan for Sunday Scriptures.

"And looking at those who sat around him, [Jesus] said,
'Here are my mother and my brothers! Whoever does the will
of God is my brother and sister and mother'"
(Mk 3:34–35).

As I have noted before, Mark wrote the first Gospel. As a result, it contains some embarrassing passages, which are softened or omitted in the later Gospels. For example, in Mark the disciples of Jesus are unsparingly presented as really dumb; in Matthew and Luke, written at a time when those same disciples had come to be regarded as "old-timers," as "pioneers," they are depicted as just a little slow.

Today's Gospel contains what is surely one of the most embarrassing moments even in Mark. Jesus' family thinks he has gone crazy, and they have arrived to institutionalize him. Matthew and Luke understandably skip this and cut immediately to Jesus' statement that his followers are his *real* family.

Nevertheless, those of us who have gone against the patterns in our families of origin may well empathize with Jesus. As Family Systems therapists insist, if only one member of a family changes behavior, a typical reaction of the rest of that family is to insist that their good old way is "sane," so the single person who has changed must be crazy.

Perhaps we can even sympathize with Jesus' family up to a point. Because of the "spiritual intoxication" he experienced at his baptism by John, he has rather suddenly become a roving preacher. He has taken literally the words of the Psalmist that Paul quotes today: "Because I believed, I spoke out." "There is talk about spiritual matters morning, noon and night." The crowds are so enthusiastic that Jesus and his disciples can't even eat. No wonder his family reacts "with apprehension, then with irritation" (BB, 128), and finally by trying to get him some professional help. Since this is the reaction of his own kin, it's understandable that his enemies are claiming that he is acting this way because he is possessed.

The point is that you have to be a little crazy to want to "do the will of God" more than anything else, more than being comfortable or respectable or "bodily and mentally" identical to your "fellows" (BB, 30). And if this "craziness" follows a "spiritual awakening," it will help a lot to have slightly crazy "brother[s] and sister[s] and mother[s]" who can be "a sufficient substitute" for the families we may have to leave behind. "[A] fellowship in [a 12-Step program] is a substitute and it is vastly more than that" (BB, 152).

Eleventh Sunday in Ordinary Time

Ez 17:22–24; 2 Cor 5:6–10; Mk 4:26–34

Note: These readings aren't used between 2001 and 2010; but I include meditations on them for communities that follow a different plan for Sunday Scriptures.

"'The kingdom of God is as if someone would scatter seed on the ground, and would sleep and rise night and day, and the seed would sprout and grow, he does not know how'"
(Mk 4:26, 27).

In today's reading from Paul, he tells us (twice) that he is "confident" here on earth, though he would "rather be . . . at home with the Lord." G. K. Chesterton once said of spiritual seekers that they were homesick even at home; the medieval Islamic mystic Rumi said of earthly life, "I don't like it here; I want to go home!"

This might seem odd to recovering people. True, *before* recovery many of us spent much of our lives feeling like we didn't belong here. We may have tried to find a "home" in "sordid places," and "[m]omentarily we did," yet this was always followed by an "awful awakening"—we were as lonely as ever (BB, 151). But then came recovery, and one of its prime benefits is finally feeling at home, at meetings to begin with, and eventually "in all our affairs." Bill W. testifies to this: "When we reached A. A., and for the first time in our lives stood among people who seemed to understand, the sense of belonging was tremendously exciting" (12 X 12, 57). Why would we want to keep traveling when we've finally gotten somewhere?

The fact is that, like spiritual people through the ages, we must always be pilgrims—we can't "rest on our laurels" (BB, 85). Bill was also aware of this spiritual truth: he speaks of 12 Steppers trudging "the Road of Happy Destiny" (BB, 164), or making "spiritual progress" (BB, 60—*progress* literally means "walking forward"). Still, if we keep moving, it helps to believe that there is someplace better up ahead. Of course, as Paul notes, "We walk by faith, not by sight." Still, our "confidence" that good things lie ahead isn't completely "blind" faith. Rather, it's rooted in all that God has already done to change our lives.

If we really have "confidence," we will imitate the farmer in the first of the two parables in this week's Gospel. We will sow our seed, we will carry our message and tell our story, and then we will "let go and let God." Fussing at the seed, repeatedly uprooting the plant to check its growth, not only doesn't help, but might harm it. The seed knows what to do, stage by stage. And we can also have "confidence" that "great events will come to pass for [us] and countless others" (BB, 164), even if our story isn't that great or that long. Very small seeds can produce very big shrubs, "big enough for the birds of the sky to build nests in its shade" (Mk). It "is only a matter of willingness, patience and labor" (BB, 163).

Twelfth Sunday in Ordinary Time

Jb 38:1, 8–11; 2 Cor 5:14–17; Mk 4:35–41

"So if anyone is in Christ, there is a new creation: everything old has passed away; see, everything has become new!"
(2 Cor 5:17).

Our first reading this Sunday is the beginning of the punch line from the Book of Job. For thirty-seven chapters, Job has been asking Rabbi Kushner's question, "Why do bad things happen to good people?" or, more personally, "Why do they happen to *me*, Job?" Job's "comforters" have voiced the conventional answers: Job must have done *something* to deserve this, or God is trying to teach Job something, or some evil power is at work. But Job hasn't bought any of it. Now God gives an answer, over four poetic chapters (38–41): there is a powerful Creator-God, and Job isn't it.

A running theme through the Hebrew Scriptures, in for example the Book of Job and in the Psalm for today, 107, is that "the waters" are a chaotic, destructive element. Only God has the power to master and make something—in fact, create everything that is—out of "the waters." So when Jesus calms a storm on a body of water, the suggestion is that Jesus shares in the Creator's power. The disciples, not depicted as very bright in Mark's Gospel, nevertheless catch this large hint: "Who can this be that the wind and the sea obey him?" can have only one answer.

But what matters most to us who call on Jesus' name is usually not his power over nature; it is rather "the power of God in human affairs" (BB, 11) that interests us. We believe that "in Christ" there can be "a new creation" (2 Cor) "in all our [human] affairs" (Step 12). What is needed to bring this "new creation" into being? Two things. The first is a cinch: "the love of Christ" for us, which is a given in the light of the way Christ selflessly died "for one's friend[s]" (Jn 15:13). The other is our response to that love. Do we have enough faith that good, "new" things can happen in our relationships, even to people like us?

Bill W. put the issue this way in speaking of his own profound spiritual awakening in late 1934: "Belief in the power of God, plus enough willingness, honesty and humility to establish and maintain the new order of things, were the essential requirements" (BB, 13–14). Like Bill, Jesus in today's Gospel tells his frightened disciples that they need to grow in "[b]elief in the power of God." We later disciples need to do this as well. And we also need to imitate Job in acknowledging, with as much "willingness, honesty and humility" as we can muster, that there is a God, and it's not us.

Note: In 2003, Roman Catholics will celebrate the Feast of Sts. Peter and Paul (June 29) on the following Sunday. See the meditation in Special Feasts.

Thirteenth Sunday in Ordinary Time

Wis 1:13–15; 2:23–24; 2 Cor 8:7–9, 13–15; Mk 5:21–43

"'My little daughter is at the point of death. Come and lay your hands on her, so that she may be made well, and live'"
(Mk 5:23).

Our Gospel this Sunday tells us something very important about Jesus: his is a hands-on ministry. He takes the hand of the little girl—rather forcefully, in Greek—to bring her back to life. The woman with the hemorrhage touches *him.*

Jesus calls her forward, "not to embarrass her," but for another purpose. The woman had to work up her courage to touch him, and then to admit publicly that she had. Why? Because her chronic menstrual flow made her "unclean," not kosher (for more on this passage, see Meditation 30 in *A 12-Step Approach to the Spiritual Exercises*).

A Pharisee would have told her that she had no business touching anyone, since she would render them unclean, too. But she had gambled that her contact with Jesus would have the opposite effect: instead of making him unclean, it would make her whole. And so Jesus insists that she come forward, come out, so that everyone else can know that healing is the *real* effect of touch, his touch and the touch of his followers.

The Greek word for "touch" is almost always used in the Christian Scriptures to describe Jesus' healing. Sometimes, as here, the word is specifically applied to Jesus' touching, or letting himself be touched by, those people the respectable consider "untouchable." The point, then, is that, in many cases, simply touching someone that everyone else avoids can work a miracle. "Healing power" jumps across the gap from person to person.

This is, of course, part of the power of 12-Step recovery, "[t]hat the man who is making the approach [to an alcoholic prospect] has had the same difficulty, that he obviously knows what he is talking about, that his whole deportment shouts at the new prospect that he is a man with a real answer, that he has no attitude of Holier Than Thou, nothing whatever except the sincere desire to be helpful . . . —these are the conditions we have found most effective. After such an approach many take up their beds and walk again" (BB, 18–19; the last sentence alludes to another of Jesus' "touch" miracles, in which he "raises up" a crippled man from his bed).

In doing 12-Step work, we should have an "attitude" like Christ's (Phil 2:5): we "should not hesitate to visit the most sordid spot"—or reach out to "the most sordid" person— "on earth" (BB, 102). With this "attitude," we can take "new prospects," "defeated drinkers," by the hand; "[m]any, we are sure, will rise to their feet and march on" (BB, 153).

Fourteen Sunday in Ordinary Time

Ez 2:2–5; 2 Cor 12:7–10; Mk 6:1–6

"So, I will boast all the more gladly of my weaknesses,
so that the power of Christ may dwell in me"
(2 Cor 12:9).

In today's Gospel, Jesus is once again "laying hands" on people and so accomplishing "miraculous deeds," as in last Sunday's reading from Mark. But since Jesus is back in his "own part of the country," near his family, whom everybody in the area knows only too well, his "deeds" fail to impress some of the locals. They knew him way back when, before this "preaching" business. They may also have heard that his own family thinks he's gone crazy. In addition, perhaps these ex-neighbors are so respectable that they are put off by all this contact that they've been told that Jesus insists on having with "lower companions"—tax collectors, prostitutes, even menstruating women. In any case, Mark says Jesus' former neighbors ". . . found him too much for them."

Their "lack of faith" seems to depress Jesus, to drain his power: the words translated "He could work no miracle there" could be more literally rendered as "He did not have the power there to do anything powerful." This dreary experience would help him to empathize that much more with powerless people, like us when we begin the recovery process—or like Paul in today's reading from 2 Corinthians.

Paul knew all about weakness. In addition to the miseries he regularly encountered on his missionary journeys, journeys to carry the message of Jesus' power to heal, he also suffered from a mysterious personal problem. No one knows exactly what it was, but he hints at its nature in today's Second Reading, comparing it to something sharp and pointed. Perhaps it was some kind of chronic pain (like not a few recovering people, I've had chronic back pain for some years;

"a thorn in the flesh" describes it pretty well). No masochist, he "begged the Lord" to take it away—"three times" is probably a symbolic number, meaning "a lot more than once."

But Paul also learned what every person who has taken a lst Step discovers: "[W]hen I am powerless, it is then that I am strong." Oddly enough it is precisely through our weaknesses, even the most personally embarrassing, that God chooses to work, to show power. By the grace of a Power greater than ourselves, our broken places are where grace and God's power shine through. "All those who have persisted have found strength not ordinarily their own. They have found wisdom beyond their usual capability. And they have increasingly found a peace of mind which can stand firm in the face of difficult circumstances" (12 X 12, 104).

Fifteenth Sunday in Ordinary Time

Am 7:12–15; Eph 1:3–14; Mk 6:7–13

*"With that, [the disciples] went off, heralding the need
for a change of attitude"*
[Mk 6:12; my own translation of two technical words,
the second of which comes from our old friend *metanoia*].

A little history is necessary for the ordinary reader to grasp this week's selection from Amos. After its zenith under Kings David and Solomon, the nation of the Jews broke into two kingdoms: Israel in the north, and Judah—much smaller, but including the city of Jerusalem—to the south. Amos was a prophet from the southern kingdom, Judah. As he insists in today's reading, before God told him to prophesy he had been an ordinary person, a shepherd. Prophecy had already become so institutionalized that there were "companies," or what we might call "unions," of prophets. But Amos was not a member; he was not officially certified by Organized Religion in any way.

By contrast, Amaziah, his opponent, is just such an official representative; he is a government-approved priest of the northern kingdom, Israel. Amos had left his own country, in the south, to denounce in God's name the injustices of the ruling class of the north. Now Amaziah is trying to throw Amos out of Bethel, the Holy Place of the north, for saying rude things about the upper class, for being a foreigner, and for violating the rules of the prophets' union. Amos's answer to Amaziah is precisely that he never claimed to be a certified religious person. Amos has come on this dangerous mission *only* because God sent him. He had asked to know God's will for him, as in the 11th Step, and "prophesy!" was God's frightening response. Amos is as free from the trappings of well-heeled religion as are the disciples whom Jesus sends out in today's Gospel. Unlike the Reverend Amaziah, who probably had quite a nice collection of sandals (domestic and foreign) and tunics (business and casual), Amos, and the disciples of Jesus, travel very light. The general effect of this would be to underscore their nonofficial status as unimportant (anonymous, even) people with an important message.

How does somebody who has had a spiritual awakening carry the message? When dealing with someone like Amaziah, a person whose "religious education and training may be far superior to yours," it's probably best to travel light—stories weigh nothing—and to keep it simple. It's also a good idea to "wear" your message on the outside, so everyone can see what you believe in the way you behave: "To be vital, faith must be accompanied by self-sacrifice and unselfish, constructive action" (BB, 93). Even stuffy people might find it hard to resist the message of people whose actions show that they are "full of love" (Eph).

Sixteenth Sunday in Ordinary Time

Jer 23:1–6; Eph 2:13–18; Mk 6:30–34

"Then I myself will gather the remnant of my flock out
of all the lands where I have driven them, and I will bring them
back to their fold, and they shall be fruitful and multiply"
(Jer 23:3).

I once took a course on "addiction and the family." The woman who taugh the course caught my attention one day when she described co-dependency as "a disease of belonging." Most people I know who have struggled with addiction (others' or their own) have wrestled with a gnawing sense of not fitting in, as I noted on Easter this year. Bill W. captures it well, in recommending Step 5: if we take this Step, "we shall get rid of that terrible sense of isolation we've always had. . . . There was always that mysterious barrier we could neither surmount nor understand" (12 X 12, 57).

Ephesians this week talks about a "barrier of hostility that kept us apart." The barrier in question here is the one between Jews and Gentiles, but the world has always been full of such barriers—only the names of the combatants change. People who feel while they're growing up like they don't belong frequently turn that sense of alienation into hatred and violence, in adulthood or even before it. They give up trying to break down the barrier, and start shooting from behind it. According to the Book of Genesis, one of the first children on earth, Cain, acted out his sense of not belonging by killing his more popular brother. And then Cain wandered for the rest of his life, never being at home.

According to Ephesians, this primordial human problem has finally been laid to rest: the "barrier" has been broken down; "enmity" has been "put to death." Jesus accomplished this by dying on the cross, a willing victim of human "hostility." Although Jesus was God's beloved Son, he nevertheless deeply experienced human "isolation" so that the entire "mysterious barrier[s]" might come down. In Christ, we have gone beyond old human divisions to be re-created as "one new human being." Jesus "pitied" all of us lost sheep, looking for a "sheepfold" where we could finally belong. And looking for a shepherd who could finally lead us "beside restful waters" (Ps 23), instead of using our conflicts to further his own ambitions.

For 12-Step people, "the good news of peace" (Eph, quoting Isaiah) comes true especially when we take the 5th Step: "[W]e talked with complete candor of our conflicts, and [we] listened to someone else do the same thing. . . [This] was the beginning of true kinship with man [and woman] and God" (12 X 12, 57). Human divisions, and the resentments that ordinarily accompany them, are "the dubious luxury of [the] normal" (BB, 66). A "spiritual awakening" (Step 12) can show us how to become "partners in a common effort" (12 X 12, 124).

Seventeenth Sunday in Ordinary Time

2 Kgs 4:42–44; Eph 4:1–6; Jn 6:1–15

". . . making every effort to maintain the unity of the Spirit
in the bond of peace"
(Eph 4:3).

This year we have been reading through the Gospel of Mark; if we were to continue this Sunday, we'd be at the story of the Miraculous Feeding of the Crowd, which all four Evangelists tell. But we are using John's version of this story, rather than Mark's. Why? Because the Gospel of John, perhaps the last to be written, typically digs much deeper into the spiritual significance of the stories it recounts. In fact, all of chapter 6 ponders this miracle, and we'll be studying that chapter for the next five weeks.

A few remarks about the story itself, specifically as John tells it. He adds a couple of important touches: Jesus feeds the crowd *near*

Passover; and the story is framed by Jesus being on, or fleeing back to, "the mountain." Passover, of course, is the Jewish feast celebrating the liberation of the children of Israel, when Moses led them out of slavery and into a new, free homeland. "The mountain," too, reminds us of Mount Sinai, where God made a covenant with the newly freed people—in fact, John's word for "mountain" here is the word used in Matthew's Sermon on the Mount, Matthew's version of Jesus' new covenant.

In short, John, like Matthew, is portraying Jesus as the new Moses, setting people free. Jesus does this by feeding them bread and fish, as Moses had called down the manna. But as Jesus' follow-up "sermon" will make clear, Jesus feeds them more significantly with his message, his word, his very self. It's especially Jesus' message that leads them to liberation, as had Moses' call to the people of Israel to leave Egypt behind. The "message" of which the 12th Step speaks also brings liberation: people who listen to it come to "know a new freedom and a new happiness" (BB, 83), which they call "recovery."

But A. A. considers recovery as just one side of the triangle that is an image of the 12-Step program. The other two sides are also relevant to our readings this Sunday. The second side is "unity," and, as Ephesians notes, this is also a product of Jesus' message: "There is but one body and one Spirit [Jesus'], just as there is but one hope given all of you by your call." The third side is "service." The theme of Jesus' Sermon on the Bread of Life will be that to give people a word, a message, of "hope" is to feed them, as he does, and as we do when we pass the message on. This is the best kind of service, as we shall see over the next several Sundays.

Note: In 2006, Roman Catholics will celebrate the Feast of the Transfiguration (August 6) on the following Sunday. See the meditation in Special Feasts.

Eighteenth Sunday in Ordinary Time

*"'Whoever comes to me will never be hungry, whoever believes
in me will never be thirsty'"*
(Jn 6:35).

Addicts have a lot of trouble with the word *enough*, even when it comes
to basic, simple matters like satisfying hunger and thirst. Bill W. sums
this up: "For thousands of years we [alcoholics] have been demanding
more than our share of security, prestige, and romance. . . . Never was
there enough of what we thought we wanted" (12 X 12, 71).

Perhaps this is because we have been looking all along for more
than something to eat and drink, more even than "security, prestige,
and romance." Bill W. believed that, "More than most people, I
think, alcoholics want to know who they are, what this life is about,
whether they have a divine origin and an appointed destiny." Alcoholics, Bill continues, are spiritual seekers who have gotten sidetracked by "the damage wrought by alcohol" (ABSI, 323), the "spiritual" effects of which are all too transient and "perishable." I've
heard it said that inside every addict is a God-shaped hole; no wonder anything short of God leaves us hungry and thirsty.

In today's Gospel, Jesus invites the people he has fed with bread
to look beyond it. Recall that one of the Temptations Jesus rejected at
the beginning of his ministry was to manipulate people into believing
him by performing tricks with bread. The crowd he has now fed
shouldn't be sidetracked just because they've been glutted with "perishable" bread; that bread is only a sign of something greater, of the
One who is the source of a new kind of life. It's what the multiplied
bread *means*, the message it carries, that really matters. The bread is a
"sign" (John organizes his Gospel around Jesus' "signs").

Like Jesus' listeners in today's Gospel, alcoholics need to look
higher: "In A. A., and in many religious approaches, alcoholics find
a great deal more of what they merely glimpsed and felt while trying to grope their way toward God in alcohol." What we need in

order to get the "heightened feeling of identification with the cosmos" (ABSI, 323) we have been seeking is—once again—*metanoia*. Today's reading from Ephesians gives another definition of *metanoia*: "a fresh, spiritual way of thinking." Twelve Steppers get this new attitude in the 2nd Step. And it's essential if we are going to go beyond (temporarily) full stomachs to (permanently) full minds and hearts and lives. Only then will we be done with the "fleshpots" (First Reading, from Exodus) of addiction.

Nineteenth Sunday in Ordinary Time

1 Kgs 19:4–8; Eph 4:30–5:2; Jn 6:41–51

". . . and live in love, as Christ loved us and gave himself up for us,
a fragrant offering and sacrifice to God"
(Eph 5:2).

In our First Reading this Sunday, we hear the story of how the prophet Elijah was given bread by God. Strengthened by that bread, Elijah retraced the steps of his Jewish forebears in the desert by taking forty days (as they had taken forty years) to reach Mount Horeb (another name for Mount Sinai). In the passage after the one we hear today, Elijah has a spiritual experience of God that reaffirms the Sinai covenant God had made in Moses' time.

Bill W. tells a folksy story about a mountain—always a symbol in the world's great stories for spiritual aspiration, always a place to meet God—and about getting distracted from spiritual hunger by earthly food. "I was brought up in a little town in Vermont, under the shadow of Mount Aeolus. An early recollection is that of looking up at this vast and mysterious mountain, wondering what it meant"—the kind of question alcoholics like to ask (see last week's meditation)—"and whether I could ever climb that high."

In other words, mountains were a symbol to Bill for spiritual aspiration from early in his life. Like many alcoholics-to-be, he wanted to "climb . . . high." What happened next? "But I was presently distracted by my aunt who, as a fourth-birthday present, made me a plate of fudge. For the next thirty-five years I pursued the fudge of life and quite forgot about the mountain" (ABSI, 100).

In today's passage from John, Jesus is once again trying to raise up his listeners from "the fudge of life." They are "murmuring"—and this word is repeatedly used in the story of the Exodus to describe the whining of the people of Israel, wanting to go back to the "fleshpots of Egypt," their version of "the fudge of life" (see last week's First Reading). "[T]he fudge of life" is another term for addiction (quite literally for those of us who find chocolate to be a mood-altering substance).

What we need to feed on is Jesus himself, the one who shows the greatest kind of love by laying down his life for his friends. Being nourished by him is the kind of spiritual experience we need to have if we wish "to eat and never die." We should follow Elijah's lead: eat, and then walk toward the Mountain of God. It may be a long "trudge" down "the Road of Happy Destiny" (BB, 164), but if we "have just now tapped into a source of power much greater than [ourselves]" (BB, 163), we know we'll be fed with every step we take.

Twentieth Sunday in Ordinary Time

Prv 9:1–6; Eph 5:15–20; Jn 6:51–58

"'Just as the living Father sent me, and I live because of the Father, so whoever eats me will live because of me'"
(Jn 6:57).

In today's Gospel, Jesus tells his listeners that they need to eat (literally, "chew" or "gnaw") his flesh and drink his blood if they want to have his life—and Abba's—in them. The bluntness of the words, as we will see next week, really bothers his followers. But Jesus is talking about making the ultimate sacrifice, laying down one's life for one's friends, and this calls for tough language. Jesus will go first, but his disciples will be expected to follow suit, in one way or another.

On a brighter note, John uses a favorite word of his, *menein* ("to make a home in"), to express the unity between Jesus and those who "eat" and "drink" him: "Those who feed on my flesh and drink my blood *remain* in me, and I in them." To love as Jesus loved is to be one with Jesus, and one with the God of Jesus, just as intimately as what we eat and drink becomes part of us. The blunt physicality of this reminds us that the kind of loving service Jesus is asking for is not some kind of vague spiritual benevolence, but rather concrete, sometimes grubby acts. Service "may mean the loss of many nights' sleep, great interference with your pleasures, interruptions to your business . . . innumerable trips to police courts, sanitariums, hospitals, jails and asylums. . . . A drunk may smash the furniture in your home, or burn a mattress. You may have to fight with him if he is violent" (BB, 97).

The selection from Ephesians gives a fuller description of people in whom Jesus "makes a home." Since they have drunk of the blood of the Lord, they are "filled"—they have enough, they have "rivers of living water" (Jn 7:38) inside them. And since they have enough, they no longer need to get "drunk on wine that leads to debauchery" (literally, "leads you to the point where you're past saving").

Instead, these satisfied people spend their time giving thanks; their lives are constant gratitude ("always and for everything"). The word for "giving thanks" here is related to Eucharist, the ceremony of sharing in one bread and one cup, at which Christians believe they somehow eat the body and drink the blood of the Lord. Those of us who are both recovering people and Christians can be doubly grateful: we really get to "[m]ake the most of the present opportunity." Stockbroker Bill W. would have loved the literal meaning of this last phrase in Greek: we get to "buy up at exactly the right moment." The love of God is ours for the taking.

Twenty-First Sunday in Ordinary Time

Jos 24:1–2, 15–17, 18; Eph 5:21–32; Jn 6:60–69

*"'Far be it from us that we should forsake the LORD to serve other
gods; for it is the LORD our God who brought us and our ancestors
up from the land of Egypt, out of the house of slavery . . .' "*
(Jos 24:16–17).

Both our First and Third Readings this Sunday are about moments
of decision. In the First Reading, the people of Israel have been
summoned by Moses' lieutenant and successor, Joshua, to decide
whether they will worship Moses' God, or whether they will worship
the gods of other peoples. Will they reaffirm the Sinai covenant,
especially since God has lived up to God's part of the deal by bringing them to the Promised Land? In the Gospel, the new people of
Israel have been summoned by Moses' successor, Jesus (see the Seventeenth Sunday in Ordinary Time, and the entire Gospel of
Matthew, for the Jesus-Moses identification). Jesus' name comes
from "Joshua," "Savior." Jesus challenges the new Israel to decide
whether they will worship his God, Abba, or whether they will break
"away and . . . not remain in [Jesus'] company any longer" (*not remain*
literally means "go backwards").

This moment of decision is a lot like Step 3. And just as with
Step 3—or any Step, for that matter—it's a good idea to review the
previous Step, Step 2, before taking the following Step. The people
of Israel do so in Joshua 24: in the events of the Exodus, they have
come to understand God as the One Who Freed Them From Slavery;
and they reason that it makes sense to turn their wills and their lives
over to the care of such a liberating God. Surely God wouldn't set
them free and then let them wander forever.

In the Gospels, Peter is often the spokesman for the other disciples; a climax in Mark and Matthew is his public assertion that Jesus
is the Messiah. Like the people of Israel under Joshua, Peter comes

to the conclusion that it would be stupid to go to someone else, because Jesus has the message of life. Peter has "come to believe" that the God whom Jesus calls Abba, the God who makes a home in people, can bring people out of slavery, just as the God of Moses once did. Just so, it only makes sense for us who have been restored to sanity to entrust our wills and our lives to the Great Restorer we have encountered. If we have been attending 12-Step meetings, "we [have] been seeing another kind of flight [Bill is thinking of the Wright brothers], a spiritual liberation from this world, people who rose above their problems. . . . We had seen spiritual release . . ." In the light of our experience, "[w]hat is our choice to be?" (BB, 55, 53).

Twenty-Second Sunday in Ordinary Time

Dt 4:1–2, 6–8; Jas 1:17–18, 21–22, 27; Mk 7:1–8, 14–15, 21–23

"Religion that is pure and undefiled before God, the Father, is this:
to care for orphans and widows in their distress,
and to keep oneself unstained by the world"
(Jas 1:27).

As I mentioned on the Third Sunday of Advent, Cycle A, the Letter of James, from which we will be reading for the next several weeks, was a favorite of Bill W.'s and Dr. Bob's. In fact, one of the suggested names for the little group that later called itself Alcoholics Anonymous was the James Movement (Bill was also quite taken with "the Bill W. Movement," but less inflated heads prevailed).

Bill and Bob particularly liked James's stress on the actions that naturally flow from faith; they were firm believers in "action and more action" (BB, 88). James's letter is cited several times in the Big Book. From the very beginning of his conversion, Bill grasped that works would have to accompany faith. Ebby T., the man who brought Bill the concept of a religious (or spiritual) experience as a key to recovery from alcoholism, told Bill that "Faith without works was dead . . .

And how appallingly true for the alcoholic! For if an alcoholic failed to perfect and enlarge his spiritual life through work and self-sacrifice for others, he could not survive the certain trials and low spots ahead. If he did not work, he would surely drink again, and if he drank, he would surely die. Then faith would be dead indeed" (BB, 14–15).

Jesus is making a related point about faith and action in the Gospel today. Pious Jews of his time believed that certain practices demonstrated a person's devoutness. Mark, writing for a non-Jewish audience, felt the need to explain these practices, not very sympathetically (Matthew, writing for a Jewish-Christian audience, is more tactful). Mark's Jesus argues that these practices, applying as they do to diet and hygiene, are only about what goes on inside a person, like James's "faith"; but it's what comes out of a person, their actions, that matter. From this point of view, whether a human being serves others in love matters more than their observance of the kosher laws.

For the purposes of 12-Step recovery, what this means is that it's not enough to work only the first 3 Steps and acquire a lot of faith; what is needed is "more action" (BB, 76; James is quoted here, too). We show the faith that we've acquired in the first three Steps by working Steps 4 through 9. We "demonstrat[e] these principles in all [our] affairs" by "work[ing] with others" (BB, 14)—in other words, by taking the 12th Step.

Twenty-Third Sunday in Ordinary Time

Is 35:4–7; Jas 2:1–5; Mk 7:31–37

"Then the eyes of the blind shall be opened, and the ears
of the deaf unstopped; then the lame shall leap like a deer,
and the tongue of the speechless sing for joy"
(Is 35:5–6).

This week's passage from Mark is another favorite of mine; I have reflected on it in Meditation 28 of *A 12-Step Approach to the Spiritual*

Exercises. For me it's associated with my younger brother, Tim, who died of AIDS some years ago. He loved working with hearing-impaired children (although not hearing impaired himself); he had a great openness to new people and new experiences, which I largely lack. When I celebrated Mass for an AIDS support group a few months after his death, this Gospel was the reading for the day. Ever since, when I hear about impairment or openness, or when I remember a line from "That's What Friends Are For," a song the proceeds from which go to AIDS research—"Well, you came and opened me / And now there's so much more I see"—I think of this cluster of associations as a tight little packet of grace.

In today's Gospel, Mark talks about a man's ears being "opened," so he can hear. Remember, Mark is writing for a non-Jewish audience. Yet he thought the word *Ephphatha* was so important that he says it in Aramaic, the language Jesus spoke, and then translates it for his Greek-speaking readers: "Be opened!"

The Christian churches in their turn have followed Mark's lead. For many centuries, when a child was baptized, the baptizer touched the child's tongue and said, "Ephphatha." Baptism means, among other things, that the child—or the adult—being baptized has come home to a loving community. So it's safe for the baptized person to be "open" to the world, as dangerous and beautiful as the world is, because the person is among friends.

Luke (in his story of the disciples on the road to Emmaus, chapter 24) uses the same Greek word to describe two disciples whose eyes Jesus "opens." We in recovery also need openness: open eyes, open ears, open hearts (A. A. uses the acronym H.O.W. for the three essentials of recovery: Honesty, Open-Mindedness, and Willingness [BB, 550]). And once we have heard the stories of those who reached recovery before us, "the bond of [our] tongue is loosened, and [we] talk straight" [my literal translation]. We talk straight when we say "what we used to be like, what happened, and what we are like now" (BB, 58). We talk straight when we admit our powerlessness; as James says, echoing Matthew's First Beatitude, it's the poor, the "beggars in filthy clothes" [literally], who have been chosen by

God to be "rich in faith and heirs of the kingdom." We talk straight when we tell our story.

Note: In 2003, Roman Catholics will celebrate the feast of the Holy Cross (September 14) on the following Sunday. See the meditation in Special Feasts.

Twenty-Fourth Sunday in Ordinary Time

Is 50:5–9; Jas 2:14–18; Mk 8:27–35

"If any want to become my followers, let them deny themselves and take up their cross and follow me'"
(Mk 8:34).

In this Sunday's Gospel, Jesus urges his followers to "deny" themselves. The word for "deny" is only used twice in the Gospels: in variations on this saying and in the story of Peter's "denial" of Jesus after Jesus is arrested. So it's a strongly negative word: Jesus is asking us to distance ourselves from ourselves as thoroughly as Peter did from Jesus. Especially these days, when people are "into" finding themselves, our response might well be "What an order! I can't go through with it" (BB, 60).

Yet Bill W. came to the conclusion that this kind of self-denial was essential for recovering people. In the Big Book, right after he first lists the 12 Steps, he tries to get at the root of the alcoholic's problem. He concludes that "the alcoholic is an extreme example of self-will run riot, though he usually doesn't think so. Above everything, we alcoholics must be rid of this selfishness. We must, or it kills us. . . . Neither could we reduce our self-centeredness much by wishing or trying on our own power. We had to have God's help" (BB, 62).

As a human being, Jesus was as tempted to this kind of selfishness as any alcoholic is. This is why he calls his close friend Peter a "satan" (tempter) in this selection from Mark: Peter is suggesting that Jesus be a Messiah on Jesus' terms, not on Abba's. Couldn't Jesus use just a *little* self-will, so that events wouldn't be so unpleasant for Jesus and his followers? Peter doesn't know it, but of course he is repeating the essence of the Temptations Jesus experienced in the desert at the beginning of his ministry, Temptations engineered by Satan with a capital S.

Interestingly, the word translated "turned around" (Jesus "turned around and . . . reprimanded Peter") means "was converted" in many other places in the Christian Scriptures. To be the kind of Messiah who would put his faith into practice, as James urges this Sunday, Jesus "had to have God's help," too. He had to let go of his own self-will, at the beginning, at the middle—which is where we are in Mark this Sunday—and at the end of his ministry, in the Garden on the night before he died.

With "God's help," recovering people also become capable of "prodig[ies] of service," as Bill W. said of the pioneering work with alcoholics of Dr. Bob and Sister Ignatia at St. Thomas Hospital, in Akron, Ohio. Bill explains this "turn-around": ". . . we are now on a different basis; the basis of trusting and relying upon God. We trust infinite God rather than our finite selves" (BB, 68). When it comes to the most basic decisions about our lives, we deny ourselves—and affirm God.

Twenty-Fifth Sunday in Ordinary Time

Wis 2:17–20; Jas 3:16–4:3; Mk 9:30–37

"Whoever wants to be first must be last of all and servant of all"
(Mk 9:35).

This week's Gospel follows up on last week's question of what kind of Messiah Jesus is. Like Peter last Sunday, the disciples are on the wrong track: Jesus keeps telling them that he is the kind of Messiah who loses big, is killed, and yet keeps going. But "they failed to understand his words" ("they didn't get it" would be a fair translation). They go on to demonstrate how very much they don't get it: once they get to where they're going, Jesus asks them what they were "discussing on the way home," and they are too embarrassed to confess that they have been "arguing about who was most important." This is the kind of question that makes no sense in terms of the kind of Messiah Jesus is; if they really "got it," they might be discussing who would be the lucky one with the grubbiest jail cell, or the worst beating by the authorities.

We addicts and compulsive people have little room to criticize the disciples for not "getting it," though. Figuring out "Who is the greatest?" accounts for most of the conversation in bars and alcoholic homes. It is not unheard of at 12-Step meetings, although the language may be cunningly altered—Bill W. uses the unmatchable term "bleeding deacons" for power freaks in A. A. (12 X 12, 135). Like the disciples, recovering people need to undergo a *metanoia* before they can fully grasp how power is going to be exercised in the fellowship, or in what Jesus called "the reign of God."

For 12 Steppers, Tradition 2 sums this up neatly: "For our group purpose there is but one ultimate authority—a loving God as He may express Himself in our group conscience. Our leaders are but trusted servants; they do not govern." The last sentence of this Tradition is especially important—so important that it was *added* to the Long Form (yes; the Short Form of Tradition 2 is *longer* than the Long Form! See Tradition 9).

For Jesus, "Messiah" and "Trusted Servant" were synonyms. This is why the early church liked to apply to Jesus the so-called Servant Songs in the second part of Isaiah (chapters 40–55; one of the Songs is used every year on the Feast of the Baptism of the Lord). Like Bill W., Jesus thought that "[s]ervice, gladly rendered" came first on the list of the "satisfactions of right living" (12 X 12, 124).

Twenty-Sixth Sunday in Ordinary Time

Nm 11:25–29; Jas 5:1–6; Mk 9:38–43, 45, 47–48

"'Would that all the LORD's people were prophets, and that the
LORD would put his spirit on them!'"
(Nm 11:29)

With this weekend's readings, we are still on the subject of power in
relationships. This time John plays the role of Dim Disciple (usually
played by Peter). He hasn't gotten what kind of Messiah Jesus is any
better than Peter has, so he smugly tells Jesus that he and the other
disciples saw an Unauthorized Person carrying the message and
inducing spiritual experiences in others. "Naturally, we cut *him* off
short" [literal translation of "we tried to stop him"]! As he has with
Peter, Jesus brings John up short for assuming that Jesus thinks
along these lines. On the contrary, Jesus believes that "anyone who
is not against us is with us."

Religious people might do well to keep Jesus' words in mind.
And recovering people might do just as well to ponder these suggestions of Bill W.'s: "If [someone you have visited on a 12th-Step
call] thinks he can do the job in some other way, or prefers some
other spiritual approach, encourage him to follow his own conscience. We have no monopoly on God; we merely have an
approach that worked with us" (BB, 95). Or, even more pointedly,
"Ministers and doctors are competent and you can learn much from
them if you wish . . . So cooperate; never criticize. To be helpful is
our only aim" (BB, 89).

The gruesome sayings that end today's Gospel should be read in
this context of tolerance and cooperation. For many of us, it is not
our hands or our feet or our eyes that give us trouble; rather,
"Selfishness—self-centeredness! That, we think, is the root of
our troubles" (BB, 62). If we want to enter the kingdom—if Jesus is
truly to be our Messiah—then we need to undergo "ego-ectomies."

"Better for you to enter the kingdom of God" with a slightly smaller self than to undergo "ten or fifteen years of literal hell" (12 X 12, 23) because your ego is too big to let you recover. We'll know our ego-surgery has worked if we stop "cutting people off short" for disagreeing with us.

Instead, we ought to emulate Moses in the passage from Numbers: even though Eldad and Medad failed to show up at the Very Important Meeting, Moses was glad that the Spirit of God came upon them. "To us, the Realm of Spirit is broad, roomy, all inclusive; never exclusive or forbidding to those who earnestly seek. It is open, we believe, to all men [and women]" (BB, 46). Even to Eldad and Medad; even to those who "prefer some other spiritual approach" than ours (BB, 95).

Twenty-Seventh Sunday in Ordinary Time

Gn 2:18–24; Heb 2:9–11; Mk 10:2–16

"It was fitting that God, for whom and through whom all things exist,
in bringing many children to glory, should make the pioneer
of their salvation perfect through sufferings"
(Heb 2:10).

When Bill W. wrote in the early 1950s about marriages in recovery, he painted a rather blithe picture: "Most married folks in A. A. have very happy homes. To a surprising extent, A. A. has offset the damage to family life brought about by years of alcoholism. . . . Permanent marriage breakups and separations . . . are unusual in A. A." (12 X 12, 117). However, when passages like these are read at meetings these days, they are sometimes met with derisive or cynical guffaws.

It's worth remembering that Bill was talking about an optimal situation, where both—or all—members of a family grow into recovery. In this best-case scenario, "[w]hether the family has spiritual convictions or not, they may do well to examine the principles by which the alcoholic member is trying to live" (BB, 130; Al-Anon was founded in the early 1950s to help people "examine the principles").

The fact is, however, that this best case often doesn't happen. Only one member embraces "spiritual convictions." Frequently the marriage or the relationship ends just as one or both members are finally taking the huge risk of being who they think they really are. A friend of mine says that he came home after taking his first, very painful 5th Step, at about six months of being sober; when he told his wife what he had just done, she responded, "Big deal! I want a divorce." Whether or not we agree with Bill that "pain [is] the touchstone of all spiritual progress" (12 X 12, 93–94), breakups like this cause enormous "suffering" (Heb).

In today's Gospel, Jesus is, like Bill W., describing the ideal, an ideal that goes back to the prototype, the "marriage" of the first human beings in the Garden of Eden. Marriages ought to resemble the healthy unity of two people ("one body") who have achieved healthy severance from everyone else ("leaves . . . father and mother")—which is what Family Systems therapists call "individuation." But like the disciples, or like 12 Steppers these days, we can't help questioning this in the light of what so often goes wrong.

Churches differ on how practically to implement Jesus' ideal. But in any case, we can take heart, because Jesus is also a person who became "perfect [that is, wholly the person he was meant to be] through suffering"; and so he can "sympathize with our weaknesses" (Heb 4:15). Encouraged by this, we can strive in our relationships to "grow by our willingness to face and rectify errors and convert them into assets" (BB, 124).

Twenty-Eighth Sunday in Ordinary Time

Wis 7:7–11; Heb 4:12–13; Mk 10:17–30

"'It is easier for a camel to go through the eye of a needle
than for someone who is rich to enter the kingdom of God'"
(Mk 10:25).

Alcoholics are excessive people—hardly a surprising statement. As
Bill W. puts it, "For thousands of years we [alcoholics] have been
demanding more than our share of security, prestige, and romance"
(12 X 12, 71). But alcoholics may not be the only people who
"dream still greater dreams" (71) about money and sex. "No human
being, however good, is exempt from these troubles. Nearly every
serious emotional problem can be seen as a case of misdirected
instinct" (12 X 12, 42).

In last Sunday's Gospel, Jesus threw cold water on people who
want more "romance" than human beings usually get; human beings
should be, he said, like Adam and Eve, two becoming one—but only
two, not seventeen. This week Jesus is being equally blunt about
money, and thus about the security it brings: it's very hard for the
rich to enter the kingdom of God, as hard as shoving a camel through
the eye of a needle (by the way, there have been plenty of misguided
attempts over the centuries to water down this saying).

Once again, as he did last week, Jesus seems to read the minds
of his disciples. "Nothing is concealed from him" (Heb). They "mar-
vel" and are "completely overwhelmed" at his remarks on money,
just as they balked at the marital ideal he proposed last week. They
had probably been hoping that, if they followed Jesus, sure, it would
be tough at first, but eventually their ministry would catch on, and
then there would be plenty of money, property, and prestige, with
thrones and castles and a certain amount of discreet sex.

The disciples came by these great expectations honestly. After
all, in the Hebrew Scriptures wealth, is often a sign of God's favor:

as today's passage from the Book of Wisdom states, "[A]ll good things together came to me in [wisdom's] company." Wisdom is no doubt better than gold, but if you're wise, you ought to be able to have the wisdom *and* the gold. "*Fools* and their money are soon parted."

As usual in Mark, the disciples are failing to get the idea that Jesus' concept of the kingdom of God is very different from these traditional ideas. Air-conditioned doghouses are not the Keys to his Kingdom. Jesus has news for them, news incorporated into the structure of 12-Step groups: they aren't going to get rich, "lest problems of money, property, and prestige divert [them] from [their] primary purpose" (Tradition 6). Their, and our, "dependence" must be "on God" (BB, 98), "with [Whom] all things are possible."

Twenty-Ninth Sunday in Ordinary Time

Is 53:10–11; Heb 4:14–16; Mk 10:35–45

> *"'. . . but whoever wishes to become great among you
> must be your servant, and whoever wishes to be first
> among you must be slave of all'"*
> (Mk 10:43–44).

Herb Caen, the late San Francisco gossip columnist, used to print an occasional item under the heading "Unclear on the Concept." For example, "the Committee to Stamp Out Alcoholism will be having a cocktail party Thursday evening at the Marin Conference Center." Today's Gospel recounts another incident in the continuing cycle of Jesus' disciples being "unclear" about the "concepts" of "Messiah" and "reign of God."

An earlier example of this occurred in the Gospel for the Twenty-Fifth Sunday in Ordinary Time. On that occasion, Jesus told the Twelve that he was going to be crucified, after which they argued about who would be greatest in the kingdom. They were "unclear" on Jesus' "concept" of "greatness," which doesn't fit well

with the form of execution especially imposed on rebelling slaves.
In this week's incident, two of Jesus' favorite disciples try to
strike a behind-the-scenes deal with him to make sure they'll get top
spots in the kingdom. Matthew's version of this event makes James
and John appear to be even sleazier: they send their *mother* to Jesus
to put the fix in. Thank God Jesus can, as Hebrews notes, "sympathize with our weakness." Instead of blowing up, he patiently goes
over the "concept" one more time: what awaits him—and the bump-
tious "Sons of Thunder" (their nickname in Mark) as well—is a
"bath of pain." Is *that* what they want? Clueless on the "concept,"
James and John burble, "Sure!" Jesus dryly notes that they'll get the
pain, all right; the thrones are another matter.

"The other ten" are having just as much trouble grasping the
"concept" that "Our leaders are but trusted servants; they do not govern" (Tradition 2). So Jesus has to spell it out for them again by
reminding them to "follow" him in service. That will mean following him to crucifixion and death, as suggested by the Isaiah passage
in the First Reading. It is from his well-known 53rd chapter, which
has always been crucial in the Christian understanding of the "concept" of Jesus as a suffering Messiah.

Service work is "the will of the Lord," which in the 11th Step
recovering people pray to know and do. As Isaiah and Bill W. might
say, "the will of the Lord [is] accomplished" in people who are willing to "see how [their] experience can benefit others . . . [n]o matter
how far down the scale [they] have gone" (BB, 84). "Clear" on the
"concept," these people "see the light in fullness of days" (Is).

Thirtieth Sunday in Ordinary Time

Jer 31:7–9; Heb 5:1–6; Mk 10:46–52

*"'Go; your faith has made you well.' Immediately [the blind man]
regained his sight and followed [Jesus] on the way"*
(Mk 10:52).

We have arrived at that moment in Mark's Gospel when Jesus is
about to enter Jerusalem to die. Very soon now anyone will be able
to see what kind of Messiah he is—everyone will become "clear on
the concept." As I mentioned on Palm Sunday this year, the "concept" will be so "clear" that even a *goy*, the Roman centurion super-
vising the crucifixion of Jesus, will be able to see that Jesus is "the
son of God!" (Mk 15:39). To foreshadow this burst of clarity, today's
Gospel, the last story from Jesus' ministry, from his time on "the
road," is about someone receiving the power to see.

The blind man calls on him as "Son of David," which is one of the
titles of the Messiah. But unlike the disciples, with their requests for
"money, property, and prestige," blind Bartimaeus understands what
kind of Messiah Jesus has decided to be. As we have seen at every step
in Mark's Gospel, Jesus has chosen, from the moment of his baptism
by John on, and especially during his temptations in the desert, to be
a peaceful Messiah. It's to this merciful Messiah, "Son of David," that
the blind man reaches out. He takes a kind of 1st Step: the essence of
this Step is "have pity on me!" All he wants to receive is sight—no
money, no power. And once he comes to believe, once his "faith"
"restores" him (Step 2), he does begin to see. Then he takes the next
indicated Step: he "follow[s] [Jesus] up the road." He has decided to
turn his will and his life over to the one who has healed him (Step 3).

The word for "road" here is important in the Christian Scriptures. In some places (especially in Acts), the "Way" (same word)
means being a Christian, following Jesus: before his conversion,
Paul (then called Saul) received "letters" empowering him to bust

any "man or woman [in Damascus], living according to the new *way*" (Acts 9:2). So what the ex-blind man does, once he can see this Jesus, Son of David, is to follow Jesus on Jesus' "Way" into Jerusalem, the place of Jesus' suffering service. Bartimaeus is on the road, and he's on the Road.

He's following a classic pattern. He could say, with Paul, and with Bill W., "Scales of pride and prejudice fell from my eyes. A new world came into view" (BB, 12). Like a 12 Stepper, Bartimaeus will in his turn carry the message down "the Road" of Happy Destiny. When he tells his story, when he works his 12th Step, all he will need to say is, "I once . . . was blind, but now I see."

Note: In 2003, Roman Catholics will celebrate the Feast of All Souls (November 2nd) on the following Sunday. See the meditation in Special Feasts. In 2008, Roman Catholics will celebrate the Feast of All Saints (November 1) on the following Sunday. See the meditation in Special Feasts.

Thirty-First Sunday in Ordinary Time

Dt 6:2–6; Heb 7:23–28; Mk 12:28–34

". . . and, 'to love him with all the heart,
and with all the understanding, and with all the strength,'
and 'to love one's neighbor as oneself'—this is much more important
than all whole burnt offerings and sacrifices"
(Mk 12:33).

Mark captures a beautiful moment in Jesus' story this Sunday. It is a few days before his death. He is involved, as so often before, in a dispute with his beloved enemies, the scribes and Pharisees; they have been arguing for two chapters. Suddenly, amid all the hostility and the trick questions, someone makes a straightforward inquiry, one that had been posed to rabbis before Jesus: "Which is the first [in importance] of all the commandments?" Jesus gives an answer that comes so profoundly from the heart of what it means for him—or for anyone—to be a Jew that his questioner agrees with him, almost in spite of himself, in a rush of spiritual fellow feeling: "Excellent, Teacher! You are right . . ."

Jesus wins this scribe's heart partly because Jesus' answer quotes the Sh'ma Yizroel. The Sh'ma is the daily prayer of Jews; it is like the Lord's Prayer for Christians or the Serenity Prayer for Recovering People. Moving stories are told of Jews reciting the Sh'ma as they went to the gas chambers during the Holocaust. This ancient prayer begins with these words: "Hear, O Israel: The LORD is our God, the LORD alone. You shall love the LORD your God with all your heart, with all your soul, [with all your mind,] and with all your might" (see Dt 6:4–5—Jesus adds "with all your mind").

When Jesus' challenger hears these sacred words, "feuds of years' standing melt away [quickly]" (BB, 78). The scribe suddenly sees, like the blind man last week. Jesus may be from the backwoods of Galilee, but he is an "[e]xcellent Teacher." Instead of comparing, the scribe identifies with Jesus, and realizes that they share "general principles common to most denominations" (BB, 94).

And what are the "spiritual principles" (BB, 93) that they share, and that they strive to "practice . . . in all their affairs"? Wholehearted love of God and service of one's neighbor. In his answer to the scribe Jesus coupled the Sh'ma (from Deuteronomy) with the "principle" of service (from Leviticus): "You shall love your neighbor as yourself" (Lv 19:18; Jesus also characteristically enlarged the meaning of "neighbor" to include non-Jews). He knew that "[e]very day is a day when we must carry the vision of God's will into all of our activities" (BB, 85). This is what "the reign of God" is about—not "money, property, or prestige," and not "win[ning] a useless argument" (12 X 12, 94).

Note: In 2003, Roman Catholics will celebrate the Feast of the Dedication of the Church of St. John Lateran (November 9) on the following Sunday. See the meditation in Special Feasts.

Thirty-Second Sunday in Ordinary Time

1 Kgs 17:10–16; Heb 9:24–28; Mk 12:38–44

"'For all of them have contributed out of their abundance;
but she out of her poverty has put in everything she had,
all she had to live on'"
(Mk 12:44).

One of the storytellers in the back of the Big Book wryly tries to com-
pute how much his "club" membership in A. A. cost him, purely in
financial terms (BB, 396–399). He arrives at a large dollar amount,
especially in the uninflated dollars of the time when he wrote his
story, but acknowledges that even this doesn't cover the "intangible
initiation fees": "the sick, sick hangovers, the remorse, guilt, broken
homes, jails, and institutions, and the mental anguish in general that
has been generated over the years. Only God as we understand [God]
can calculate these" (399).

Our Gospel today tells the story of a woman who also paid a
high price—indeed, "all she had to live on"—but for a very different
purpose. She is a "widow." Widows are a special class in the fellowship of God's people, both in the Hebrew and the Christian
Scriptures. In a patriarchal society, widows without grown sons are
completely powerless: they do not have a man in their lives to support and protect them (it was all but impossible during Jesus' time
for a woman to be "self-supporting through [her] own contribu-
tions"). The widow of Zarephath in the First Reading is typically
destitute.

But the powerlessness of widows made them that much more
important to the rest of the Jewish or Christian communities, since
they so clearly lived out dependence on the Higher Power. The rest of
us are dependent, too, but we tend to forget it, and the widows remind
us, and also give us a chance to do service work by helping them.

Jesus is praising this widow, then, for working a very thorough 3rd Step. She could reasonably claim that the fellowship should be helping her, rather than her making any kind of contribution. Instead, she is turning over all that she has to God as she understands God. Mark could well add the earlier words of Jesus, ". . . whoever does not receive the kingdom of God as a little child will never enter" (Mk 10:15). This widow knows a great spiritual secret: we have to "giv[e] away the entire product" of the spiritual gold mine we have found in order to keep it (BB, 128–29). Clearly, she has had such a powerful spiritual experience that "[f]ear of . . . economic insecurity [has left her]" (BB, 84). The point is so obvious that Jesus doesn't spell it out: blessed is this widow, for "the reign of God is [hers]" (Mt 5:3).

Thirty-Third Sunday in Ordinary Time

Dn 12:1–3; Heb 10:11–14, 18; Mk 13:24–32

"'Heaven and earth will pass away, but my words
will not pass away'"
(Mk 13:31).

As I mentioned around this time last year, our Gospels on these Sundays, as we end another church cycle of Scripture readings, reflect on the end of all things. For Christians, Jesus' return is the longed-for end of the story of God's people. In fact, the early Christians, contemporaries of Mark and Paul, cheerfully believed that Jesus would be back very soon (in Mark, Jesus says, "This generation will not pass away until all these things take place"; see also the meditation for the Thirty-Second Sunday in Ordinary Time, Cycle A). In the later Gospels there is a growing sense that it may be a while until Jesus returns, and that the fellowship needs to create some Traditions so it can be ready for what may be a long wait (see, for example, Matthew's Community Discourse, chapter 18 in his Gospel).

Even back in the early days, "trusted servants" like Mark also offered some cautions about Jesus' "imminent" return. Then—and now—people could easily become so obsessed with it that they would "rest on [their] laurels" (BB, 85) instead of carrying the message—or holding down a job. Even worse, some, who had a "grouch" or a "brainstorm" ("the dubious luxury of [the] normal"—BB, 66), began to make lists for the returning Jesus of those who, in their judgment, ought to be placed on the left side of Jesus' trial bench, with the goats (see Mt 25:31–46). It's partly to calm down these excitable types that Mark quotes Jesus to the effect that only Abba—and not even Jesus himself—knows the time for the coming of "the Son of Man."

Unfortunately, even this blunt statement hasn't stopped a lot of people over the centuries from trying to second guess Abba (frequently with an eye to getting some "money, property, and prestige" by frightening people). They turn up especially at times like the present. If people like these have been getting to you, bear in mind that the usual message of God to people at Jesus' first Advent was "Do not be afraid." A better strategy for people who are "trudg[ing] the Road of Happy Destiny" (BB, 164) is to remember a few simple slogans: "Easy Does It"; "One Day at a Time" (or, as Thoreau reportedly said on his deathbed, "One world at a time"); and ". . . remember, I am with you always, to the end of the age" (the last line of Matthew's Gospel, 28:20).

Feast of Christ the King

Dn 7:13–14; Rv 1:5–8; Jn 18:33–37

"To him who loves us and freed us from our sins by his blood,
and made us to be a kingdom, priests serving his God and Father,
to him be glory and dominion forever and ever. Amen"
(Rv 1:5–6).

This Sunday brings Cycle B, during which we have been reading through the Gospel of Mark, to a close. From the very beginning of those readings last January until now, the great theme has been the reign, the kingdom, of God. Especially over the last several weeks, Jesus has been trying to help his friends, including us, to understand that he is the Messiah (Anointed One, the Ruler) of a different kind of reign than most human beings, and particularly his Jewish contemporaries, can only imagine.

On this last Sunday we celebrate that reign, and Jesus as that ruler. The reading from Daniel suggests that Jesus is the Son of Humanity (Son of Man)—or the Son of Us All, as a friend of mine puts it. Jesus the Ruler is not different from the rest of us. Along the same lines, the Letter to the Hebrews has been insisting for weeks that Jesus is a great high priest precisely because he sympathizes so deeply with his human sisters and brothers, because he learned to be a priest through what he suffered.

Today's Gospel, from John the Theologian, not from Mark, gives us Jesus' final words about the reign. At this climactic moment Jesus is not with his dim but well-intentioned friends; he is face to face with the authorities (for more on this passage, see Meditation 41 in *A 12-Step Approach to the Spiritual Exercises*). But even to Pilate, the Roman governor, Jesus can only say what he has been saying all along: "My kingdom is not here."

We can tell how different his kingdom is because only his blood is being shed in loving service. "If my kingdom were of this world, my subjects would be fighting"—slaughtering and being slaughtered—"to save me from being handed over" (Jn). In all earthly kingdoms, "[T]he struggle for wealth, power, and prestige [tears] humanity apart." Addicts, and the people who love them, are not the only human beings who are "victim[s] of the delusion that [they] can wrest satisfaction and happiness out of this world if [they] only manage well" (BB, 61).

But Jesus' kingdom is not of this world. As Jesus puts it, very simply, at the Last Supper (in Luke), "But not so with you"—"you" being anyone who wants to follow him (Lk 22:26). In his death, Jesus is giving his last and greatest lesson about "how best to live and work together as groups" (12 X 12, 130). His Way is this: "God makes [it] possible . . . [to] be rid of . . . selfishness" (BB, 62).

CYCLE C

December 2003–2004

December 2006–2007

December 2009–2010

✛

Advent
and Christmas

First Sunday of Advent

Jer 33:14–16; 1 Thes 3:12–4:2; Lk 21:25–28, 34–36

"And may he [God] so strengthen your hearts in holiness
that you may be blameless before our God and Father
at the coming of our Lord Jesus with all his saints"
(1 Thes 3:13).

During Advent, when we remember the First Coming ("advent") of Jesus, we also look forward to his Second Coming—and we *do* look forward, with anticipation, not dread. Of course the language used in today's selection from Luke, our Gospel of choice in Cycle C, seems pretty dreadful at first glance—"nations will be in anguish, distraught at the roaring of the seas," "people will die of fright," and so on. This sounds more like a Wes Craven film than like "good news."

Some Bible history can help here: this kind of religious language and thought has been popular from time to time through the centuries, and appears in parts of the Bible (Daniel in the Hebrew Scriptures, Revelation in the Christian Scriptures, as well as parts of Matthew, Mark, and Luke). It's called *apocalyptic*, from the Greek word for "uncover," "disclose"; it's rather similar to fantasy literature in its vivid language and imagery, including dragons, battles, plenty of blood and fire. Its purpose in the Bible, however, is more than just an imaginative escape; biblical apocalyptic is meant to give hope to a persecuted community by assuring the members that God is secretly on their side, however grim things may look just at the present. What is "uncovered" is the fact that God will come through for God's overwhelmed people. Frequently the lurid, mysterious language is meant to keep the authorities from catching on should these "subversive" writings fall into the wrong hands.

So the Book of Daniel was written to sustain the Jews during a persecution conducted by Antiochus Epiphanes, the *goy* king of neighboring Syria. This "apocalyptic" book claims to describe

192

events from five hundred years earlier, but if you know how to "uncover" it, you will grasp that it really predicts that the Jews (including the Maccabeean freedom fighters) who are resisting the evil foreigner will overcome in the end, with God's help. In the same way, Revelation was meant to assure early Christians during a ferocious persecution by the Roman Empire that all would be well if they kept the faith; the mighty empire would be the surprise loser in this struggle.

What should our reaction to these "apocalyptic" parts of the Bible be? Luke says we shouldn't get drunk over them (21:34), a warning suitable for more than alcoholics: many other people get intoxicated with "apocalyptic" because of the angry rush it can give them. But feeling persecuted, like feeling resentful, is "the dubious luxury of normal [people]" (BB, 66), as well as the very "dubious luxury" of the paranoid. Better to focus in "the coming days" on what is true for us: in God we "shall be safe and . . . shall dwell secure" (Jer).

Second Sunday of Advent

Bar 5:1–9; Phil 1: 4–6, 8–11; Lk 3:1–6

"[John the Baptist] went into all the region around the Jordan, proclaiming a baptism of repentance for the forgiveness of sins . . ."
(Lk 3:3).

Mona Simpson gets the title for her wonderful novel *Anywhere But Here* from a passage of Emerson's that she quotes as an epigraph: "There are three wants which can never be satisfied: that of the rich wanting more, that of the sick wanting something different, and that of the traveler who says, 'anywhere but here.'" Addicts and co-dependents know all about "can't get no satisfaction," know about "wanting more," "wanting something different," wanting to be "anywhere but here."

In today's Gospel, Luke solemnly announces when and where Jesus' adult story began. "B.C." (and B.C.E.) and "A.D." weren't used until long after the Gospels were written, so "when" had to be indicated by the reigns of kings and chiefs. Almost with audible trumpet fanfares, Luke proclaims: "In the fifteenth year of the rule of Tiberius Caesar, when Pontius Pilate was procurator of Judea, Herod tetrarch of Galilee, Philip his brother tetrarch of the region of Ituraea and Trachonitis, and Lysanias tetrarch of Abilene, during the high-priesthood of Annas and Caiaphas, the word of God was spoken to John son of Zechariah in the desert."

These then are the people—some of them terrible (Herod, Annas, Caiaphas), some of them pretty good (Philip), some of them unknown (Lysanias)—who were the powers-that-be when John the Baptist became a precursor of Jesus' ministry. And "the salvation of God," God's reign, became visible "to all humankind" (Lk, quoting Is). Yet these earth-changing events happened largely in places about which the Roman emperor, Tiberius, the first-named and most important earthly ruler on Luke's list, would have known little and cared less.

What matters about this, I think, is that Jesus was born and served God and neighbor in a very particular place and time. The power of God shone forth in this particular human being, who lived in an obscure place and was (at the time) an unknown compared to the political figures Luke cites. And Jesus was content—he did not want to be "anywhere but here," did not want to have more, to be different. What we addicts and compulsive people need is not some other place or time; what we need is "a change in attitude" (*metanoia*—translated "baptism of *repentance*" in today's Gospel). Only by "learn[ing] to value the things that really matter" (Phil) can we move from the "discontent" that characterizes the "dry" alcoholic (BB, xxvi) to a "newfound peace [that] is a price-less gift" (12 X 12, 74). And this change of heart is what John son of Zechariah proclaimed in the desert, there and then.

Third Sunday of Advent

Zep 3:14–18; Phil 4:4–7; Lk 3:10–18

*"The LORD, your God, is in your midst, a warrior who gives victory;
he will rejoice over you with gladness, he will renew you in his love"*
(Zep 3:17).

As I noted on the First Sunday of Advent, during this church year
(Cycle C) we are reading from the Gospel of Luke. On this Third
Sunday in Advent, associated each year with John the Baptist, our
gospel selection introduces two important themes.

First, Luke's has often been called the Gospel of the Poor. Luke
is the Evangelist, for instance, who tells us that the first people to
hear the good news of Jesus' birth were poor shepherds. When Jesus
is taken by his parents for the first time to the Jerusalem Temple,
they meet two old people, one of whom is a widow. And in today's
reading John preaches, not only to "the crowds," but even to "tax
collectors" and to "soldiers."

These latter two classes of people were roundly hated by most of
John's (and Jesus') Jewish contemporaries because they drew their
power from the occupying Romans, and because they abused that
power. As I mentioned on the Tenth Sunday in Ordinary Time, Cycle
A, tax collectors made their profit from what they could extort over
and above the tax rate. And soldiers backed them up, by "bully[ing]"
(literally "shaking thoroughly," or, as we might say, "shaking
down") the taxpayers, or by informing on them (for example, "This
old man has a goat out back he didn't list on his return").

That John is willing to talk to such people says a lot about God's
mercy to the "poor," in the broad sense of "people that decent people consider scum." Even more pointedly, John is harsher to the
respectable "crowds," whom he calls "brood of vipers," than he is to
the outcast tax collectors and soldiers. He doesn't tell the tax collectors and soldiers to get some vocational rehabilitation; instead, he

tells them they can keep their jobs, but need to get a *metanoia* about how they perform them.

Perhaps as a result of this focus on the "poor," Luke's is also known as the Gospel of Joy. Luke uses the word a lot; only Philippians (as in today's selection) uses it as frequently. So Luke's is a good Gospel for recovering people: we know all about declaring our poverty, our powerlessness. The 1st Step implicitly asks the question of the tax collectors to John: "[W]hat are we to do?" If we follow John's advice—essentially "[T]rust in God and clean house" (BB, 98)—we can find a way to become "happy, *joyous*, and free" (BB, 133; my italics).

Fourth Sunday of Advent

Mic 5:1–4; Heb 10:5–10; Lk 1:39–45

". . . Mary set out and went with haste to a Judean town
in the hill country, where she entered the house of Zechariah
and greeted Elizabeth"
(Lk 1:39–40).

This Fourth and final Sunday of Advent is always Mary's. This year's Gospel, from Luke, tells the story of what has come to be called the Visitation (this overlaps with the Gospel for the Assumption, August 15 in Special Feasts). Mary has just learned that she is pregnant with the Messiah. As part of the angel's message, she has also learned that her older relative Elizabeth is six months pregnant. Mary "gets up" (literally) and goes "in haste" to be of service to the older woman, whose first (and only) child this will be. Mary will "visit" Elizabeth, but not as a social call.

There is a clear message here about helping others, even at cost to oneself—Mary, too, is pregnant, and in the early stages, perhaps with morning sickness and other discomforts. And this is a message recovering people need to hear, particularly during the holidays.

American culture glibly assures us that Christmas is about getting things. Alcoholics, according to Bill W., "eat, drink, and grab for more of everything than we need, fearing we shall never have enough" (12 X 12, 49). So an American alcoholic, even a sober one, may find the winter holidays an unusually difficult time.

It might help to "restore us to sanity" (Step 2) in these matters if we recall that the Gospel of Luke—the source for much of our information about the *first* Christmas—insists that Christmas is about giving service, particularly to the poor, as Mary's "visitation" demonstrates. We are summoned, this time of year as every time of year, to follow Christ in "the offering of the body" (Heb), an offering that characterized him from the moment he "[came] into the world."

And if we offer our bodies in service to the poor? Then we can expect what Micah promises us: the Messiah not only gives peace, the Messiah *is* peace. A 12-Step way of making this point is, "Practical experience shows that nothing will so much insure immunity from drinking as intensive work with other alcoholics" (BB, 89; from chapter 7, "Working with Others"). And nothing will so much insure the "priceless gift" (12 X 12, 74) of "peace" as "proceeding in haste" to provide loving service. In turn, peace leads to "joy"— Elizabeth's baby jumps for joy, and, as I noted last week, recovering people "are sure God wants us to be happy, joyous, and free" (BB, 133). Doing God's will in service is our part of the deal.

Christmas, Mass during the Day

Is 52:7–10; Heb 1:1–6; Jn 1:1–18

*"And the Word became flesh and lived among us
[literally, 'pitched his tent,'] and we have seen his glory . . ."*
(Jn 1:14).

As we have seen in Cycles A and B, the services at midnight and at dawn on Christmas use passages from Luke to depict the birth of

Jesus. Typical of Luke's Gospel, these passages emphasize joy coming to the poor—to shepherds and to homeless (temporarily) people like Mary and Joseph. This year, when we consider the readings for the Mass during the day, we reflect, with John the Theologian, on the deepest meaning of these humble events. And we conclude with him that within this all-too-everyday story lays the meaning of everything that is: God has entered the world through these ordinary, fumbling people.

Luke called these events a "word" (*rhema*—see the Christmas meditation from Cycle B). John, in commenting on them, uses a different Greek word—*logos*—which also means "word." But *logos* has other connotations: it also suggests "order," or "meaning," or even "story." In both Jewish and Gentile (specifically Stoic) thought, *logos* was an important philosophical term for "wisdom," especially wisdom as discovered in the beauty and order of "a starlit night" (BB, 46).

In our time, Viktor Frankl, a psychiatrist and a survivor of Auschwitz, called his brand of psychic healing "*logo*therapy" (see his book significantly titled *Man's Search for Meaning*). He believed that he and the other survivors made it through—lived to tell the tale—because they thought that what was happening to them could mean something. They felt that even the terrible events of the Holocaust could be the raw materials of a story.

Elie Wiesel, another Holocaust survivor, sums this all up: "God made human beings because God loves stories" (see the Fifteenth Sunday in Ordinary Time, Cycle A). Recovering people especially know the power of story; it is "our stories [that] disclose in a general way what we used to be like, what happened, and what we are like now" (BB, 58). When newcomers first attend 12-Step meetings, they don't think they have a story—they think they have a scattered heap of events connected only by the "excitement, depression [and] anxiety" (12 X 12, 74) that characterize the lives of alcoholics. But if the newcomers stay, in time the old-timers will, by sharing their stories, teach the newcomers to see their lives as stories, too. Twelve-Step meetings are storytelling schools.

What we celebrate on this Christmas Day is that "God, [who] spoke in fragmentary and varied ways to our forebears through the prophets" (Heb) chose this day to tell us a much more coherent story. It begins, "Once upon a time there was a baby in a homeless shelter."

Holy Family

Sir 3:2–6, 12–14; Col 3:12–21; Lk 2:41–52

"Bear with one another and, if anyone has a complaint against another, forgive each other; just as the Lord has forgiven you . . ."
(Col 3:13).

My friend Tom Weston, S.J., likes to tell people who think their families are a hopeless mess about a climactic incident in the story of St. Francis of Assisi. When Francis was a young man, he began to have "sudden and spectacular . . . religious experiences" (BB, 568). He felt called to follow Jesus by jettisoning all "money, property, and prestige" (the 6th Tradition urges A. A. to do the same). He quarreled bitterly with his father, the financially successful merchant Pietro Bernardone, about the younger man's life path. The father finally insisted that Francis should either follow him in the family business or return everything Pietro had given him. So Francis calmly stripped off every stitch he had on and walked out on to the street outside his father's house, naked. Tom Weston's characteristic comment: "This is a little hostile. And it probably stirred up a lot of hard feelings. But if this ferocious family conflict had not occurred, we would have ended up with just another Italian businessman. Instead we got a saint."

Our Gospel today, on this Feast of the Holy Family, commemorates a similar painful event from the story of Jesus and his parents. Jesus is twelve: he is at the brink of his teenage years, which are usually the hardest for parents and children. This is also the age when a Jewish boy has his bar mitzvah, the ceremony during which he demonstrates knowledge of God's Law as a sign of his growing maturity. Jesus does just that, and does so in the Temple at Jerusalem (see Meditation 23 in *A 12-Step Approach to the Spiritual Exercises* for more on this incident).

His parents, though, like most parents, are not that impressed; rather, they are (again, like most parents at such a moment) more sad than proud. For one thing, like many teenagers, Jesus had neglected to tell them where he was going or what he was going to do. Mary can only ask why Jesus has pained them so. And, like most teenagers, Jesus answers mysteriously—commentators disagree about what "in my Father's house" means, and Jesus' parents "did not grasp" it, either. They could only keep "all these things in memory," and, like Signor Bernardone, watch their son trudge off down the road of his own destiny.

What destiny? "We cannot be sure. God will determine that" (BB, 164). Those of us in recovery who are either children or parents might do well to ponder these stories in order to "[b]ear with one another [and] forgive whatever grievances you have against one another" (Col).

January 1, New Year's Day

Nm 6:22–27; Gal 4:4–7; Lk 2:16–21

"But when the fullness of time had come, God sent his Son, born of a woman, . . . so that we might receive adoption as children" (Gal 4:4–5).

On previous New Year's Days I have studied the Gospel and the First Reading for today. This New Year's Day let's focus on the reading from Paul's Letter to the Galatians. As I have mentioned elsewhere, many Scripture scholars believe that "Abba" was Jesus' special name for God. To Jesus, God was an affectionate parent, comfortable with pet names. Yet the word *Abba* is used only three times in the Christian Scriptures: once in Mark's account of Jesus' Agony in the Garden of Gethsemane on the night before his death, and twice in Paul.

Here in Galatians, Paul uses the Aramaic word like this: "The proof that you are children [of God] is the fact that God has sent forth into our hearts the spirit of God's Son which cries out 'Abba!' ('Father!')." The other Pauline passage, Romans 8:14–17, is very close to these verses from Galatians, but in Romans Paul comes to a slightly different conclusion: ". . . and if children, then heirs, heirs of God and joint heirs with Christ—if, in fact, we suffer with him so that we may also be glorified with him" (Rom 8:17; this passage contains several of the *syn* ["with"] words that Paul is fond of—see Trinity, Cycle B).

As "co-heirs" with Jesus, then, we who follow him have a mixed heritage. Like him, we are "born of a woman"—this is a Hebrew way of saying "human." (On January 1, Roman Catholics also remember Jesus' long-suffering mother, Mary.) And to be human is to suffer, among other things. But on the other side of our heritage, we are adopted children of Abba, as Jesus was Abba's "natural" child. Because of this, our suffering has a meaning, a purpose, a *logos* (see Christmas), even if that purpose is as hard to discern and to accept as it was for Jesus in Gethsemane. Right after Jesus invokes "Abba" in Mark's account of the Passion, Jesus works an 11th Step: ". . . yet, not what I want, but what you [Abba] want" (Mk 14:36). This is also the prayer of God's adopted children; it is quoted three times in the Big Book (63, 85, 88).

As we begin a new year, let us rejoice in the "new freedom and the new happiness" that this "adoption" gives us, a freedom to realize some of the Promises: "We will not regret the past nor wish to shut the door on it. . . . No matter how far down the scale we have gone, we will see how our experience"—and particularly our suffering—"can benefit others" (BB, 83–84).

Epiphany

Is 60:1–6; Eph 3:2–3, 5–6; Mt 2:1–12

"On entering the house, [the wise men] saw the child with Mary
his mother; and they knelt down and paid him homage.
Then, opening their treasure chests, they offered him gifts
of gold, frankincense, and myrrh"
(Mt 2:11).

On the Feast of Epiphany this year, I'd like to draw out some implications of the gifts that the "astrologers from the east" offer Mary's
child. The old carol "We Three Kings of Orient Are" does something
similar: it includes three verses in which each of the "kings" comments on the gift he presents to Jesus.

The first king brings gold, which is, as the old saying goes, "a gift
fit for a king": "Born a King on Bethlehem's plain, / Gold I bring to
crown him again, / King for ever, ceasing never / Over us all to reign."
By listing gold as the first gift, Matthew may also want in this gospel
passage to remind us of "the wealth of nations," which Isaiah believed
would come to Jerusalem some day. *Nations* means Gentiles, *goyim*;
if their gold is coming to Jerusalem, it means the membership requirements for God's people have changed, and anyone can become a
"member of the same body and a sharer of the promise" (Eph). In any
case, this gift reminds us that Jesus' mission was first and always to
proclaim "the kingdom of God."

The second "king" brings "frankincense": "Frankincense to
offer have I, / Incense owns [that is, points to] a Deity nigh, / Prayer
and praising, All men raising, / Worship him, God on high." *Frank*
here is from an Old French word that means "rich" or "expensive."
In giving such an exalted gift, this king is hinting strongly that
there's more to Mary's child than meets the eye. No wonder the three
"astrologers" "prostrated themselves and did [Jesus] homage"—
there's something divine about this child. (By the way, the word in

the Greek Scriptures for "step" [as in 12 Steps] comes from a verb that means "to come as a suppliant": when we take Steps, we too "own a deity nigh.")

The third king offers "myrrh": "Myrrh is mine; its bitter perfume / Breathes a life of gathering gloom; / Sorrowing, sighing, bleeding, dying, / Sealed in the stone-cold tomb." The only other time that "myrrh" appears in the Christian Scriptures is in John's Gospel: women friends of Jesus will use "myrrh" to prepare his body for burial after he has "laid down his life for his friends." This final gift foretells a life—and a death—of loving service.

All three gifts, then, are "epiphanies," in James Joyce's understanding of the term: places where meaning shines through. Jesus' life is about the kingdom of God, a kingdom not of this earth, in which loving service and self-sacrifice, not power, "are the permanent and legitimate satisfactions of right living for which no amount of pomp and circumstance, no heap of material possessions"—including gold and frankincense—"could possibly be substitutes" (12 X 12, 124).

Note: In 2007, the Feast of the Baptism of the Lord is not celebrated on a Sunday; go straight from Epiphany to the Second Sunday in Ordinary Time.

Baptism of the Lord

Is 42:1–4, 6–7; Acts 10:34–38; Lk 3:15–15, 21–22

"I have taken you by the hand and kept you;
. . . to bring out the prisoners from the dungeon,
from the prison those who sit in darkness"
(Is 42:6, 7).

The Advent-Christmas season ends each year with this feast. This year we read Luke's version of Jesus' baptism. By Luke's time this story had gotten to be an embarrassment to Jesus' followers, since it seemed to suggest that John the Baptist was somehow superior to Jesus. So Luke muffles the event: "When all the people were baptized, and Jesus was at prayer after likewise being baptized"—notice that John isn't even mentioned, and Jesus is lost in a large crowd—"the skies opened and the Holy Spirit descended on him in visible form like a dove." Jesus has been baptized off camera, so to speak.

Luke focuses instead on the descent of the Holy Spirit "like a dove." Why a dove? In the Hebrew Scriptures doves are a symbol, not of the Spirit, but of God's people, Israel. So Luke's point is that Jesus' baptism is not just a "spiritual awakening" for him. The "voice [is] heard," not just by Jesus, but apparently by "all the people." Of course no real "spiritual awakening" is meant just for the person who receives it; it is meant to be "carried" to others. What happens to Jesus at his baptism changes his life, true; but it will later change millions of other lives, too.

The word *spirit*, as I've pointed out before, literally means "wind" or "breath," in all three languages—Hebrew, Greek, and Latin—in which Christians do much of their religious thinking. These words are metaphorically connected because winds are invisible but powerful, and so the wind has often been invoked to describe internal experiences that change people's lives. Bill W. used this image to communicate his *metanoia*: "Suddenly the [hospital] room lit up with a great white light. . . . It seemed to me, in the mind's eye, that I was on a mountain and that a wind not of air but of spirit was blowing. And then it burst upon me that I was a free man" (AACA, 63). At his baptism "it burst upon" Jesus, too, that he was "a free man," "beloved" by God. From that moment on, he "went about doing good works" (Acts)—he "practiced these principles in all [his] affairs" (12th Step).

As the Big Book notes (in Appendix II, "Spiritual Experience," 569–570), "transformations" as dramatic as Jesus' or Bill W.'s, "though frequent, are by no means the rule." But even an "educational" *metanoia* can be surprisingly sturdy. Bill put it this way, paraphrasing this week's Servant Song from Isaiah 42: "What seemed at first a flimsy reed, has proved to be the loving and powerful hand of God" (BB, 28).

✣

Lent
and Easter

First Week of Lent

Dt 26:4–10; Rom 10:8–13; Lk 4:1–13

"For there is no distinction between Jew and Greek; the same Lord is Lord of all and is generous to all who call on him"
(Rom 10:12).

The First Sunday of Lent each year tells the story of Jesus' temptations. Luke's version, which we read this year, is similar to Matthew's (Year A), except that Luke interchanges Matthew's Temptations # 2 and # 3—in Luke it's the Kingdoms of the World (power), *then* the death-defying, God-tempting stunt from the top of the Temple. Luke must see something climactic in this last temptation.

Note that the devil prefaces the first, as well as the climactic, temptation with *"If* you are the Son of God." This seems like an odd proviso: in Matthew, Mark, and Luke, Jesus enters the desert immediately following his baptism in the Jordan River by John, during which a voice from heaven has proclaimed, according to Luke, "You are my beloved Son." After such an overwhelming spiritual experience, *not* of the "educational variety" (BB, 569), surely there can be no doubt that Jesus is the Son of God.

Instead, what the devil is trying to get Jesus to do, especially in the Third Temptation, is to decide *for himself* what it means to be "Son of God," to take matters into his own hands. The gist of this temptation is, "Don't worry about 'knowledge of God's will for' you [Step 11]—just do this, take the plunge off the temple spire, and present God with the accomplished fact!" Jesus replies that that's no way to be God's child; instead, "in this drama of life, God [is] going to be [the] Director" (BB, 62). As I have said on previous Temptation Sundays, Jesus answers the Tempter by taking a kind of 3rd Step. Bill W. puts this negatively: "First of all, we had to quit playing God" (BB, 62). Jesus, following the lead of Moses in Deuteronomy, phrases it positively: "The LORD your God you shall fear; him you shall serve, and by his name alone you shall swear" (Dt 6:13).

For Jesus—and for us—taking a 3rd Step is not a once-and-for-all gesture. In Matthew, at the end of the Temptations, angels comfort Jesus for all that he's just gone through. But in Luke, Jesus ends up alone: the devil has merely backed off "to await another opportunity" (literally, "to await the right time"). Jesus will have to fight this battle again, and especially when he comes face to face in Gethsemane with "God's will for" him (see the 11th Step). "God's will for" Jesus turns out to be a miserable death—and a wild hope, as wild as the hopes for liberation and for a new land that sustained the "maltreated and oppressed," "wandering" ancestors of Jesus in Egypt and in the desert.

Second Week of Lent

Gn 15:5–12, 17–18; Phil 3:17–4:1; Lk 9:28–36

"I am the LORD who brought you from Ur of the Chaldeans,
to give you this land to possess"
(Gn 15:7).

The Second Sunday of Lent each year focuses on the Transfiguration of Jesus, when "the pattern of his glorified body" briefly showed through his "lowly body" (Phil—I have studied this gospel passage in Meditation 32 of *A 12-Step Approach to the Spiritual Exercises*). The suddenly "dazzling" Jesus is conversing, presumably as an equal, with two of the greatest figures from Jewish history: Moses, the bringer of the Law; and Elijah, the great prophet.

One of the small—but significant—details added by Luke in his version of this story is the subject of Jesus' conversation with Moses and Elijah: "They . . . spoke of his passage which he was about to fulfill in Jerusalem." The Greek word translated "passage" is *exodos*; it's the sort of conversational topic one would bring up with Moses, the hero of the Book of Exodus in the Hebrew Scriptures. Jesus was talking with these two giants of his people about his own personal "exodus," his own journey to freedom, in which he was going to reenact the pilgrimage that had made his people the People of Yahweh. It's an exodus that he will "fulfill" in Jerusalem: the Transfiguration story in Luke comes just before a long section (chapters 9–18) that Luke has organized around Jesus' final journey to Jerusalem.

Exodus literally means "the way out." The Book of Exodus tells the story of how God empowered Moses to show his people "the way out" of slavery in Egypt. Jesus' death and glorification will show the people of the new covenant "the way out" of enslavement to human divisions and violence. And one of the suggested titles of the Big Book was *The Way Out*, because it described "a common solution" for alcoholism, "a way out on which we can absolutely agree" (BB, 17).

Lent and Easter form that spiritual season, around the beginning of spring, when human beings join nature in celebrating the ways out of death we have perennially found. The "lowly body" of plants assumes a "new form" as they blossom once again. The "lowly body" of Jesus, which is put to death and buried, returns to his friends in a "new form." On the other side of addiction, once they have found "the way out," the "lowly body" of powerless people with unmanageable lives is remade into a "new form." As with Peter, James, and John in today's Gospel, "[q]uite often friends of the newcomer are aware of the difference long before [the newcomer] is . . ." (BB, 569). But whenever this awareness dawns, Peter's reaction is the right one: "[H]ow good it is for us to be here."

Third Week of Lent

Ex 3:1–8, 13–15; 1 Cor 10:1–6, 10–12; Lk 13:1–9

"'No, I tell you; but unless you repent,
you will all perish just as they did [metanoesete]'"
(Lk 13:5).

I was once celebrating Sunday Mass in a large suburban parish. During my homily, I mentioned in passing my work with recovering alcoholics. After Mass, as I was greeting people at the church door, a couple in their late fifties came up to me. The man stated gruffly that he once had a drinking problem, but didn't drink excessively anymore—"not usually," he added hastily. Then he angrily asserted, "The *real* problem with the world these days is that all the young people aren't acting like they should!"

In our Lenten Gospel today, Jesus warns his listeners not to fall into the trap of taking the moral inventory of other people. It's all too easy, he notes, to assume that when bad things happen to people—other people, that is—they must somehow have deserved it. Those people who were massacred by the Roman troops? Must have deserved it! The people crushed by a falling tower? Deserved it! This kind of thing, of course, still goes on: a priest friend told me that, just after the Loma Prieta earthquake in the San Francisco Bay area in 1989, he met several people on a retreat who claimed to know exactly what the people of the Bay area had done to deserve it.

This is smug. But even worse, for recovering people it's a poor substitute for doing what we really need to do, which, as Jesus notes twice in this passage, is to "reform"—that is, reform *ourselves*. In Greek this is our old friend *metanoia*, "undergo a complete psychic change." Bill W. makes the same point, very simply: as part of 12-Step recovery, it is suggested that we make a "searching and fearless moral inventory of *ourselves*" (4th Step—my emphasis). In case we haven't gotten the idea, Bill tersely notes that "The inventory [is] ours, not the other [person's]" (BB, 67).

Obsession with the (perceived) misbehavior of others is the essence of a dry drunk. Like the man I met after Mass, "dry" people aren't "happy about [their] sobriety" (BB, 152), and have fallen back on the addict's second favorite defense mechanism, projection (#1 is denial): "If I'm not happy, it must be someone else's fault." Then they round up the usual suspects: young people, old people, women, men, gay people, straight people, people of any color at all as long as it's not the color I am, and so on. During Lent—or any time of the year, if we want to be sober and grow spiritually (same thing)—we need to "improve our conscious contact with God as we understand God" (Step 11). We need to enhance our *metanoia* by taking a good look at our own fig tree, not somebody else's.

Fourth Week of Lent

Jos 5:9, 10–12; 2 Cor 5:17–21; Lk 15:1–3, 11–32

"So if anyone is in Christ, there is a new creation: everything old has passed away; see, everything has become new! All this is from God, who reconciled us to himself through Christ, and has given us the ministry of reconciliation"
(2 Cor 5:17–18).

This Sunday's Gospel is the story of the Prodigal Son, one of the greatest stories ever told. Recovering people will have no trouble identifying with the Prodigal. We know all about making parents miserable by our poor choices. We also know a lot about "squander[ing our] money on dissolute living," especially those of us who have done more expensive drugs, like cocaine. The word translated *dissolute* can also be translated "debauched" or "profligate"; literally it means "beyond saving." Curiously, many people widely believed to be "unsavable" have nevertheless found a Higher Power that could restore them to sanity (2nd Step). Like the Prodigal, they came "to [their] senses" (literally, "came to themselves") and went home.

However, much of the brilliance of this story lies in the fact that it doesn't end with the "rebirth" of the Prodigal; instead, it goes on to the bitter reaction of the Elder Brother. The Elder Brother makes a case for himself, and we have no reason to doubt a word of it: "For years now I have slaved for you. I never disobeyed one of your orders . . . Then, when this son of yours [he won't say 'my brother'] returns after having gone through your property with loose women, you kill the fatted calf for him." He is right; this is grossly unfair. Measured by ordinary human rules, love is always unfair. We who listen to this story need to realize that we are *both* brothers. Nothing is more common than this turn of events: someone who has miraculously turned out to be savable gets back on his or her feet. Six months after falling off a bar stool and into A. A., this person is eager to take the inventory of the people who are still "out there," the brothers and sisters who have not yet "come to their senses." By the same token, people who have put up with an addict for years may be furious when the addict finally gets clean because the addict has gotten away, figuratively, with murder. Al-Anon is for, among others, Elder Brothers (and Elder Sisters).

In Luke, Jesus aims this story at his beloved enemies, the Pharisees, many of whom were Elder Brothers, taking a dim view of prodigal types, like most of Jesus' followers. But the trip from Prodigal to Pharisee can be a very short one, unless we remember, as in last week's Gospel, to "reform" ourselves. Let's also remember where we came from, and remember to imitate the Higher Power, who welcomed us home with a kiss.

Fifth Week of Lent

Is 43:16–21; Phil 3:8–14; Jn 8:1–11

". . . I regard everything as loss because of the surpassing value
of knowing Christ Jesus my Lord"
(Phil 3:8).

This Sunday's Gospel continues our Lenten theme this year: "[R]elief never [comes] by confessing the sins of other people. Everybody [has] to confess his [or her] own" (12 X 12, 56). This theme bears repetition, because "[t]his subtle and elusive kind of self-righteousness can underlie the smallest act or thought" (12 X 12, 94–95).

"The scribes and the Pharisees" of Jerusalem have pounced on a woman who has committed adultery. They decide to use her as bait to trap Jesus, the upstart rabbi from the boondocks. Perhaps they have heard that he proclaims a loving and forgiving God, and that he numbers women among his closest friends. Just the sort of person to set aside a literal interpretation of the Law, which requires stoning for adulterous women (it's uncertain whether people actually did this at the time of Jesus). If he recommends mercy for the woman, they can attack him as weak on family values.

The trap fails. Jesus does nothing at all for a while, which defuses the crisis a bit. Pushed by his adversaries, he finally responds, but very briefly—only eight words in Greek. Then he goes back to doodling. In the 1927 *King of Kings*, Cecil B. DeMille had Jesus write in the dirt the sins of the would-be stoners. Pure Hollywood; and it garbles the whole point of the story. That point—again—is that everybody should confess their own sins, or "Let the sinless of you throw at her first" (my literal translation of Jesus' words). Of course everybody leaves, "beginning with the elders," presumably because they were wiser, not more sinful.

When the accusers have all left, Jesus has a moment alone with the woman. He gently asks her a rhetorical question: "Has no one condemned you?" She replies "No one, sir." The word for "sir" here also means "Lord" in the Christian Scriptures, a frequent title for Christ. So even in this brief and miserable encounter, she has somehow come "to know Christ" as the Messiah, someone with power to set people on a path to a new life. Jesus is a "Lord" who doesn't need "to feel superior by pulling [others] down" (12 X 12, 94). So he can do "something new" (Is). "Lack of power, that was our dilemma" (BB, 45); perhaps that was the woman's dilemma as well. But to meet Jesus is to feel "the power flowing from his resurrection" (Phil), a power by which "we [are] reborn" (BB, 63).

Palm Sunday, Procession

Lk 19:28–40; Mass: Is 50:4–7; Phil 2:6–11;
St. Luke Passion, Lk 22:14–23:56

"[Jesus] replied, 'Truly I tell you,
today you will be with me in Paradise'"
(Lk 23:43).

Luke's is the Gospel of compassion, the Gospel of the poor. So when on this Palm Sunday we read Luke's account of Jesus' suffering and death, it's not surprising that the tone is gentler, less brutal, than in Mark's version. For example, in Luke Jesus says, "Father, forgive them; they do not know what they are doing."

Then, too, Luke is the Evangelist who lets us hear from the Two Criminals who were crucified with the gentle Messiah (see also Meditation 43 in *A 12-Step Approach to the Spiritual Exercises*). When Jesus was born, the first to hear the good news were shepherds; now, as Jesus is dying, the last to guess the good news is a condemned man.

The Two Criminals differ in the way they see their predicament—as differently as life and death. One attacks Jesus. Like "the alcoholic who has lost all and is locked up," he still refuses to acknowledge his part in what has happened to him. Instead, the Bad Thief, like "the outlaw safe cracker," and like many practicing addicts, "thinks society has wronged him" (BB, 62). He will blame others, take their inventory rather than his own, to the bitter end. But the other criminal takes an emergency 5th Step with Jesus: the Good Thief—this is an oxymoron, like "sober alcoholic"—asks himself, "Where were we to blame?" (BB, 67), and answers, "We are only paying the price for what we've done."

As any recovering person will recognize, being able to "admit your faults to [God] and to your fellows" (BB, 164) is one of the first and biggest signs of grace: it is "the beginning of true kinship with man and God" (12 X 12, 57). And grace always opens the door to wild hopes. So this Good Thief goes on to say, to another dying criminal, "Jesus, remember me when you enter upon your reign." Even at this impossibly low bottom, Jesus is somehow still carrying the message of "the reign of God," 12th-Stepping to the very end.

The result? "What seemed at first a flimsy reed, has proved to be the loving and powerful hand of God" (BB, 28). Jesus, out of his deep faith in Abba, has the confidence to reply, "Truly I tell you, today you will be with me in Paradise" (Lk 23:43). And if we believe Jesus, we will believe that the Good Thief "found much of heaven [when he was] rocketed into a fourth dimension of existence of which [he] had not even dreamed" (BB, 25).

Note: I haven't included meditations for Holy Thursday or Good Friday. For Holy Thursday you may want to consult the meditation for Corpus Christi, at the end of this Lent-Easter section, since on that feast Roman Catholics celebrate the gift of the Lord's Supper in a special way.

Easter, Mass during the Day

Acts 10:34, 37–43; 1 Cor 5:6–8; Lk 24:13–35

This year I have chosen to study the Gospel that is suggested for an evening Mass on Easter Sunday. I am also studying the alternative Second Reading, from 1 Corinthians.

> *"[The two disciples] got up and returned to Jerusalem; and they found the eleven and their companions gathered together. . . . Then they told what had happened on the road . . ."*
> (Lk 24:33, 35).

As I mentioned when the Emmaus story came up before (the Third Sunday of Easter, Year A), it's one I'm particularly fond of. What I especially like about it is that it shows Jesus going after a couple of real quitters. They want to "go out"—12-Step slang for "give up on recovery"—but Jesus won't let them go. Even though most of his friends are in Jerusalem, and he has a lot to do there, he takes the time to chase down two peripheral disciples, off in the hinterlands, far from the action.

Like these disciples, I have always been rather "on the depressive side" (12 X 12, 45), as Bill W. puts it. It wasn't the 1st Step that gave me trouble, it was the 2nd. Perhaps, like so much else, this is genetic: my father said, literally on his deathbed, that in living his life he had tried to follow *his* father's [deadly] advice: "If you can't do something right, don't even try." Like my forebears, I'm only too ready to admit defeat.

And that's what these two disciples are doing. They had been "hoping that [Jesus] was the one who would set Israel free," but what kind of Messiah would end up like Jesus did? Even the rumors of a resurrection that morning hadn't fazed them; they're going home, presumably to return to their old jobs and their old relationships and their "old ideas" (BB, 58). But Paul urges people like them, and people like me, to throw out everything old, as the Jews threw out the "old yeast" at Passover. In doing so Jews imitate their ancestors, Moses' followers: when the children of Israel were in a hurry to hit the desert road for a new land, they had no time for yeast. Why should we lug along "old ideas," especially since "[o]ur ideas did not work. But the God idea did" (BB, 52)?

As we saw in Mark last year, Jesus was patient a long time with his followers, even though they were "slow . . . to believe." But on this Easter Day, when everything can become new, he is more forceful: "What little sense you have!" And his going the extra mile after these lost sheep pays off: their hearts burn within them. More practically, even though it is night and they had originally planned to stay home—forever—instead, they get back on the Road of Happy Destiny at once. Have they got a story to tell.

Second Sunday of Easter

Acts 5:12–16; Rv 1:9–11, 12–13, 17–19; Jn 20:19–31

"Now Jesus did many other signs in the presence of his disciples,
which are not written in this book.
But these are written so that you may come to believe . . .
and that . . . you may have life in his name"
(Jn 20:30, 31).

Our readings this Sunday invite us to consider the question, "What does it take for us to 'come to believe'?" Doubting Thomas in the Gospel is an example of someone for whom coming to believe "was a tedious process" (BB, 48): he insisted on seeing something first. But as I noted on this Sunday in Year A, once he saw something, he "came to believe in a Higher Power, and [he] began to talk of God" (12 X 12, on Step 2, 28). For the crowds in today's reading from Acts, seeing was also believing: they saw the "signs and wonders" that the apostles were bringing about, and so came to be "added to the Lord." And the First Reading, from Revelation, begins with "John, your brother" having a vision of—seeing—"the One who lives."

Still, Jesus often urges people to go beyond just what they can see. Once, when a man asked Jesus to save his son's life, Jesus replied, "Unless you see signs and wonders you will not believe" (Jn 4:48). And after the resurrection Jesus responded to Thomas's seeing-based act of faith by adding one last Beatitude to the eight in Matthew: "Blest are they who have not seen and have believed."

Still, the point is to "come to believe," whatever it takes. Jesus went ahead and healed the man's son anyway; and Jesus does not deduct points from Thomas's score because Thomas had to see to believe. "We found that God does not make too hard terms with those who seek [God]" (BB, 46).

One of the things that can make coming to believe easier is that part of recovery is seeing miracles every day, seeing people who "once [were] dead but now . . . live." Dr. William Silkworth, an early friend of A. A., had just such an experience: "[A] trembling, despairing, nervous wreck" of a man came to his hospital, "a case of pathological mental deterioration." While in the hospital, the man "accepted the plan outlined in this book [the Big Book]." A year later the man returned, so transformed that the doctor "was not able to bring myself to feel that I had known him before" (BB, xxix). "What is this but a miracle of healing?" (BB, 57). Such miracles are "recorded"— and recounted at 12-Step meetings—"to help you believe . . . so that through this faith you may have life . . ." (Jn).

Third Sunday of Easter

Acts 5:27–32, 40–41; Rv 5:11–14; Jn 21:1–19

"Peter felt hurt because [Jesus] said to him the third time, 'Do you love me?' And he said to him, 'Lord, you know everything; you know that I love you.' Jesus said to him, 'Feed my sheep'"
(Jn 21:17).

Scholars have recently suggested that we consider the lakeside meeting of several important disciples with Jesus in today's Gospel as one of several versions of the *first* appearance of the risen Jesus to them (for more on different traditions about the risen Jesus, some focused on Jerusalem, some on Galilee, see Meditation 48 in *A 12-Step Approach to the Spiritual Exercises*). This would explain some puzzling features: for example, why are the disciples back at their old jobs in Galilee? Perhaps they had given up, like the disciples returning to Emmaus in Luke, because the risen Jesus had not yet visited them. Again, why don't the disciples recognize Jesus when he does appear? Maybe this was the first time they had seen the New Jesus.

If we buy this notion, it makes the scene between Jesus and Peter much more poignant: if this is their first meeting since the crucifixion, it's the first time they've spoken since Peter confirmed Jesus' sad prophecy by betraying his Master. Characteristically, Peter seems not to have thought about that when he first realized on the boat that it was Jesus on the shore. Instead, he was so glad to see Jesus that he dove into the water to reach him sooner. But when he gets close to Jesus, his ardor to do a 9th Step seems to dribble away. Peter would naturally prefer "to skip the more humiliating and dreaded meetings" (12 X 12, 85).

Just as characteristically, Jesus takes the lead and helps Peter with Peter's amends. "The Lord"—this is especially the title of the risen Jesus—does not make Peter confess his failing; he simply makes Peter acknowledge his love, three times for three denials. Why do such 9th Steps have to happen? "Our real purpose is to fit ourselves to be of maximum service to God and the people about us" (BB, 77). In other words, "Feed my sheep." Peter's amends did "fit" him to serve God.

Look at him in today's reading from Acts, in which he is being interrogated by the very authorities who had once frightened him into betraying Jesus. The new Peter, who has "commence[d] to out-grow fear" (BB, 68) with a vengeance, stoutly testifies: "Better for us to obey God than human beings! . . . . We testify to [Jesus the Savior]. So too does the Holy Spirit . . . " If we follow Peter's example by working the 9th Step, "we will be amazed before we are half way through": "As God's people we [will] stand on our feet," and so "Fear of people . . . will leave us" (BB, 83, 84).

Fourth Sunday of Easter

Acts 13:14, 43–52; Rv 7:9, 14–17; Jn 10:27–30

"'I give them eternal life, and they will never perish.
No one will snatch them out of my hand'"
(Jn 10:28).

A friend of mine recently told me something I hadn't known about sheep. Jesus speaks in other Gospels of a shepherd carrying a sheep on his shoulders. This sheep had gotten lost—the only member of the flock to wander off—but then was found again by the painstaking shepherd. In this Sunday's gospel passage from John, Jesus identifies with this shepherd: no one is going to "snatch [the sheep] out of my hand." But why is Jesus, or any shepherd, *carrying* the sheep? I had always assumed that it was because the sheep had fallen, or gotten caught in brambles, and was too banged up to walk. But my friend assured me that sheep need community very badly, rather like the sheep in the movie *Babe*. If they get lost, they become so frightened, like alcoholics, by "that terrible sense of isolation" (12 X 12, 47) that they freeze, become paralyzed. The shepherd has to carry them because they can't walk, until the fear wears off, I suppose. Once they "commence to outgrow fear" (BB, 68), however, I presume they can take steps, just like the other sheep.

It's mildly embarrassing, but I can see myself in this feature of "sheeply" life. I'm one of those alcoholics for whom fear "was an evil and corroding thread . . . [shot through] the fabric of our existence" (BB, 67). Pretty early in my drinking I had brushes with real panic, and alcohol was never the same to me afterwards—it was always a tranquilizer. When I got frightened—of the usual things, death and insanity and heights and failure and imperfection and success, and finally the fear of having another panic attack—I tended to freeze up.

In fact, according to my colleague Dr. Dave Scratchley, a pharmacological psychologist, all anxiety is freezing up. In the presence of great fear, like powerless animals, human beings hold very still. This may have helped keep our ancestors alive during very frightening times. I believed for a long time that only alcohol could get me moving again. But in recovery I have come to believe afresh in "the Lamb" (Rv) who is my shepherd. To carry me back to the fold, I need a Higher Power who has felt what I've felt, fear and all, yet still goes on. A Higher Power who doesn't mind going after strays like the Emmaus disciples. And finally, a Higher Power with a very strong grip.

Fifth Sunday of Easter

Acts 14:21–27; Rv 21:1–5; Jn 13:31–33, 34–35

"'[God] will wipe every tear from their eyes.
Death will be no more; mourning and crying
and pain will be no more, for the first things have passed away'"
(Rv 21:4).

If last Sunday was Sheep Sunday, this Sunday's readings would justify us in calling it New Sunday. Everything is new—new heavens
and a new earth, and a New Jerusalem, in the reading from
Revelation; and a new commandment of love in the gospel. When
better to celebrate all that is new than spring?

Celebration is especially in order if we contrast all that is new
with some of "our old ideas," which we may insist on "hold[ing] on
to" despite the fact that "the result" of sticking to these "old ideas"
is "nil" (BB, 58). One of my favorite "old ideas," which as a student
of literature I found particularly seductive, was that adulthood means
accepting that life is tragic. Often, when I was in my cups, I had a
deep sense that life is "really" about "death" and "mourning" and
"crying out" and "pain," as Revelation puts it. After an evening of
drinking, I could somehow reach these insights even while watching
reruns of *The Love Boat.* However, once I entered recovery, I con-
cluded that what I had really meant by "Life is tragic" was "Why am
I having such a rotten time?" Recovery changed all that.

People in recovery experience much that is new: a "new attitude" (BB, 72, 85, 99, 150), which is a good translation of the word
metanoia in the Christian Scriptures; "a new freedom and a new happiness" (BB, 83), according to one of the Promises; and finally "a
new life" (BB, 28, 99). But in what sense is Jesus the one who
"make[s] all things new"?

The answer lies in the strange beginning of this Sunday's Gospel.
Judas has just left the Last Supper, to betray Jesus, to set in motion

horrible events. Why does Jesus say "*Now* is the Son of Man glorified"? What is so glorious about what Jesus is beginning to undergo? The glorious part lies in the fact that Jesus is going to be the first to live up to the "new commandment" that he is announcing to his disciples. In a world where people suffer unjust, cruel deaths all the time, it is new, it is "glorious," voluntarily to lay down your life for your friends. In a world where people mostly "retaliate, snatching all they can get out of the show" (BB, 61), it is new to "love one another." This is a "message," this is a piece of "good news," that we would do well to "carry," and "to practice in all our affairs" (Step 12).

Sixth Sunday of Easter

Acts 14:21–27; Rv 21:10–14, 22–23; Jn 14:23–29

*"'But the Advocate, the Holy Spirit, whom the Father will send
in my name, will teach you everything, and remind you
of all that I have said to you'"*
(Jn 14:26).

In the 12 X 12 (139–45), Bill W. describes some of A. A.'s early struggles with membership requirements, struggles that eventually led to the very inclusive Tradition 3 (which I have cited before, for example, the Twenty-Third and Thirtieth Sundays in Ordinary Time, Cycle A): "The only requirement for A. A. membership is a desire to stop drinking." In particular, he mentions a newcomer seeking admittance to the fellowship early in its history, an alcoholic with another "difficulty . . . worse stigmatized than alcoholism" (142).

The historical context: "In our early time, nothing seemed so fragile, so easily breakable as an A. A. group. . . . On the A. A. calendar it was Year Two" (12 X 12, 139, 141). I have been told on good authority that the newcomer was a gay man. A. A. at this early point was almost exclusively male, and males not necessarily liberal, even by the standards of the time. Nevertheless, the early members, for all their hesitancy, finally consulted this principle: "What would the Master do?" Bill's comment: "Not another word was said. What more indeed *could* be said?" (Bill's italics) The result? "Overjoyed, the newcomer plunged into 12th-Step work. Tirelessly he laid A. A.'s message before scores of people. Since this was a very early group, those scores have since multiplied themselves into thousands" (12 X 12, 142). Many years after Bill wrote these words, in the early 1950s—in fact, some years after Bill's own death in 1971—the "newcomer" himself died—sober. The thousands had "multiplied themselves into"—who knows how many!

In today's reading from Acts, we hear the story of the early Christians, faced with an equally crucial decision about membership. The Church had begun within the Temple, within Judaism. Yet in some places, particularly the city of Antioch, outside Palestine, Gentiles had come into the Church without spending an interim phase as Jews, and without honoring some important elements of Judaism, like the kosher laws. "This created dissension and much controversy . . ." (Acts; Paul recounts this "controversy" in his Letter to the Galatians, the Ninth and Tenth Sundays in Ordinary Time, Cycle C).

At a summit meeting in Jerusalem, members of *this* fellowship also asked, "What would the Master do?" They got in touch with "the Master's" Spirit, which he had stated would "instruct" and "remind" them of him (Jn). And the "decision of the Holy Spirit"—the Spirit of a "loving God" (Tradition 2)—was to include, not exclude. As Pentecost approaches, let's ask that this Spirit may always govern us "in all our affairs," and especially when we are discussing requirements for membership. ". . . [I]n God's sight all human beings are important . . ." (12 X 12, 124).

Feast of the Ascension

Acts 1:1–11; Eph 1:17–23; Lk 24:46–53

Note: Many communities celebrate the Feast of the Ascension on the Thursday before the Seventh Sunday of Easter. If your community does, read this meditation on Thursday and the next meditation on the following Sunday.

"I pray that the God of our Lord Jesus Christ, the Father of glory,
may give you a spirit of wisdom and revelation as you come
to know him, so that, with the eyes of your heart enlightened,
you may know what is the hope to which he has called you,
what are the riches of his glorious inheritance among the saints . . ."
(Eph 1:17–18).

A much-loved passage in the Big Book (83–84) lists some "promises" that recovering people can reasonably expect to be "fulfilled . . . if we work for them." In this year's First and Third Readings, both by Luke, for the Feast of the Ascension, the feast of Jesus' Farewell, Jesus, too, speaks of a "promise." After his departure, the fellowship that has sprung up around him needs to stay in Jerusalem until Abba fulfills this promise.

What exactly is Abba promising? The key element in this promise is "power," which appears in all three readings today. In the First Reading, the account of the Ascension from Acts, Jesus tells his group, "You will receive power when the Holy Spirit comes down on you . . ." The Second Reading prays that members of the Ephesian fellowship "may know . . . the immeasurable scope of [God's] power in us who believe." Note that this "power" is also a kind of clearer "vision," is a source of "great hope," and is true "wealth . . . to be distributed among the members," which neatly summarizes Steps 2 and 12. Finally, in the gospel passage, which is the ending of Luke's Gospel, Jesus says his friends are to "[r]emain here in [Jerusalem] until you are clothed with power from on high."

Remember, "power" in Luke is more or less synonymous with "the Holy Spirit." So we will see Jesus' "promise" "materialize" (BB, 84) on the Feast of Pentecost, when the disciples' "lack of power" (BB, 45) will end with a bang, with the arrival of a "great, clean wind" (BB, 14). They won't be naked and powerless anymore.

Power to do what, exactly? In Luke, it's power to be "witnesses," to carry the message "to the ends of the earth." Power, in other words, to do 12th-Step work. The Promises in the Big Book, although they don't use the word *power*, mention some other things that someone doing 12th-Step work will surely need: "a new freedom and a new happiness," "see[ing] how our experience can benefit others," "know[ing] how to handle situations which used to baffle us," "realiz[ing] that God is doing for us what we could not do for ourselves," and so on. While these Promises may not "materialize" as dramatically as Abba's promise did on Pentecost, "[t]hey are being fulfilled among us [recovering people]—sometimes quickly, sometimes slowly" (BB, 83–84).

Seventh Sunday of Easter

Acts 7:55–60; Rv 22:12–14, 16–17, 20; Jn 17:20–26

"And let everyone who is thirsty come.
Let anyone who wishes take the water of life as a gift"
(Rv 22:17).

In this Sunday's Gospel, we have the third and final part of Jesus' Prayer of Consecration, the conclusion of his Last Supper Discourse in John. On the Seventh Sunday of Easter, Cycle A, Jesus talked about his relationship to God; on the same Sunday in Cycle B he talked about his relationship with his immediate friends; in this passage he talks about his relationship with "those who will believe in me through [the] word [of his friends]." The key concept in this third section is unity: all three sets of relationships are really just one relationship, spreading out in circles. The word *menein* ("live in"), of which John is so fond (see the Seventh Sunday of Easter, Cycle B), is another way to express that unity.

Unity is also the focus of the First Tradition: "Our common welfare should come first; personal recovery depends upon A. A. unity." When Bill W. comments on this Tradition, he is at pains to make clear that it does not envision some kind of totalitarian group, in which the individual is casually sacrificed to some notion of the common good. This kind of brutality is in fact the hallmark of dysfunctional families and dysfunctional governments, in which diversity is seen as the enemy of unity. What is missing in these groups is the notion of love, and particularly love in John's and Jesus' sense of the word: being willing to lay down one's life for one's friends (*not* to have it ripped out of one's grasp).

In John's writings, *the world* is often his term for the violent place where love needs to come to birth. In explaining why loving unity is necessary for recovery, Bill employs the same term: "In the world about us we saw personalities destroying whole peoples [the Traditions were put together, with much trial and error, during the 1940s]. The struggle for wealth, power, and prestige was tearing humanity apart as never before. If strong people were stalemated in the search for peace and harmony, what was to become of our erratic band of alcoholics?" (12 X 12, 130) What saved this "erratic band" was precisely that they were not "strong people"; in their common powerlessness they found a "common solution, . . . a way out on which we can absolutely agree" (BB, 17).

Bill ends his commentary on Tradition 1 with the story of U. S. naval airmen shot down in the Pacific during World War II. Most survived, plainly because "*they* saw that their common welfare came first" (Bill's italics). He adds a comment on the airmen in which John the Evangelist would have seen a world of meaning: "None might become selfish of water or bread" (12 X 12, 131). Christians and 12 Steppers alike should love enough that no one need ever go hungry or thirsty, physically or spiritually.

Pentecost, Mass of the Day

Gn 11:1-9; Rom 8:22-27; Jn 7:37–39

"When the day of Pentecost had come, they were all together in one place. . . . All of them were filled with the Holy Spirit . . . "
(Acts 2:1, 4).

The Feast of Pentecost celebrates the coming of the Spirit on a group gathered for spiritual purposes. The word *spirit* is a play on the words for "wind" and "breath" (true in Hebrew, Greek, and Latin). This is why in Acts the arrival of the Spirit is signaled by "a noise like a strong, driving wind." And this is why in John's Gospel, where Jesus' resurrection-ascension and the sending of the Spirit all occur on one glorious Sunday, Jesus "breathe[s]" on his disciples as he says "Receive the Holy Spirit." They are receiving his "spirit," what gives him life; and, as the readings for this Easter season have made very clear, what gives Jesus life and "fire" is love. When he greets his disciples after the resurrection, wishing them "peace," "he show[s] them his hands and his side," not to shock them or to make them feel guilty, but to remind them that love, of God and of them, is his "breath."

The Greek word for "breathes on" comes from two roots. *Breathes* can mean "blows up," "inflates," as one might pump up a limp balloon. And certainly the disciples in John need inflating: they are limply hiding behind closed doors, full of fear. By contrast, when the Spirit "fills" the disciples in Acts, they fling open the doors and go outside, carrying the message with "bold proclamation."

The limp phase the disciples went through after Jesus' death is important in the spiritual life. Inspired by his reading of William James, Bill W. believed that, for alcoholics to enter recovery,

"Complete hopelessness and deflation at depth were almost always required to make the recipient ready" (AACA, 64). In other words, you have to be deflated, and let all the "old ideas" (BB, 58) wheeze out of you, before you can be "blown up" with fresher air and new ideas. "Deflation at depth" opens up a space that the Wind of God can fill with "different gifts" (1 Cor), or "simple gifts," as the old Shaker hymn puts it (see the meditation for Corpus Christi). We are no longer "prideful balloons, . . . float[ing] above the rest of the folks on our brainpower alone" (12 X 12, Step 2, 29); instead, the Spirit "help[s] us to get down to our right size" (30). Once we're "right size," we can recover, and can use what the Spirit has uniquely given us "for the common good" (1 Cor).

Trinity

Prv 8:22–31; Rom 5:1–5; Jn 16:12–15

Note: Some Christian communities do not celebrate Trinity Sunday, because they feel that every time we worship, we honor the God who is somehow Three-in-One (Triune). If your community is one of these, please go to the readings for Sundays in Ordinary Time (2004, Tenth; 2007, Ninth; 2010, Ninth).

". . . and hope does not disappoint us, because God's love
has been poured into our hearts through
the Holy Spirit that has been given to us"
(Rom 5:5).

Our First Reading on this Feast of the Trinity talks about Wisdom, the last and most important thing we ask for when we say the Serenity Prayer. In this passage from Proverbs, Wisdom is a "crafts-man," helping God build the world. The Big Book notes that a lot of people have gotten a deep sense of God from this world God has made. Chapter 4, "We Agnostics," describes such an encounter with

Creating Wisdom: "[W]e found ourselves thinking, when enchanted by a starlit night, 'Who, then, made all this?' There was a feeling of awe and wonder" (BB, 46).

I wish I were one of these "enchanted" people; but too often I forget to look at starlit nights because I'm too busy brooding on "the wrong-doing of others, fancied or real" (BB, 66). Or, if not crooning over my resentments, "starlit nights" may only make me wish for a warm fire and cable TV. Luckily, "God does not make too hard terms with those who seek [God]" (BB, 46). For folks like me, God is more easily found in human relationships, and especially in the stories we tell one another about those relationships. As Proverbs puts it, Wisdom is also to be found "playing on the surface of the earth," delighted to be with the human race.

While God is a Creator, we celebrate on this feast the fact that God is also a relationship. Within God love goes on between Abba and Jesus: "All that the Father has belongs to me" (Jn). And the Spirit "receives" things from Jesus. As we tell children, it's nice to share.

What goes on within God also spills over, as love will: God's relationship to us, as Paul notes, is also all about love, love that is "poured out." The word translated here says two important things about the love of God: this word can connote lavishness or even wastefulness—when it comes to loving, God is a Prodigal Father. But it is also often used in the Christian Scriptures of the "pouring out" of blood, of one's life, in loving sacrifice. Jesus uses the word this way at the Last Supper.

Either way, this is the kind of love that 12 Steppers need: "'Freely ye have received; freely give . . .' is the core of [the first] part of Step Twelve" (12 X 12, 110; Bill W. is quoting Matthew's Missionary Discourse, 10:8). When anyone loves like this, they are showing the world who God is, just as Jesus did, and just as he promised that his Spirit would enable his followers to do.

Corpus Christi

Gn 14:18–20; 1 Cor 11:23–26; Lk 9:11–17

Note: On this Sunday Roman Catholics celebrate the gift to us of the Lord's Supper (Corpus Christi equals Body of Christ). This special feast was created because medieval Christians felt that, with so much going on at the Holy Thursday celebration, the gift of bread and wine, and the fellowship that they symbolize, might get neglected in the larger drama. You may prefer to read this meditation on Holy Thursday, and to read on this Sunday the meditation for the appropriate Sunday in Ordinary Time.

"[The disciples] did so and made them all sit down [literally, 'bending down']. . . . *And all ate and were filled"* (Lk 9:15, 17).

A couple of weeks ago, on Pentecost, I cited the Shaker hymn "Simple Gifts," the melody of which Aaron Copland put to good use in his ballet score *Appalachian Spring.* If I recall, the chorus of this hymn runs like this: "When true simplicity is gained / To bow and to bend we shan't be ashamed; / To turn, turn, will be our delight / Till by turning, turning, we come round right." The Shakers, a Christian fellowship, were so nicknamed because they danced while they prayed and sang—"to bow and to bend" and "turning, turning" indicate dance steps. Twelve dance steps?

This comes to mind because Luke's version of the Feeding of the Five Thousand in this Sunday's Gospel is full of variations of "bowing" and "bending." For example, the words translated "Have them sit down in groups of fifty or so" literally means "Bend them down in bendings of around fifty." This is a typically Lucan effect; his is the Gospel of humility, of graceful bending and bowing.

Apparently Jesus had a distinctive way of saying grace, of saying the Jewish meal blessing, when he broke bread with his friends.

The language Luke uses here—"Jesus raised his eyes to heaven, pronounced a blessing over [the bread and the fish], broke them, and gave them to his disciples"—is remarkably similar to the language he uses in chapter 24 to describe the down-to-earth meal Jesus shares at Emmaus with the runaway disciples. Something about the way he did this opened their eyes so that they "had been made known to [him] in the breaking of the bread" (Lk 24:35). Perhaps Jesus' trademark was a certain simplicity, a certain humility, in the way he blessed the bread.

Naturally this simplicity was at a later day a characteristic of Christian Eucharist meals, at which Jesus was remembered and proclaimed. Or at any rate they were supposed to be simple. In fact, Paul chides his contentious Corinthian friends because their pre-meeting potlucks have become far from humble—the rich don't share with the poor, some people bring the equivalent of salmon mousse, and Perrier in Gucci canteens. Some people even get drunk. Paul has to remind them to keep it simple.

This same Shaker spirit ought to characterize 12-Step meetings (with or without food). A spirit without "intolerance," a spirit of "informality" and "genuine democracy," can let a newcomer know that "here [is] haven at last" (BB, 160), what the hymn calls "the place just right." And surely people who have undergone a conversion—literally, people who have "turned" and "turned"—should realize that humility is not "a forced feeding on humble pie," but rather "the nourishing ingredient which can give us serenity" (12 X 12, 74).

✛

Ordinary
Time

Second Sunday in Ordinary Time

Is 62:1–5; 1 Cor 12:4–11; Jn 2:1–12

"As a young man marries a young woman, so shall your builder
marry you, and as the bridegroom rejoices over the bride,
so shall your God rejoice over you"
(Is 62:5).

The former American poet laureate Richard Wilbur wrote a lovely poem called "A Wedding Toast" on the occasion of his son's marriage. In it he alludes to the story of the Wedding Feast at Cana, the story in today's Gospel. Wilbur cites this story to make a point about love. As the story goes, Jesus and his disciples, including his mother, went to a wedding reception (which, as the First Reading, from Isaiah, reminds us is a favorite image in the Hebrew Scriptures of God's loving relationship with God's people). When a crisis occurred, not only did Jesus turn water into wine so that the celebration could continue, but he made a whole lot of wine, somewhere between 90 to 125 gallons. Even those of us who are recovering alcoholics might consider this just about enough for us and for a handful of good friends, and *enough*, as I have remarked, is a word that alcoholics do not use lightly.

Wilbur concludes about Jesus' munificence that "[i]t made no earthly sense, unless to show / How whatsoever love elects [chooses] to bless / Brims to a sweet excess / That can without depletion overflow." Like Bill W.'s miner who "has struck something better than gold," those who have "struck" love—and recovery—"insist on giving away the entire product" (BB, 129). And as we "give freely of what [we] find" (BB, 164), we discover that the supply is never depleted—the more we give, the more it "overflow[s]."

This reckless generosity, this "sweet excess," is especially appropriate when we are dispensing the "different gifts" that we bring to the fellowship, whether that fellowship is a 12-Step group or a church community. The scrappy Corinthians naturally had turned their community into a Battle of the Gifts, which Paul is trying to resolve in this section of 1 Corinthians. Note that he lists "faith" as a gift, which might seem pretty commonplace compared to more attention-getting gifts like "healing" and "tongues" and "miraculous powers." This hints at Paul's solution to the squabble: all the gifts are useful, and all come from the same Spirit, so people with more sensational gifts have no call to be so impressed with themselves.

As we shall see in a couple of Sundays, Paul's final solution is even better: *love* is the best gift, "service, gladly rendered" is the goal of "true ambition" (12 X 12, 124). So aim for love, if only because it doesn't ask stupid questions like "Whose gift is greatest?" or "What if we run out?"

Third Sunday in Ordinary Time

Neh 8:2–4, 5-6, 8–10; 1 Cor 12:12–30;
Lk 1:1–4, 4:14–21

"'. . . do not be grieved, for the joy of the LORD is your strength!'"
(Neh 8:10)

This is the time of year when U.S. presidents are sworn into office (January 20 is the official date). On this occasion, incoming presidents deliver an inaugural address, setting forth the aspirations and goals for the time they will be in office. In today's Gospel, Luke gives a short inaugural address by Jesus, spoken in his hometown synagogue at the beginning of his ministry. Jesus tells the crowd—which is friendly so far—his goals for his term of service.

He has received a strong sense of those goals, of his mission, at his baptism (see the Gospel for the Feast of the Baptism of the Lord). He has wrestled with the Tempter over just how he will realize that mission (see the First Sunday in Lent). As we saw last year in the

Gospel of Mark, Jesus will also have to struggle during his ministry with his disciples, to get them to see what a different kind of Messiah he felt called to be.

But just now, in the synagogue at Nazareth, Jesus is fresh from defeating the Tempter. Having fought in the desert for his vision of his ministry, he now confidently inaugurates it. He tells his listeners that he will be the sort of kindly ruler (Messiah) who will "bring glad tidings to the poor, . . . liberty to captives, [r]ecovery of sight to the blind and release to prisoners."

The word translated *prisoners* in his inaugural address literally means "those who have been broken into pieces." Anyone who has dealt with addictions can identify. The 1st Step describes that brokenness with merciful understatement: "our lives had become unmanageable." What broken people need is "conscious contact" with a person, with a Messiah, who has a gentle Spirit. This contact can in turn put our lives back together again. Beyond that, it can make us, as Paul suggests in today's reading from 1 Corinthians, a contented "member" of a larger "body" "constructed" by "God."

Remember that Paul was trying to warn the Corinthian Group # 1 to "honor" all its "members." Characteristically, the group was battling over which members had the most important gifts—the secretaries or the coffee-makers or the cake-lady, to put it in 12-Step terms. For that group, and for all spiritual groups, "personal recovery"—or individual spiritual growth—"depends upon . . . unity [of the fellowship]" (Tradition 1). Every gift is essential—some of the humbler gifts are absolutely essential. Without group unity, we will stay "broken into pieces," "prisoners" of our own egos.

Fourth Sunday in Ordinary Time

Jer 1:4–5, 17–19; 1 Cor 12:31–13:13; Lk 4:21–30

"But strive for the greater gifts. And I will show you
a still more excellent way. . . . the greatest of these is love"
(1 Cor 12:31, 13:13).

In this Sunday's Gospel, we pick up exactly where we left off last week. Very suddenly the hometown crowd turns on Jesus, and Jesus tartly quotes the proverb about prophets not finding acceptance among their own people (a story we considered in Mark's version, the Fourteenth Sunday in Ordinary Time, Cycle B). Was it *this* sudden? In fact the commentators believe that Luke has stitched together separate visits of Jesus to Nazareth; his ex-neighbors did reject him, but it took a while for them to work up enough of a resentment. (Addicts can generally accomplish these things faster.) Of course, as Mark informs us, Jesus' own family thought he was crazy, so perhaps it's understandable that his neighbors would, in Mark's typically blunt expression, "[find Jesus] too much for them" (6:3).

This human orneriness in the Gospel seems to strike a note very different from the beautiful hymn to love in the reading from Paul. But keep in mind that Paul cites this much-quoted (especially at weddings) love song in order to end an unloving squabble among the quarrelsome Corinthian congregation. The Corinthians had been feuding particularly about which of them had reserved the biggest gifts from God. Over the last couple of Sundays, Paul has been arguing that *all* the gifts have their place in the Body; this week he goes (literally) to the heart of the matter by pointing out that love is the best gift. Love is the gift that provides the impetus for the services provided by all the other gifts, the little no less than the great.

This is the area covered by Tradition 8, which insists that there should be no professional class in A. A., no special set of gifts that distinguishes one group of members from everybody else. It is—or it should be—a "well-understood fact that in God's sight all human beings are important" (12 X 12, 124). And so we cannot afford to do without a single gift that anyone has; "and the greatest of these is love." Twelve Steppers should especially "set your hearts on" love because "[love] is not irritable or resentful" (1 Cor 13:5). Bill W. felt that, "with the alcoholic, whose hope is the maintenance and growth of a spiritual experience, this business of resentment is infinitely grave. We found that it is fatal. For when harboring such feelings we shut ourselves off from the sunlight of the Spirit" (BB, 66). As John the Evangelist would be the first to point out, for human beings love and light and life pretty much all come to the same thing.

Fifth Sunday in Ordinary Time

Is 6:1–2, 3–8; 1 Cor 15:1–11; Lk 5:1–11

"Then I heard the voice of the Lord saying, 'Whom shall I send, and who will go for us?' And I said, 'Here am I; send me!'"
(Is 6:8)

In our Gospel this Sunday, Jesus takes Simon Peter, who will become one of his best friends, through the Steps in a hurry (I have studied this gospel passage in Meditation 26 of *A 12-Step Approach to Spiritual Exercises*). Luke has already described Peter as being in some loose way Jesus' disciple, but Peter has kept his day job, as a fisherman. As 12 Steppers say, Peter is "of the fellowship," but not "in the fellowship." In this week's Gospel, Jesus first creatively uses Peter's boat as a nautical podium. Then he provides Peter with a spiritual experience the fisherman can hardly miss: with the power of Jesus helping him, Peter makes an unimaginably large catch of fish.

Peter reacts by coming to believe in a hurry. But his 2nd Step is intertwined with a combined 1st and 4th Step realization: if Jesus has this kind of power, he must know the "exact nature of [Peter's] wrongs"—every wretched thing Peter has ever done or wished he could do. So he assumes the 1st Step position: he "[falls] at the knees of Jesus saying, 'Leave me, Lord. I am a sinful man.'" The word for "falls" is used in Mark and Luke to refer to the really desperate people who come to Jesus—the woman who couldn't stop bleeding, the man so full of devils he lived in caves (see the Meditation for Thanksgiving Day, in Special Feasts). Like a good sponsor hearing a 5th Step, Jesus picks Peter up; and then he promises him a life of going on 12th Step calls: "Do not be afraid. From now on you will be catching human beings."

This is not the first time in Luke someone has been told not to fear. Angels said this to Zechariah (the father of John the Baptist), to Mary, the mother of Jesus, and to the shepherds on Christmas night. Each of them was being asked to "carry" (in several senses) a frighteningly big message. They all needed to hear an encouraging word. If, like them, and like Peter in today's Gospel, we hear the word, leave everything, and follow Jesus in carrying the message, then fear will no longer be "an evil and corroding thread [in] the fabric of our existence . . . we [will] commence to outgrow fear" (BB, 67, 68). Like the prophet Isaiah, whose "spiritual awakening" is depicted in today's First Reading, we will quickly move from the 1st Step ("Woe is me, I am doomed!") to Steps 4 through 9 ("I am a man of unclean lips . . . [Y]our wickedness is removed") to the 12th Step ("Here I am, [Lord] . . . send me").

Sixth Sunday in Ordinary Time

Jer 17:5–8; 1 Cor 15:12, 16–20; Lk 6:17, 20–26

"[Jesus] came down with them and stood on a level place,
with a great crowd of his disciples and a great multitude of people.
. . . Then, he looked up at his disciples and said:
'Blessed are you who are poor . . . '"
(Lk 6:17, 20).

Like Matthew, Luke has Jesus deliver a Great Sermon near the beginning of his ministry, a sermon in the first part of which he declares blessed those who are aware of their powerlessness (both sermons are studied at greater length in Meditation 27 of *A 12-Step Approach to the Spiritual Exercises*). Matthew places his Sermon on a mount: Jesus is the new Moses for Matthew's Jewish-Christian audience, and Moses met God on Mount Sinai. Bill W., who didn't have a small ego, also thought of mountaintops at the moment of his big spiritual experience: "I felt lifted up, as though the great clean wind of a mountaintop blew through and through. . . . It seemed to me, in the mind's eye, that I was on a mountain and that a wind not of air but of spirit was blowing" (BB [1939], 14; AACA [1957], 63).

But in the Gospel of Luke, "the Gospel of the Poor," Jesus delivers this Sermon on a plain. Some of Luke's material overlaps with Matthew's, although in slightly different form (for example, 4 Beatitudes and 4 Woes versus Matthew's 8 Beatitudes). But the site is a crucial difference: the word translated "level stretch" in the quotation above is related to words for "[flat] earth" and for "foot." In other words, Jesus' message is down to earth. Like the early members of A. A., Jesus "believe[s] [God] would like us to keep our heads in the clouds with [God], but that our feet ought to be firmly planted on earth" (BB, 130).

This advice is perennially useful for anyone who wants to "carry" a "message." It's better to tell your story in a plain way to most people, and it's certainly a good idea to take this tack with alcoholics: "Never talk down to an alcoholic from any moral or spiritual hilltop; simply lay out the kit of spiritual tools for his [or her] inspection" (BB, 95). Not every spiritual tradition began on a "mountaintop": the Buddha achieved enlightenment beneath a tree, and Zen Buddhism, according to Robert Pirsig, author of the American classic, *Zen and the Art of Motorcycle Maintenance*, is often called "the Spirit of the Valley." Mountain air is clean, but a bit thin; we may also want to learn from Jeremiah's "tree planted beside the waters that stretches out its root to the stream." This tree, down in the valley, does very well: "In the year of drought it shows no distress, but still bears fruit."

In 2010, go next week to the First Week of Lent. After Corpus Christi, return to the Eleventh Sunday in Ordinary Time.

Seventh Sunday in Ordinary Time

1 Sm 26:2, 7–9, 12–13, 22–23; 1 Cor 15:45–49; Lk 6:27–38

"'. . . do not condemn, and you will not be condemned.
Forgive, and you will be forgiven; give, and it will be given to you'"
(Lk 6:37–38).

The Gospel this Sunday continues with Jesus' Sermon on the Plain. This week's passage includes the injunction to "be compassionate, as your Father is compassionate." I want to make two points about this statement.

First, as I noted on the Seventh Sunday in Ordinary Time, Cycle A, Matthew quotes the same command, but uses "perfect" rather than "compassionate." However, Jesus is not telling us to be "perfect" in the sense of rigidly sitting still so that we never risk a mistake. Rather, "perfect" in Matthew means "having become what you were created to be"; and for human beings, to become what we were meant to be is to become "compassionate." Matthew and Luke are saying the same thing.

Second, the word in Luke translated "compassionate" is one of several Greek words for "merciful." It's somewhat less frequent in the Christian Scriptures than its synonyms. One of the other, more common words for "merciful" envisions a situation where a person with power is asked to "have mercy" on a person who lacks power—for example, a blind man asks Jesus to "have mercy" on him. But our less usual word today—*oiktirmos*, translated "compassionate"—depicts a moment when one person says "Oy!" because that person's life is unmanageable, and somebody else empathizes enough to say "Oy!" along with the sufferer. "Oy," of course, is in Yiddish (as well as in Greek) a cry from a troubled heart; we could call it a 1st-Step cry, except that alcoholism is comparatively uncommon among Jews and Greeks.

Oiktirmos suggests another principle for recovering people to keep in mind when working with others. "Conditions" are "most effective" for carrying the message when the person "who is making the approach has had the same difficulty" and "has no attitude of Holier than Thou" (BB, 18–19). As Tom Weston puts it, "Recovery works when someone who's been there reaches out to someone who is there." *Oiktirmos* also fits well with the spirit of Luke's Sermon on the Plain; when it comes to powerlessness and unmanageability, we're all on a level playing field.

I agree with my friend Father Charlie Shelton, S.J., who has written well about moral development, especially among adolescents: the foundation of morality, and of moral development, is empathy, the ability to feel another's *schmerz* (Yiddish for "pain," "woe"). So 12 Steppers would do well to cultivate the spirit of *oiktirmos*, since 12-Step recovery is founded on ongoing moral development (Dr. Silkworth, an early student of A. A., called the program "moral psychology" [BB, xxv]). But in the end, compassion makes sense for all human beings, because we are all children of Adam. Say "Oy!" with someone else today, because you may need them to say "Oy!" with you tomorrow.

In 2004, go next week to the First Week of Lent. After Corpus Christi, return to the Twelfth Sunday in Ordinary Time. In 2007, go next week to the First Week of Lent. After Corpus Christi, return to the Eleventh Sunday in Ordinary Time.

Eighth Sunday in Ordinary Time

Sir 27:4–7; 1 Cor 15:54–58; Lk 6:39–45

" 'No good tree bears bad fruit,
nor again does a bad tree bear good fruit' "
(Lk 6:43).

An important appendix to the Big Book describes the "spiritual experience" that A. A. believes is crucial in recovery. The main point this appendix makes is that such experiences are sometimes "sudden and spectacular upheavals," but more frequently are gradual and all but imperceptible: "Most of our experiences are [of] . . . the 'educational variety' because they develop slowly over a period of time. Quite often friends of the newcomer are aware of the difference long before he [or she] is." But this appendix doesn't spell out what "the difference" is: how can you tell if someone has had a "spiritual experience," sudden or "educational"? (By the way, no one has ever been able to find the exact phrase "educational variety" in James's *Varieties of Religious Experience*, despite the reference to James in this passage from the Big Book.)

In this week's installment from the Sermon on the Plain, Jesus gives a telling answer to this very question: "A good tree does not produce decayed fruit any more than a decayed tree produces good fruit. Each tree is known by its yield." Paul offers a relevant list of what he calls the "fruits" (same word as "yield" in this week's Gospel) of the Spirit: "love, joy, peace, patience, kindness, generosity, faithfulness, gentleness, and self-control" (Gal 5:22). This list is an equivalent in Paul's writings to the Promises in the Big Book (83–84), which attempt to sketch the "fruits" of recovery.

If someone has had a contact with a Higher Power, they should be making progress toward "fruits" like these. In the early days of A. A., newcomers were attracted by the "fruits" they sensed in the early members, "fruits" like "the very practical approach to [newcomers'] problems, the absence of intolerance of any kind, the informality, the genuine democracy, the uncanny understanding" (BB, 160). As Paul commented about his list of fruits, "Against such there is no law!"

At this point some readers may be thinking of intolerant members of the fellowships they attend. They may even be considering photocopying my remarks here and thoughtfully sending the copy to the offending members so the latter can make more spiritual progress and become more like these thoughtful folks. If your thoughts are drifting that way, you would do well to read *slowly* the section in today's Gospel about "specks" and "beams." And, for good measure, you might want to ponder these words of Bill W.: "We talked of intolerance, while we ourselves were intolerant" (BB, 50).

Ninth Sunday in Ordinary Time

1 Kgs 8:41–43; Gal 1:1–2, 6–10; Lk 7:1–10

Note: These readings aren't used between 2001 and 2010; but I include meditations on them for communities that follow a different plan for Sunday Scriptures.

> *"[Solomon prayed to God,] '. . . do according*
> *to all that the foreigner calls to you,*
> *so that all the peoples of the earth may know your name*
> *and fear you, as do your people Israel,*
> *and so that they may know that your name has been invoked*
> *on this house that I have built'"*
> (1 Kgs 8:43).

Our readings for this Sunday invite us to consider the inclusiveness of the reign of God that Jesus announced, particularly in his Great Sermon, which is the Charter for the Reign. Shortly after that sermon—right after in Luke—Jesus is contacted by a Gentile, a *goy*. This Roman centurion asks Jesus to cure a servant of his, and assumes that Jesus, like the officer himself, has power great enough to make small work of a miracle of healing. The point Jesus draws from this is that Gentiles sometimes seem to have more faith than do members of God's chosen people. Therefore, Gentiles should be heard by God, as in the First Reading, in which Solomon prays that God would "listen from your heavenly dwelling" to the *goyim*. Specifically, since it follows hard on Luke's Sermon on the Plain, the story of the centurion suggests that Gentiles with faith are as eligible for the reign as are Jesus' fellow Jews.

This principle of inclusiveness was severely tested in the early Christian church. Our Second Reading this Sunday is from the opening of Paul's Letter to the Galatians, in which Paul launches a fiery defense of inclusiveness. He means business: in today's reading, he puts a curse on anybody who disagrees with him on this point. The first church council, described in Galatians and in Acts 15, had ruled in Paul's favor; the Jerusalem leaders had agreed that Gentiles could enter the Christian fellowship without becoming Jews. Further on in Galatians, Paul will even recount a story in which, in the name of inclusiveness, he holds out against Peter, a leader in the Church, when Peter seems to Paul to be waffling on this point.

One of the most attractive features of 12-Step groups is their inclusiveness. This was largely true from the beginning, and on spiritual grounds. In the Big Book (published in 1939, four years after the fellowship began), Bill W. outlines a principle the early members tried to practice: "To us, the Realm of Spirit is broad, roomy, all inclusive; never exclusive or forbidding to those who earnestly seek. It is open, we believe, to all men [and women]" (BB, 46). At the first A. A. "council," the International Convention held in Cleveland in 1950, this principle was codified in Tradition 3: "The only requirement for A. A. membership is a desire to stop drinking."

Members of both Christian and 12-Step fellowships owe it to the fierce struggles of the pioneers to keep alive these traditions of inclusiveness. Bill puts it simply and memorably: "Love and tolerance of others is our code" (BB, 84).

Tenth Sunday in Ordinary Time

1 Kgs 17:17–24; Gal 1:11–19; Lk 7:11–17

Note: These readings aren't used between 2001 and 2010, but I include meditations on them for communities that follow a different plan for Sunday Scriptures.

"Fear seized all of them; and they glorified God, saying,
'A great prophet has risen among us!'
and 'God has looked favorably on his people!'"
(Lk 7:16)

In today's selection from Galatians, we have Paul's "pitch," in which he describes "what happened" (BB, 58) to change him from a persecutor of "the Church of God" to one of its most devoted "spread[ers] [of] . . . the good tidings concerning [God's Son]." His account here of his *metanoia* is less colorful than Luke's version in Acts, chapter 9, but Paul gives enough information for us to perceive that his was, like Bill W.'s, a "religious experience[s] . . . in the nature of [a] sudden and spectacular upheaval[s]" (BB, 569). In Paul's case, "upheaval" is especially apt, since, according to Luke, God's revelation of Jesus to Saul (as Paul was then called) knocked him off his horse.

However, while Bill's "spiritual awakening" was "sudden," it's also possible to trace some of the events in his life and the traits in his character—mostly disastrous—that led up to it, as he does in chapter 1 of the Big Book, "Bill's Story." Paul also gives a brief hint in this passage from Galatians—"Paul's Story"—of "what [he] used to be like" (BB, 58). He tells his readers, "I advanced in Judaism beyond many among my people of the same age, for I was more zealous for the traditions of my ancestors" (Gal 1:14). Can we detect any powerlessness or unmanageability in Paul's self-description?

Perhaps I'm only projecting one of my own salient defects of character, but I pick up a strong whiff of perfectionism in Paul's "inventory" of himself. He claims not just "spiritual progress" but something much like "spiritual perfection" (BB, 60): "I went *to extremes* in persecuting the Church," "I made progress . . . *far beyond most* of my contemporaries, in my *excess* of zeal . . ." (my emphasis). He sounds rather like the young Bill W., who "fashion[ed]" out of his childhood sense of inferiority "another sort of boomerang, one that almost killed me later on. . . . I was the leader and lead I must—or else. So it went. All or nothing. I must be Number One" (AACA, 53).

No wonder Paul and Bill readily speak of God's "favor" (Gal). God gave them both a break from this self-destructive urge toward "spiritual [and other] perfection" (BB, 60). We who follow on their paths may also feel "reborn" (BB, 63), like the son of the widow of Naim, when we "suddenly realize that God is doing for us what we could not do for ourselves" (BB, 84). In the spiritual life, "[t]he only urgent thing is that we make a beginning, and keep trying" (12 X 12, 68).

Eleventh Sunday in Ordinary Time

2 Sm 12:7–10, 13; Gal 2:16, 19–21; Lk 7:36–8:3

"I do not nullify the grace of God; for if justification comes through the law, then Christ died for nothing"
(Gal 2:21).

A line in today's Gospel needs close attention: Jesus says, "[T]hat is why her many sins are forgiven—because of her great love." This may sound like "God forgave her because she did a really nice thing in anointing my feet." But that isn't the point of the little story about the "moneylender" that Jesus tells his rude host. In fact, this story makes the opposite point: you love somebody who has forgiven you a lot. Forgiveness first, then love in return out of a sense of gratitude. So what Jesus is actually saying is, "You can tell she had a lot of sins forgiven—look at how much she has loved in return!"

Paul makes a similar point in today's reading from Galatians. Maybe the central spiritual idea of Paul's life was this: How It Works is *not* that we do really good things, like keeping the Law of Moses, and then God rewards us for our virtue. If this is a loving God (as in Tradition 2), then we shouldn't have to resort to manipulation or wheedling to win God's affection. No, it's the other way around: Paul lives a life of faith, a life of love, a life of grateful service to others, *because* "the Son of God . . . loved me and gave himself for me."

Perhaps Paul was particularly relieved to let go of his "old idea" about pleasing God because he'd tried it and found it didn't work. As he described himself last week, "I advanced in Judaism beyond many among my people of the same age, for I was more zealous for the traditions of my ancestors" (Gal 1:13, 14). Paul sounds like one kind of person who balks at the 2nd Step, the kind whose "religious observance is scrupulous." Bill diagnoses the problem of these perfectionists: "[The] answer has to do with the quality of faith rather than its quantity . . . We supposed we had humility when really we hadn't" (12 X 12, 32). In Paul's case, it took a devastating experience of powerlessness for him to change his "old ideas."

Paul can make his "new idea" sound very complicated (especially in the Letter to the Romans). John typically keeps it simple: "We love because he [God] first loved us" (1 Jn 4:19). This makes sense in terms of human nature, and particularly in terms of addicted human nature: it's a lot easier to love out of a sense of gratitude than out of a sense of duty. So I'd suggest this as a closing jingle for 12-Step meetings: not "Keep coming back—it works"; but "Keep coming back—God loves."

Note: In 2007, Roman Catholics will celebrate the Feast of St. John the Baptist (June 24) on the following Sunday. See the meditation in Special Feasts.

Twelfth Sunday in Ordinary Time

Zec 12:10–11; Gal 3:26–29; Lk 9:18–24

". . . all of you are one in Christ Jesus"
(Gal 3:28).

Today's reading from Paul contains one of the most radical statements in the Christian Scriptures. Bear in mind the kind of world in which Jesus lived and died and rose again, the world in which Paul proclaims Jesus as Christ (Messiah). Socially the distinctions between people were sharply drawn and rigidly observed. It was a society in which there were many slaves, who had little hope that they or their children would ever be free. It was a society in which women were possessions of men; women without men, like childless widows, were regarded as non-persons.

And of course Paul had spent much of his life Before Christ as a devout Pharisaic Jew, for whom another distinction, the difference between Jews and Gentiles, was fundamental. Despite all this, Paul can tell the Galatians that in Christ none of these distinctions matter anymore—that in Jesus-the-Messiah there is no "Jew or Greek, slave or free, male or female." Paul's statement draws out the radical implications of Jesus' vision of the reign of God. Having found "in Christ Jesus" "a new freedom and a new happiness" (BB, 83), Paul believes that "the Realm of Spirit is broad, roomy, all inclusive" (BB, 46).

However, Jesus' way of being Messiah is so radically new that you have to undergo a complete psychic change, as Paul did on the outskirts of Damascus, to "get" Jesus' idea. The Gospel for today is Luke's accounting of Peter's bold assertion that he has "come to believe" that Jesus is the Messiah. So far so good. But, as in Mark and Matthew—particularly Mark, where this is a central theme—Jesus "strictly forbade" his disciples from spreading Peter's insight, precisely because the disciples hadn't had this kind of sweeping psychic change yet.

So Jesus begins at once to educate them. If he is going to be his kind of Messiah, he, and they as well, will have to "take up [their] cross." To combine the concepts "suffering" and "Messiah," they will have to let go of their "old ideas." But if they can "get" Jesus' radical vision of the reign of God, it will be "the beginning of the end of [their] old life, and the beginning of [their] emergence into a new one" (12 X 12, 26). "Taking up the cross" is a price worth paying, because, in Jesus' new reign of God, "[a]ll are one."

"This should be very encouraging news" (12 X 12, on Step 11, 105) for addicted and compulsive Christians. We have spent much of our lives feeling alone, on the wrong side of "that mysterious barrier" between us and other people. But if we can experience "a psychic change" (BB, xxvii), we can attain "the surety that we . . . can fit and belong in God's scheme of things" (12 X 12, 124).

Thirteenth Sunday in Ordinary Time

1 Kgs 19:16, 19–21; Gal 5:1, 13–18; Lk 9:51–62

"When the days drew near for him to be taken up, he set his face to go to Jerusalem. And he sent messengers ahead of him"
(Lk 9:51–52).

In our Gospel this Sunday, Luke employs the solemn language just quoted. These words announce that Jesus is setting out on his Road of Destiny, which will lead to the Holy City, through death, and then back "up" to Abba. Luke organizes the next nine chapters, roughly the middle third of his Gospel, around this motif of Christ's journey. (A person's spiritual life is often thought of as a journey or pilgrimage, as on p. 164 of the Big Book.)

In the light of Luke's loud rhetorical fanfare, it's no wonder that James and John—whom Jesus nicknamed Sons of Thunder, according to Mark—got angry when the Samaritans wouldn't welcome Jesus and his followers as they began this solemn journey. James and

John were particularly incensed because, like most of their contemporaries, they thought the Samaritans were barely Jews at all. As so often happens with family feuds, this was because of incidents that had occurred centuries before. One need not know the specific history; it's just another instance of people drawing lines that leave out other people. Underneath the "historic" rationalizations for this behavior, the "true motive" is "to feel superior by pulling [them] down" (12 X 12, 94).

In any event, John and James, feeling very "superior," believed that these outcast Samaritans ought to be grateful for any spiritual crumbs thrown their way by this indulgent Messiah. When the Samaritans don't "welcome him," naturally these two become "angry, indignant, self-pitying" (BB, 61), like alcoholics who haven't gotten their own way. Didn't the Samaritans realize how important Jesus (and they) was? Like alcoholics, these disciples helpfully propose the "obvious" (to them) solution to this little disagreement: "Lord, would you not have us call down fire from heaven to destroy them?" Note by the way that *they* get to call down the fire; perhaps they thought Jesus might be too squeamish, so they offer to take the job off his hands. *They* are not that sensitive.

I'm reminded of my friend Patricia: she believed she had genuinely entered recovery when she had a flat tire and thought of calling Triple A, not Suicide Prevention. Addicted people have trouble seeing anything but the most apocalyptic solutions to problems, which is one reason why they should read the Christian Scriptures in order (Revelation comes last). Jesus, the new kind of Messiah (see last week's Gospel), does not buy the Thunderboys' "solution." Instead, he proposes an alternative that probably hadn't occurred to them. Rather than destroy the Samaritans, why don't they just "set off for another town"? James and John: "Oh . . . yeah, well I guess we could do that."

Fourteenth Sunday in Ordinary Time

Is 66:10–14; Gal 6:14–18; Lk 10:1–12, 17–20

"Whatever house you enter, first say, 'Peace to this house!'
And if anyone is there who shares in peace,
your peace will rest on that person . . ."
(Lk 10:5–6).

This week's Gospel picks up where last Sunday's left off. There Jesus, on his way up to Jerusalem, "sent messengers on ahead of him." This Sunday he does the same thing, but a bit more formally: he "appoint[s] a further seventy [some ancient manuscripts say seventy-two], and send[s] them in pairs before him." What sort of attitude are these "messengers," these 12th Steppers, supposed to have?

After the fiasco with James and John last week, no wonder Jesus' charge to the seventy is "Keep It Simple, Storytellers." They are to travel light—not even sandals (in Mark they can wear sandals). As the Sixth Tradition observes, money, property, and prestige can sour people's attitudes. People with extra sandals may start thinking, for instance, that "fire from heaven" is the best tactic with the resistant client.

It can't be that way with Jesus' disciples; unlike John the Baptist, he is neither gloomy nor threatening, and they shouldn't be, either. Instead, his traveling disciples are to use the everyday greeting, "Peace" (*shalom* in Hebrew), but in a more than conventional way—their peace, their serenity, is to "rest" on the people they 12th Step. Again, no "fire from heaven"—maybe a little dust, but no fire.

Finally, they go "in pairs." It's always been the custom in A. A. for people on a 12th-Step call to go in pairs, too. Why? Well, alcoholics don't always want peace, and things can get very hectic; and then it can be pretty disheartening work—many need sobriety, few want it. Furthermore, alcohol is "cunning, baffling, powerful" (BB, 58–59), so sending in a team can help, sort of like the two-priest squad in *The Exorcist*. One-on-one interventions rarely work; addictions simply don't fight clean. Most important, perhaps, if you have two people, you have the basic requisites for a meeting: a storyteller and a story listener (taking turns, of course). You can thus act out the fact that recovery is a "we" business.

Jesus' advice to missionaries may or may not be philosophically striking. But, as with 12-Step work, intellectual elegance is not the goal. Rather, as the seventy gleefully attest when they return from their mass 12th-Step call, "It works—it really does" (BB, 88). We know that "The reign of God is at hand" when people start having "deep and effective spiritual experiences which . . . revolutionize [their] whole attitude toward life, toward [their] fellows, and toward God's universe" (BB, 25).

Fifteenth Sunday in Ordinary Time

Dt 30:10–14; Col 1:15–20; Lk 10:25–37

"'[T]he neighbor to the man who fell into the hands
of the robbers [was] [t]he one who showed him mercy'"
(Lk 10:36, 37).

I was told this story at fifth- or sixth-hand: an alcoholic priest has recently checked into a treatment center for Catholic clergy. He's still shaky and green when his turn to celebrate the Sunday Mass comes up. The Gospel is this Sunday's, the story of the Good Samaritan. The point of the priest's sermon that day is this: "I studied this story and tried to identify with the people in it. But I'm not the priest who passes by, and I'm not the Levite. And I'm not the Samaritan either—I'm not in good enough shape to be much help to anybody. No—I'm the guy in the ditch."

I wish I'd heard this story before I went to treatment myself. I opted to go to a treatment center for "ordinary" people, not for my fellow clergy. On balance it was a good idea, but one problem with this setup was that it made it easier for me to take "professional" care of all the other patients, and to forget that I was "the guy in the ditch." The treatment counselors—the real ones, not the eager volunteers like me—finally brought me forcibly to a halt, which is an embarrassing story for another occasion.

Anyone who has ever taken a 1st Step has made an admission like this priest's. Whether it was our own addiction or the addiction of someone we cared about, eventually it left us feeling naked, beaten, and left for "half-dead." Addiction "robs" people of everything, more thoroughly than any human mugger could, and then leaves them in a literal or metaphorical "ditch."

Curiously, if you asked most people what the moral of the story of the Good Samaritan is, I think they'd probably say, "Help others like the Good Samaritan did." In this view, the Good Samaritan is the Father of All 12th-Step workers, which is why they name hospitals after him. But Jesus tells this story in answer to an unfriendly question, "Who is this neighbor God wants me to love?" The one we are supposed to love is the one who shows up when we're in the ditch—that's our neighbor, the one who 12th-Steps us, not the one we help.

It makes it that much more pointed that the helper in the story is a "good Samaritan." Recall, there was an ancient family feud between Jews and Samaritans, and "good Samaritan" would have sounded to Jesus' audience like an oxymoron. But when you're "the guy in the ditch," you don't get to decide who will show up to help. It may even be someone you've always despised. That's the beauty of being in ditches.

Sixteenth Sunday in Ordinary Time

Gn 18:1–10; Col 1:24–28; Lk 10:38–42

"'[Y]ou are worried and distracted by many things;
there is need of only one thing'"
(Lk 10:41–42).

In today's reading from the Letter to the Colossians, Paul (or a follower of Paul) makes a bold statement: he doesn't mind the pain he encounters in the service work he does, because his task is to "fill up what is lacking in the sufferings of Christ." Could anything be lacking in the sufferings of Christ? What can God need of us? A brief answer lies in the old story of the statue of Jesus damaged in Italy during World War II. American soldiers reassembled as many of the fragments as they could, but they couldn't find two important pieces. So when the troops moved on, a G.I. hung a sign on the statue that said "Christ has no hands but yours."

The "sufferings" of Jesus also get "filled up" in a way familiar to 12 Steppers. It's a common belief among them that, as they meet other people on the Road of Happy Destiny, they may be the first—or the only—Big Book that someone comes across. So they tell their stories, with the laughter and the pain: "For [the newcomer's] sake, we do recount and almost relive the horrors of our past" (BB, 132).

And sometimes the person with whom they share their story will respond, "Yes, I am one of them too; I must have this thing" (BB, 29). But whether or not a particular listener wants what they have, *they* can always sense that, "No matter how far down the scale we have gone, . . . our experience can benefit others" (BB, 84). Grace happens when we see that our sufferings can heal others; and in this way the story of Jesus laying down his life for his friends gets reenacted, every day, everywhere. Jesus' "sufferings" get "filled up."

Still, it's a good idea to hold on to a certain amount of "worldliness and levity" (BB, 16) as we work at building the kingdom of

God. "[T]hose of us who have tried to shoulder the entire burden and trouble of others find we are soon overcome by them" (BB, 132). As compulsive people, we can easily get too "busy with all the details," like Martha, and forget the one "required" thing. What is that one thing we most need to remember? "We relax and take it easy. We don't struggle [because] God is doing for us what we could not do for ourselves" (BB, 86, 84).

Seventeenth Sunday in Ordinary Time

Gn 18:20–32; Col 2:12–14; Lk 11:1–13

"'For everyone who asks receives, and everyone who searches finds, and for everyone who knocks, the door will be opened'"
(Lk 11:10).

Luke's version of the Lord's Prayer appears in this Sunday's Gospel. At the end of 12-Step meetings, it is often the custom to recite this prayer. I have noticed on some retreats I have given that some 12-Step people have been toying with the words, and I have to admit that it made me a bit nervous. But of course there's a precedent for this. Matthew was the first to tinker with it—he added several pieces to Luke's version. It's in fact Matthew's "improved" Lord's Prayer that we've said for centuries.

Still, I prefer Matthew's and Luke's "daily bread" to the "daily strength" that some folks have inserted. Sure, as people who lack power, we may well feel that getting strength is just the ticket. But we need so much more than strength; we are hungry and thirsty, too, and with a hunger and thirst that never seems to get satisfied. I've heard it said that alcoholics are people who want more of anything than there is. Bill W. certainly thought so: "Never was there enough of what we [alcoholics] thought we wanted" (12 X 12, 71), and this was true of much more than alcohol. "Our liquor was but a symptom" (BB, 64) of this deep-down hunger.

By the same token, I have never been very interested in the mythical pill to cure alcoholism, about which we hear rumors from time to time. I am fairly certain that, even if such a pill appeared, I would fill a prescription for a lifetime supply of it and then go through it in three weeks. So what's the best way to feed someone like me, someone who's capable of waking people up in the middle of the night when I'm hungry, like the obnoxious neighbor in the Gospel? The best arrangement is to give me bread—and wisdom—one day at a time.

And it won't hurt for the Giver occasionally to check on whether I am passing my "bread" on to friends who have "come in from a journey" on the Road of Happy Destiny. I need to feed others as freely as I have been fed. I'll be able to do this if I receive "the Holy Spirit" one day at a time. For this is specifically the Spirit of the generous Jesus; generosity is one of the "fruits" of his Spirit (Gal 5:22). As the First Reading, from Genesis, amply demonstrates, God is determined never to lose a generosity contest.

Eighteenth Sunday In Ordinary Time

Ecc 1:2; 2:21–23; Col 3:1–5, 9–11; Lk 12:13–21

"Put to death, therefore, whatever in you is earthly: fornication,
impurity, passion, evil, desire, and greed (which is idolatry). . . .
Do not lie to one another . . . "
(Col 3:5, 9).

Paul uses a vivid phrase in this Sunday's reading from Colossians to describe the "old self," the self we were before "having had a spiritual awakening as the result of these Steps" (Step 12). The old self is characterized by "that lust which is idolatry." The word for "lust" here is a term that Plato, and other philosophers, used; it refers to the desires of someone who has, or claims to have, or insists on having, more than their share of something.

This is true of most addicts, who, as I mentioned last week, want more of everything than other people seem to need or get. Addicts never have enough of anything, especially their drug; they make idols of their insatiable needs. Gerald May uses the old spiritual term *attachment* for "addiction" (in his *Addiction and Grace*; for more on "addiction" as "attachment," particularly in the spiritual thought of Ignatius Loyola, see *A 12-Step Approach to the Spiritual Exercises*). But *idolatry* is an even older word for the same behavior.

Bill W. insists that alcoholics, even vehemently anti-religious alcoholics, have lots of "idols": "We found, too, that we had been worshippers. What a state of mental goose-flesh that used to bring on! Had we not variously worshipped people, sentiment, things, money, and ourselves?" (BB, 54). For most people, to claim they aren't "worshippers" is to "[lie] to one another" (Col), and to themselves as well.

As chapter 5 of the Big Book states, what is needed is honesty. If we honestly look at this world full of "worshippers," this is what we see: "What usually happens? The show doesn't come off very well" when one person wants to "wrest satisfaction and happiness out of this world" at the expense of others (BB, 61). Sooner or later though, if addicts and other "worshippers" are lucky, some dark night arrives when they realize that they've been fools, like the rich farmer in the Gospel this week.

"[E]ither God is everything or else [God] is nothing" (BB, 53). Anything less than God, no matter how much of that thing we have, is an idol, and will inevitably let us down in the end. Oddly enough, even on such a dark night, if grace happens, this "sorrow and grief" (Eccl) can lead to "serenity" and "peace" (BB, 84). Our "new self" (Col) can leave idolatry behind by humbly recognizing that it is God who gives us "our daily bread."

Nineteenth Sunday in Ordinary Time

Wis 18:6–9; Heb 11:1–2, 8–19; Lk 12:32–48

"'. . . be like those who are waiting for their master to return from the wedding banquet, so that they may open the door for him as soon as he comes and knocks'"
(Lk 12:36).

One of my favorite stories by the great Christian fabulist Flannery O'Connor is "A Good Man Is Hard to Find." In it a very ordinary suburban family is on a car trip to Florida. They're rather like the Simpsons—dim father, long-suffering mother, bratty children—with the addition of a ditsy grandmother, who has vague pretensions of being a Southern belle along the lines of Scarlett O'Hara. She nags "Homer" into going into the backwoods of Georgia to look for a Tara-esque plantation she thinks (wrongly, as it happens) is in the area. The family has a car accident, caused by the grandmother's cat getting loose; against orders, she had snuck the cat into the car in a picnic basket. Banged up, the family encounters the Misfit, a sociopath and an escaped convict, and his gang. The grandmother, a tireless scanner of the tabloids, at once recognizes the Misfit and shrieks his name, thereby dooming her entire family. One by one the members of the family are taken offstage into the woods and shot.

The grandmother is the last alive. Trying to suppress her rising hysteria, she natters inanely about religion with the Misfit, hoping to persuade him to spare her life. Like a lot of practicing addicts, the Misfit feels like he belongs nowhere, as his name suggests. However, unlike Abraham the Wanderer in today's reading from Hebrews, the Misfit wanders without faith, so her appeals to his "niceness" make no impression on him. Finally, grace happens even to this pathetic old woman, and in a sudden burst of dignity she tries physically to touch the Misfit, to bring him into the circle of humanity: "Why you're one of my babies," she cries. He of course instantly blows her away. His mordant epitaph on the grandmother: "She would of been a good woman . . . if it had been somebody there to shoot her every minute of her life" (p. 133).

Jesus makes a similar point, more mildly, of course, in the Gospel this Sunday: "Be on guard." Our lives can have meaning and dignity if we take a little time every day to recall that our choices matter. And especially the biggest choice: "God either is, or [God] isn't. What [is] our choice to be?" (BB, 53). This is a call to faith, to "conviction about things we do not see" (Heb). In the end, recovering people may be a bit luckier than "normies" (non-addicts), because, at "every minute of [our lives,]" a little reflection will "remind [us] we are no longer running the show" (BB, 87–88).

Note: In 2004 and 2010, Roman Catholics will celebrate the Feast of the Assumption (August 15) on the following Sunday. See the meditation in Special Feasts.

Twentieth Sunday in Ordinary Time

Jer 38:4–6, 8–10; Heb 12:1–4; Lk 12:49–53

"Therefore, since we are surrounded by so great a cloud of witnesses,
let us lay aside every weight and the sin that clings so closely,
and let us run with perseverance the race that is set before us"
(Heb 12:1).

Recovering people may have to read today's Gospel twice to get the point. When we hear dark warnings like "a household of five will be divided three against two and two against three; father will be split against son and son against father, mother against daughter and daughter against mother, mother-in-law against daughter-in-law, daughter-in-law against mother-in-law," our reaction may well be "Been there, done that. So what's your point?" Those of us who grew up in addicted families are all too accustomed to people choosing up sides. We need to bear in mind that Jesus is talking as a first-century Jew, as someone for whom being cut off from a close-knit and supportive extended family would be unusual, and terribly painful. Jesus' point is that someone who has begun a spiritual journey has often had to leave home and family behind, as have the people of faith, the "cloud of witnesses," in Hebrews. We have to keep looking forward, as Abraham and Sarah did on their travels, as Jesus did in his journey to the cross. If we keep looking backward on the Road of Happy Destiny, we might forget that "[n]ever [can] we recapture the great moments of the past" (BB, 151).

This doesn't mean that we "shut the door" on the past (BB, 83). In the 8th and 9th Steps, we have to acknowledge our part in what went on in the past. But having done so, we let the past be past. Unfortunately, not every member of an addicted family is going to be willing or able to let the past go, maybe for now, maybe forever. Non-recovering members may react as angrily to the 12 Stepper as Jeremiah's people did to him: "[Jeremiah] demoralizes . . . all the people, by speaking such things to them." Tellers of unpalatable truths often end up, like Jeremiah, in the mud.

The key to healing such divisions, at least on our side of them, lies in the Al-Anon concept of detachment with love—affectionately letting people go their own journey: parents, children, siblings, and in-laws. We may also want to "keep our eyes fixed on Jesus, who inspires and perfects our faith." When Jesus' family told people that they thought he'd gone crazy, he did not denounce his kin. Instead, he found other people who shared his vision, and declared that they were his family. "[D]o not grow despondent or abandon the struggle" of recovery (Heb): there are people who can "draw" you out of the mud.

Twenty-First Sunday in Ordinary Time

Is 66:18–21; Heb 12:5–7, 11–13; Lk 13:22–30

". . . I am coming to gather all nations and tongues;
and they shall come and shall see my glory"
(Is 66:18).

I have always been reluctant to quote statistics on who gets sober and who stays sober. In early recovery, I was confidently informed by people, including some treatment professionals, that only 1 in 34 ever makes it; so, they insisted, I had better "work to achieve my [recovery] with fear and trembling" (Phil 2:12). But statistics about recovery are notoriously hard to obtain, and hard to evaluate—"34" what? drunks? treated drunks? treated drunks who also attend 12-Step meetings? And people who dispense statistics are sometimes using them as a scare tactic. But this is counterproductive with folks "on the depressive side" (12 X 12, 45) like me, since fear only makes us drink *more*. "Depressive" people "may even sink to such a point of despair that nothing but oblivion looks possible as a solution" (12 X 12, 45).

What does work with people like me is what I heard a recovering alcoholic say when I was newly sober. He was willing to grant that the "door," to use Jesus' term, might be "narrow." But his response was that, if only a few people were going to "get in," he was going to take Steps to make sure he was one of them. This has always seemed to me the better approach; too often when addicted people hear others say that most of us won't make it, we think they're asking for volunteers. Instead, recovering people need to remember that every Step they take changes the odds in their favor.

In any event, the reading from Isaiah and the end of today's Gospel take a view very different from the "narrow door" approach. In these passages, all kinds of unlikely people "will take their place at the feast in the kingdom of God." These colorful folks come from regions that Palestinian Jews would have considered the boondocks, including Tarshish (in Spain), Put and Lud (somewhere in Africa), and Javan (Greece, more or less). Nobody knows where "Mosoch" was. So you might think of it as a name for whatever place your addiction took you to. The name sounds ugly to me somehow. But even "Mosoch," and more sordid places, have not only sent some people—after a detour through the Steps—to "the feast in the kingdom of God" with Abraham and the prophets. These watering holes have also produced a priest or a Levite or two, just as Isaiah predicted.

Twenty-Second Sunday in Ordinary Time

Sir 3:17–18, 20, 28–29; Heb 12:18–19, 22–24; Lk 14:1, 7–14

"The greater you are, the more you must humble yourself;
so you will find favour in the sight of the Lord"
(Sir 3:18).

"Were entirely ready to have God remove
all these defects of character. Humbly asked [God]
to remove our shortcomings"
(Steps 6 and 7).

"Revelation" is another marvelous story by Flannery O'Connor, one of the last she wrote before her most untimely death at thirty-nine from lupus (see also the Nineteenth Sunday in Ordinary Time). In this story, a very decent woman, much like the "leading Pharisee" who is Jesus' host in today's reading from Luke, has a disturbing encounter with a college girl while both are waiting outside a doctor's office. The "nice lady," Ruby Turpin, has just been burbling about how nice "Negroes" are—Ruby thinks some "Negroes" may even be a lot nicer than "white trash," for instance. After a longish stretch of this cheery smugness, the college girl, the sort of crazed prophet O'Connor often inserts in her stories, erupts. She chucks the thick psychology text she's been reading at Ruby's head and calls her "a warthog from hell." The crazy girl is subdued by the bystanders and taken somewhere for a long sabbatical; Ruby, offended and baffled, goes home with her husband.

At the end of the story, the Good Woman is resentfully pondering this "message" from God as she surveys her immaculate pig farm—and it *is* immaculate, because Ruby is a Nice Person. Then she has her "revelation": she imagines a host of disreputable people, "white trash" and "battalions of freaks and lunatics shouting and clapping and leaping like frogs," messily entering heaven. "Bringing up the end of the procession" are dignified folk like Ruby and her husband, "shocked" because they realize that "even their virtues [are] being burned away" (p. 508).

The Jesus of Luke's Gospel would love O'Connor's vision of heaven. In fact in today's reading he goes it one better: he suggests that we be proactive and invite just such ragtag people, "battalions of freaks and lunatics," to our parties. Bill W. urges the same principle in terms of who should be included on the guest list at any 12-Step "reception." Tradition 3 insures that at any given meeting we may meet "beggars, tramps, asylum inmates, prisoners, queers, plain crackpots, and fallen women" (12 X 12, 140).

Under the terms of the "new covenant" announced by Jesus, these unlikely people are "the assembly of the first-born enrolled in heaven" (Heb). Our best response when we encounter such people? "Yes, I am one of them too; I must have this thing" (BB, 29). If you're a warthog, "[a]dmit [it] . . . and join us" (BB, 164). Then you can at least be a sober warthog.

Twenty-Third Sunday in Ordinary Time

Wis 9:13–18; Phln 9–10, 12–17; Lk 14:25–33

"I have indeed received much joy and encouragement
from your love, because the hearts of the saints have been
refreshed through you, my brother. . . . yet I would rather appeal
to you on the basis of love . . . "
(Phlm 7, 9).

There's a story well worth retelling behind our reading from Paul this Sunday. Paul is writing to Philemon, a wealthy Christian and a slave owner. This is the only letter of Paul's we have that is written to an individual rather than to a whole group. This "personal" letter was preserved, and included in the Bible, because it says beautiful and important things about the relationship between love and freedom.

The occasion for the letter: one of Philemon's slaves, Onesimus, had run away from his master and joined Paul, who was at the time under house arrest. Onesimus then became a Christian and acted as Paul's servant. Paul, as Onesimus's "sponsor," has decided that the slave owes his master an amends, particularly since Onesimus stole something as he was hitting the road.

Paul does not attempt to give Philemon an order about how to receive Onesimus's amends. Instead, Paul delicately mentions the love that Philemon (whose name means "Beloved") owes him: Paul had converted, had "12th-Stepped," Philemon. And Paul quietly stresses that Onesimus is now a member of the fellowship with Philemon. Onesimus is "more than a slave" now—he is "a beloved brother." Indeed, he is "more than a brother," because Philemon now knows him both as a human being and "in the Lord."

Paul even makes an affectionate joke, perhaps to soften Philemon a little more. The word *onesimus* means "Useful," and Paul says that the slave, "who was formerly useless to you is now useful indeed both to you and to me." This may recall one of the Promises:

"That feeling of uselessness and self-pity will disappear" (BB, 83–84). The Promises are supposed to kick in "before we are half way through" Step 9, the "amends" Step, which Onesimus will be taking with his master.

To sum up the Letter to Philemon: the message of the gospel, the good news, which both Philemon and Onesimus have heard and accepted, is that love is now the standard for their lives, master as well as slave. Or, to use Bill W.'s words, "Love and tolerance of others is our code" (BB, 84). And since that is the case, if we accept this "code," all of us, slave and free, "are going to know a new freedom and a new happiness." As Gandhi observed, it takes enormous energy to keep someone else enslaved—the master is a slave, too, to his own "misuse of willpower" (12 X 12, 40). Freedom, for both slave and master, can come only from letting go: "We do not tire so easily, for we are not burning up energy foolishly as we did when we were trying to arrange life to suit ourselves" (BB, 88).

Twenty-Fourth Sunday in Ordinary Time

Ex 32:7–11, 13–14; 1 Tim 1:12–17; Lk 15:1–32

"But I received mercy because I had acted ignorantly in unbelief,
and the grace of our Lord overflowed for me
with the faith and love that are in Christ Jesus"
(1 Tim 1:13–14).

We looked at the second part of this Sunday's Gospel, the Prodigal Son last Lent (Fourth Week of Lent). This week let's focus on two stories that form a package with the Prodigal Son, stories meant to make the same point, that God, who is "loving" (Tradition 2) and stubborn, refuses to throw away any human being.

A human being might be more wasteful than God. For example, it would have been easy, when the Prodigal returned, for his father to get on his high horse and say, "Son? I have only one son, and he's at home!" Fathers in trashy TV melodramas utter clichés like this all the time. And really, if you still have 99 sheep, wouldn't it make more sense to do a cost-benefit analysis and write the 100th off as "slippage," or whatever the insurance term might be? Finally, a poor woman might well worry about the disappearance of 10 percent of her savings, but having the neighbors over to celebrate seems excessive.

Yet God and God's angels in heaven are in fact excessive, and refuse to deal with human beings on the basis of sound business principles. They hate to lose anyone. Even if God gets angry, God can change God's mind, as Moses persuades God to do in the reading from Exodus. All Moses has to do to bring God around is to remind God that, in the relationship between God and "God's own people," God is the one "with such great power and with so strong a hand." As the stronger, God can afford to be big about this conflict. Why should God throw away what God made in love?

Take Paul, for example. In today's reading from 1 Timothy we get a taste of Paul's 5th Step: before his conversion, he was "a blasphemer, a persecutor, a man filled with arrogance." Yet out of this "wreckage" (BB, 164), God cleverly salvaged a "faithful servant."

Or take a bunch of "unlovely creature[s]" (BB, 16), described by one of their own as "self-centered in the extreme," as "childish, emotionally sensitive, and grandiose" (12 X 12, 24, 123). God made of this seedy bunch "a new instrument for social action" with "a new therapy based on the kinship of common suffering" (Lasker Prize, 1951, awarded to A. A.: BB, 573). The conclusion is inescapable: as Tom Weston puts it, "God is big and God has skills." "To . . . God be honor and glory forever and ever" (1 Tim).

Twenty-Fifth Sunday in Ordinary Time

Am 8:4–7; 1 Tim 2:1–8; Lk 16:1–13

"'. . . since then the good news of the kingdom of God
is proclaimed, and everyone tries to enter it by force'"
(Lk 16:16).

The story of the Cunning Steward in today's Gospel has always puzzled its listeners and readers. Maybe it even puzzled Luke. After he recounts the story, he seems to offer several different morals, none of which fits this parable very well and some of which seem to contradict each other. For example, is the point of this story "The worldly take more initiative than the otherworldly when it comes to dealing with their own kind"? So we should imitate the Cunning Steward? Or is the point, "If you cannot be trusted with elusive wealth, who will trust you with lasting?" So *don't* imitate the Cunning Steward? Or is the moral, "You cannot give yourself to God and money"? So stay away from money, then; but how does this fit with Moral # 2?

I've heard a lot of preachers over the years try to solve the riddle of what a rotten person like this Steward can tell us about "God's kingdom." I've even heard brain-numbing sermons on first-century Palestinian accounting techniques. My current hunch is that the story makes the same point as a verse, quoted above, from later in this chapter of Luke's Gospel: "[P]eople of every sort are forcing their way in[to God's kingdom]."

In other words, the point of the story about the Steward lies in a quality he has, a quality captured perfectly in the Yiddish word *chutzpah*. It takes chutzpah to do what the Steward does. Is the boss about to fire you for small stuff? Pull a really big swindle on him! Somehow his chutzpah works. Maybe the owner can't help but admire the breathtaking nerve of this, even though the owner is the loser by it. Some con jobs are so majestic you just have to admire them, even grudgingly, as in *The Sting*.

The moral of the story, then, is that, if you need to use chutzpah to get into the kingdom, use it—beg, borrow, or steal, as we say. Good manners may be something that alcoholics, who are "dying helplessly like people in a sinking ship," (BB, 152) can't afford. Studies suggest that extroverts do better in A. A. than introverts, perhaps because extroverts "have the [crucial] capacity to be honest" (BB, 58), as well as the equally important "capacity" to be loud about what's going on inside them (I speak as a stone introvert myself). So "Easy Does It" (BB, 135)—but a little chutzpah never hurt.

Twenty-Sixth Sunday in Ordinary Time

Am 6:1, 4–7; 1 Tim 6:11–16; Lk 16:19–31

"He said, 'No, father Abraham; but if someone goes to them from the dead, they will repent'"
(Lk 16:30).

For the last several weeks, the readings from Luke have been full of stories with surprise endings. Wastrel sons get welcomed home; the good boys who stayed home and tended the family business turn out to be mean and full of long-standing resentments. Crooked business managers give lessons on how to get into heaven. This Sunday's Gospel offers another instance: Lazarus the Street Man goes to heaven; the Rich Guy, who seemed to have it all together, goes to a place where his thirst will never be quenched (alcoholics, be warned).

The surprising fates of the Rich Man and Lazarus are actually not a surprise if you really know the mind of Jesus. As his mother chanted when she was carrying him, ". . . he has filled the hungry with good things, and sent the rich away empty" (Lk 1:53). That's how it works in the reign of God.

Now you might think that recovering people could skip the story of the Rich Man and Lazarus. When we were hitting bottom, we may have spent some time in the gutter ourselves. We may have gone to the dogs, whether we did this literally, or whether, as is more often the case with addicts, Skid Row was between our ears. Surely we of all people ought to be able to empathize with down-and-outers like Lazarus, the homeless man who "lay"—passed out?—at the rich man's gate. We could never be as thoughtless as the Rich Man, who "feasted splendidly every day."

However—and this is a surprise, too, a nasty one—even people who are themselves ex-Lazaruses can easily forget what it was like to be "the guy in the ditch." That's why we need Step 12. Twelfth-Step work helps us stay sober—and grateful—by frequently taking us back to the beginning of our climb back up from the dogs. "Having had a spiritual awakening," our task thereafter is to "recount and almost relive the horrors of the past" (BB, 132) so that others may "benefit [from] our experience" (BB, 84). This is our way of "bearing witness," which Paul enjoins on Timothy in today's Second Reading.

Despite what Father Abraham says in Luke, *some* people may "get it" if ex-drunks rise from the dead to tell their story. And even if in a particular instance Abraham is right, and the "[brothers] will not be convinced," the 12th Step does the ex-drunk a world of good. As I have stated before, recovery is about growth in compassion; and Lazarus can help us in this effort.

Twenty-Seventh Sunday in Ordinary Time

Heb 1:2–3, 2:2–4; 2 Tim 1:6–8, 13–14; Lk 17:5–10

". . . for God did not give us a spirit of cowardice,
but rather a spirit of power and of love and of self-discipline"
(2 Tim 1:7).

I have always found this Sunday's Gospel infuriating. How can Jesus tell me to announce that I am a "useless servant"? Here I've been "plowing" and "herding" all day, and now I have to "cook" and "wait table"? Haven't I been working hard at recovery and helping others and carrying the message? You call *that* "only carrying out . . . orders," "no more than [my] duty"?

When I listen to myself talking in this strain, I realize I sound a lot like the Elder Brother in the story of the Prodigal Son. He, too, was very clear on how hard he had "worked" for his father (the word can mean "slaved"), and how unappreciated he felt. When I am focused on how virtuously I am doing my duty, I have forgotten love and gratitude, as the Elder Brother has—his father had to remind him that "all that is mine is yours" (Lk 15:31). I need to be reminded that, if it weren't for the gift of recovery, I wouldn't even be able to wait on tables—I'd be under them.

Being focused more on duty and rights than gratitude can make it hard to forgive others. Today's gospel passage comes just after Jesus tells his disciples to forgive others "seven times a day." The disciples find this prospect pretty gruesome, and that is why they ask Jesus to "increase our faith." They correctly guess that forgiving people to this extent will require more than a sense of duty. Like the Elder Brother, they're going to need a faith booster, an influx of grace, if they really are going to forgive their brothers (and sisters) seven times a day.

Growing faith is necessary for a growing ability to forgive. It also helps us to forgive others if we remember that we have needed to be forgiven, as the Lord's Prayer and the 9th Step remind us. Finally, with forgiveness as with other spiritual practices, we should keep in mind that we do not "claim" to be perfect "servants." Rather, we are trying to make "spiritual progress" (BB, 60) in that direction.

The Second Reading offers some traits by which we can measure our "spiritual progress": those who have received the Spirit of Jesus are "strong, loving and wise" (2 Tim). For much of my life I thought "strong" and "loving" were mutually exclusive qualities: strong people are so often brutal and loving people so often weak. It takes "wisdom," which we ask for in the Serenity Prayer, to combine love and strength, as they are combined in God's Spirit. People who have this strong and loving Spirit also have the humility to "be able to receive forgiveness and give it, too" (12 X 12, 58; on the 5th Step).

Twenty-Eighth Sunday in Ordinary Time

2 Kgs 5:14–17; 2 Tim 2:8–13; Lk 17:11–19

"'Were not ten made clean? . . . Was none of them found to return
and give praise to God except this foreigner?'"
(Lk 17:17, 18).

Hugh R., an A. A. friend of mine, used to sum up recovery very simply: "I need to remember to be grateful." Our gospel story this week is about nine people who forgot, and one who remembered.

The kicker, of course, is that the one who remembered was a Samaritan. In this section of Luke, there are plenty of stories in which the Bad Guys—Tax Collectors, Corrupt Judges and Cunning Stewards, Samaritans—turn out to be good. This week's "Good Samaritan" doesn't give first aid to "the guy in the ditch," or arrange to pay for that crime victim's long-term care. No, this Samaritan *is* a "guy in the ditch," since he's a leper. Lepers were severely quarantined under the Jewish law, no doubt from a fear that leprosy might be contagious. And, as we have seen before, there was old, bad blood between Jews and Samaritans.

This man takes the first three Steps together with the other nine lepers. They all ask a Power greater than themselves to "have pity on us!" (Step 1). And they believe he has power to restore them to health (Step 2). So they turn their wills and their lives—if you can call them lives—over to him (Step 3). They then show they have taken these steps by moving into action, by following directions: they head off to the priests, as Jesus tells them to. With the priests, they would all work a kind of 5th Step: in the Law of Moses, priests officially readmit ex-lepers to "true kinship with man and God," which is one benefit of Step 5 (12 X 12, 57).

But only one ex-leper "remembers to be grateful." Even before his official reinstatement as a human being, he returns to Jesus to finish the steps by working Step 12. He alone carries the message by "com[ing] back" to the place where he had found healing, "praising God in a loud voice." Interesting that Jesus merely notes the difference between this *goy* ["foreigner"] and "the other nine." There may be ironic laughter in his voice; in calling this Good Guy a *goy*, he is echoing and so mocking the anti-Samaritan prejudices of his contemporaries.

If it were me, of course, I'd do more than laugh off the display of rudeness by the other nine. I'd give their leprosy back to them and see if *that* taught them some manners. Lucky that there's a God who isn't me, one who "still remain[s] faithful" even "if we are unfaithful" (2 Tim).

Twenty-Ninth Sunday in Ordinary Time

Ex 17:8–13; 2 Tim 3:14–4:2; Lk 18:1–8

"But as for you, continue in what you have learned and firmly believed, knowing from whom you learned it . . ."
(2 Tim 3:14).

The story of the Unjust Judge in today's Gospel is directed to those who "los[e] heart" about praying. One of the most moving passages Bill W. ever wrote gives wonderful advice to people who are thoroughly tired of praying. It occurs in the 12 X 12, written when Bill, although sober, had been struggling for years with clinical depression: "All of us, without exception, pass through times when we can pray only with the greatest exertion of will. Occasionally we go even further than this. We are seized with a rebellion so sickening that we simply won't pray" (12 X 12, 105).

What should we do when prayer dries up? As addicts, albeit recovering addicts, we may fall back on "old ideas," (BB, 58), and the oldest idea of any addict is that if something has stopped working, it means we need to do a lot more of it. So should we will ourselves to pray? Bill disagrees, so strongly in fact that he expresses his disagreement in italics: *"Our whole trouble had been the misuse of willpower. We had tried to bombard our problems with it instead of attempting to bring it into agreement with God's intention for us"* (12 X 12, 40).

But if willpower isn't the answer, what should we do when we "lose heart"? Bill gives this gentle suggestion: "... [W]e should not think too ill of ourselves. We should simply resume prayer as soon as we can, doing what we know to be good for us" (12 X 12, 105). "Think[ing] ill of ourselves" is the *second* oldest idea that addicts haplessly fall back on. The fact is, as Bill notes, that "losing heart" is something that happens to *"all of us*, without exception" (my emphasis), who are on a spiritual journey. The Spanish mystic John of the Cross called it "the dark night of the soul."

Jesus reminds us that, no matter how distant God seems at such times, God is actually still on our side. Even the Mean Judge finally listens to the powerless widow: as he (literally) says, "Since she's giving me a pain, this widow here, I'll rule in her favor, or she'll end up in my face [literally, 'giving me a black eye']"—and this from a person who despises the weak. But God, especially in Luke, frankly has a soft spot for the powerless; prefers them even. So "resume prayer as soon as [you] can," because "when we turn to [God], all will be well with us" (12 X 12, 105).

Thirtieth Sunday in Ordinary Time

Sir 35:12–14, 16–18; 2 Tim 4:6–8, 16–18; Lk 18:9–14

"But the tax-collector, standing far off, would not even look up to heaven, but was beating his breast and saying, 'God, be merciful to me, a sinner!' I tell you, this man went down to his home justified . . ."
(Lk 18:13–14).

Once again in this Sunday's Gospel we have the voice of the Elder Brother, reminding God of all the fine things he has done. Unlike the Elder Brother in the Prodigal Son, however, this fellow, a Pharisee, is in a good mood. When he spots the tax collector off in a back corner of the Temple, it only makes him feel that much smarmier, probably because this preening guy has no clue about Abba's taste in friends. He would have done well to ponder this week's First Reading, from Sirach: "The Lord is a God of justice, who knows no favorites." Instead, the Preener utters the kind of fatuous prayer that is like a fingernail on a blackboard to God: "I give you thanks, O God, that I am not like everyone else . . . [and especially] this tax collector."

As I have remarked when the subject of "tax collectors" has come up before, Jesus' contemporaries despised them because they helped the occupying Roman (Gentile) army extort money. Think in terms of a lieutenant in the Mob. Or, better still, insert the name of whatever group *you* despise. Some people might even say, "I give you thanks, O God, that I am not like those alcoholics, those addicts." Some recovering people might say, "I give you thanks, O God, that I am not like those phony religious people."

The point of this week's parable is that the best way to pray is to remember the 1st Step. The Preener is not a hypocrite—he really does "fast twice a week" and "pay tithes," he really isn't "grasping, crooked, [or] adulterous." But since he's already doing so well, what need of God does he have? Once again, Sirach could give him a clue: "The prayer of the *lowly* pierces the clouds; it does not rest till it reaches its goal."

By contrast, the Rotten Guy leaves God all the room in the world to make changes in him, and that's really the only way God can work, without people jiggling God's hand or offering God uninformed advice. Of course the Rotten Guy will need to take "action and more action" (BB, 88) as he follows up on this 1st Step—but we'll hear all about that next Sunday, when Jesus runs into a typical tax collector, who's nevertheless trying to go straight.

Thirty-First Sunday in Ordinary Time

Wis 11:22–12:1; 2 Thes 1:11–2: 2; Lk 19:1–10

*"When Jesus came to the place, he looked up and said to him,
'Zacchaeus, hurry and come down; for I must stay
at your house today'"*
(Lk 19:5).

In this Sunday's Gospel, Jesus takes a tax collector, like the man in last Sunday's Gospel who worked a good 1st Step, through the rest of the Steps. What did it take for Zacchaeus's complete psychic change to get rolling? Apparently only this: Zacchaeus had to have the "willingness" (BB, 76) to do something that would make him look pretty stupid in the eyes of the crowd. Imagine one of those sleazy characters that Danny DeVito often plays in movies climbing a tree. "No person likes to admit he is bodily and mentally different from his fellows" (BB, 30), and the height-challenged Zacchaeus surely didn't. But *metanoia* takes what it takes, and if climbing trees proves to you how unmanageable your life is, go climb a tree.

However, the most essential Step in the process of this tax collector's "overhauling" (BB, 68), it turns out, is Step 9. Bill W. offers some suggestions for people who owe financial amends: "Most alcoholics owe money. We do not dodge our creditors. . . . Arranging the best deal we can we let these people know we are sorry" (BB, 78). The tax collector meets these requirements, and then some: "Zacchaeus stood his ground and said to the Lord: 'I give half my belongings, Lord, to the poor. If I have defrauded any in the least, I pay them back fourfold.'"

And "before [he] is half way through" his 9th Step, "half way through" the restitution he has offered to make, he comes "to know a new freedom and a new happiness" (BB, 83). Jesus remarks, "Today salvation has come to this house": Zacchaeus is "a son of Abraham" again, that is, a member of the Jewish community in good standing. He has "the surety that [he] need no longer be [a] square peg in [a] round hole but can fit and belong in God's scheme of things" (12 X 12, 124). Unlike the Rotten Guy—the tax collector in last week's parable—he has a name, Zacchaeus, which means "the pure, the innocent one." Now he can live up to his name, now he can stand tall.

What the adventure of Zacchaeus tells us about God is the core of the Gospels, "the good news" (BB, 158). The beautiful passage from Wisdom in the First Reading foreshadows it: "For you [God] love all things that are . . .; for what you hated, you would not have fashioned." This was the good news that Jesus came to proclaim: "The Son of Man has come to search out and save what was lost."

Thirty-Second Sunday in Ordinary Time

2 Macc 7:1–2, 9–14; 2 Thes 2:16–3: 5; Lk 20:27–38

"Now may our Lord Jesus Christ himself and our Father,
who loved us and through grace gave us eternal comfort
and good hope, comfort your hearts and strengthen them
in every good work and word"
(2 Thes 2:16–17).

In the Gospels, Jesus often wrestles with the Pharisees. It's important to recall that he was pretty close to them, socially and religiously. The Pharisees were middle-class, devout Jews who tried very hard—too hard, in Jesus' estimation—to work a spiritual program. Jesus' affectionate—at first—quarrel with them arose because he thought they focused too much on their work and not enough on God's grace. The quarrel was that much more painful because the Pharisees and Jesus had so much in common.

This Sunday we have a different group going head to head with Jesus. The Sadducees were upper-class members of the priestly clans; Jesus only encounters them at this late point in Luke because he has finally reached Jerusalem, the center of Saducee power.

They would have spent little time in the boondocks, among the grungy people who formed Jesus' band.

Religiously, the Sadducees were more conservative than the Pharisees. You might want to imagine someone like William F. Buckley in the role of the Sadducees's spokesman. These aristocrats didn't believe in individual resurrection from the dead, for instance, because it isn't mentioned in the older Hebrew Scriptures; hence, "Mr. Buckley's" ridiculous question, intended to make a fool of Jesus, about the Serial Wife with Seven Husbands.

Contrast the staunch belief in resurrection in 2 Maccabees, from which our First Reading is drawn, a book written not too long before the time of Jesus. Of course, the Sadducees had little personal incentive to believe in individual resurrection, since they were *already* rich, this time around, so who needed an afterlife? It couldn't get any better than what they already had, unlike the lives of the desperate people whom Jesus felt especially close to.

"Mr. Buckley's" question is meant to be stupid, but the answer Jesus gives is far from stupid. His point is that resurrection is not about people being a certain way or possessing a certain something (the Sadducees knew all about possessing). Instead, Jesus claims that we are "children of the resurrection" because we are in a relationship with a Higher Power, the essence of whom is life. We can "turn our will and our lives over" (Step 3) to such a Vital Power with confidence, not just about "today" and "tomorrow," but even about "the hereafter" (BB, 63).

Abraham Lincoln gave his wife, Mary Todd, a wedding ring which was inscribed, "Love is eternal." Whatever changes we may undergo, we believe that beneath all changes is "a loving God" (Tradition 2) who lives and "keeps faith" (2 Thes).

Thirty-Third Sunday in Ordinary Time

Mal 3:19–20; 2 Thes 3:7–12; Lk 21:5–19

*"'. . . do not be terrified . . . So make up your minds not to prepare
your defence in advance; for I will give you words and a wisdom . . .
By your endurance you will gain your souls'"*
(Lk 21:9, 14–15, 19).

We began Cycle C last Advent with the second half of chapter 21 in
Luke. Today, almost a year later, we get the first half, and so round
off the story. You might recall what I said last year about apocalyptic literature: it's very strong spiritual medicine, and people need to
read the label carefully before they take it. Addicts generally read
labels *after* they have chugged half the bottle, or scooped up a handful of tablets and swallowed them, so my warning about apocalyptic
Scriptures bears repetition. Above all, apocalyptic "medicine" is pre-
scribed to give pain relief to people suffering terrible persecutions.
People who are not in fact being persecuted will get very loaded on
apocalyptic, and before long will *feel* like they're being persecuted,
which justifies their taking larger doses of apocalyptic, and so on.

This Sunday's passage from Luke is in any event not primarily
about the end of the world; it's about the fall of Jerusalem, which the
Romans devastated in 70 A.D. Jesus probably predicted this, many
years before it took place. But when Luke's Gospel was written, it
was already well in the past. So what had actually occurred probably
colors Luke's account of it. The Romans, with their usual thorough-
ness, did not leave "one stone . . . on another" in Jerusalem, the
social, political, and religious focal point of Jesus' people.

For us, so many centuries later, what still matters in these readings is the injunction to hang on to "patient endurance." 2 Thessalonians gives a good description of what can happen when people lose
patience and get carried away with apocalyptic ideas: lacking any
"good orderly direction," they just "wander around"; instead of

working, they just "work around" (literal translations of "are unruly" and "acting like busybodies"). In other words, they run around like chickens with their heads cut off, or they "work grudgingly and under half steam" (12 X 12, 49). Either way, they give up on building the kingdom.

This is always the temptation with apocalyptic, to lose patience with history and community and relationships, because everything is so wicked—as the apocalyptic people understand wickedness—that God must be about to tear it all down. Especially now, just after the turn of the millennium, the world needs people who can patiently work a good One-Day-at-a-Time program. *Work* is the key word here; as 2 Thessalonians puts it, what are needed now "in the Lord Jesus Christ" is people who "earn the food they eat by working quietly." Each of us can seek to be "one in a family, to be a friend among friends, to be a worker among workers, to be a useful member of society" (12 X 12, 53).

Feast of Christ the King

2 Sm 5:1–3; Col 1:12–20; Lk 23:35–43

". . . giving thanks to the Father, who has enabled you to share
in the inheritance of the saints in the light.
He has rescued us from the power of darkness
and transferred us into the kingdom of his beloved Son . . ."
(Col 1:12, 13).

We studied this gospel passage on Palm Sunday of this year. As usual, Luke focuses on the desperate and poor members of society; in this case, one of the Rotten Guys being executed with Jesus. Like the tax collector praying in the Temple a few weeks ago, this criminal utters a short, but profoundly honest, prayer: "Jesus, remember me when you come into your kingdom."

Today, on the Feast of Christ the King, we may wonder what kind of kingdom this is (see also the Meditations on the Kingdom of Christ, #18–19 in *A 12-Step Approach to the Spiritual Exercises*). In fact, the whole Gospel of Luke, which we have been studying this year, has been answering the question, "Who belongs in the kingdom?" So, one last time: criminals are some of the first people to get in. People who have plunged deeply into the darkness are quicker to grasp a ray of light from "the kingdom of God's beloved Son" (Col).

This gives us the "who" of the kingdom, but what of the "where" and "when"? Consider a passage earlier in Luke, in which the Pharisees ask Jesus when the kingdom will come. Jesus answers cryptically that "the kingdom of God is among you." For centuries people have tried to figure out what he meant by "among you." Some interpreters believe it means "inside you"; as the Big Book puts it, "[D]eep down in every man, woman, and child, is the fundamental idea of God" (BB, 55).

However, while recovery may begin as an inside job, sooner or later it needs to show up outside as well. The kingdom is out there, in the world, as well as inside us—this is the other interpretation of "the kingdom of God is among you." Recovering people "practice [the] principles [of the 12 Steps] in *all* [their] affairs" (Step 12; my emphasis). And so they need Traditions quite as much as they need Steps.

Significantly, Jesus replies to the man with whom he is being executed that "this day" he (Jesus) is "com[ing] into [his] kingdom," a "kingdom" this criminal will share. So where and when is the kingdom? Here and now—as Jesus lays down his life in love, when he *acts* upon his "decision to turn [his] will and [his] life over to the care of God as [he] understood [God]" (Step 3). Even in these miserable events—*especially* in these miserable events—"the kingdom of God is among you" (Lk 17:21).

All that remains for us is to "[g]ive thanks to the Father for having made you worthy to share the lot of the saints in light" (Col; see the Meditation for Thanksgiving in Special Feasts).

✛

Special
Feasts

There are a few feasts in the course of the Roman Catholic Church year that are considered so special that, in years when they happen to fall on a Sunday, they outrank the Sunday celebration and its readings. Years when this happens between 1999 and 2010 have already been indicated among the Sunday meditations. Meditations for those feasts are given here. If your church does not follow this regimen, please read the Sunday meditations on those dates. Of course, you can also feel free to browse in these "extra" meditations.

February 2

The Presentation of the Lord

Mal 3:1–4; Heb 2:14–18; Lk 2:22–40

(The Gospel Reading for today is also used on the Feast
of the Holy Family, Year B.)

"[The old man Simeon said:] '. . . for my eyes have seen
your [God's] salvation, which you have prepared in the presence
of all peoples, a light for revelation to the Gentiles
and for glory to your people Israel"
(Lk 2:30–32).

This feast commemorates the day when Jesus, the "messenger of the
covenant" (Mal), was ceremonially "presented" to God in the Temple
in Jerusalem. There Jesus and his parents are met by two people who,
as I noted in Meditation 23 of *A 12-Step Approach to the Spiritual*
Exercises, represent all the powerless people, totally dependent on a
power greater than themselves, who had been awaiting the Messiah,
"the Anointed of the Lord." Anna is a widow, a class of needy people
specially protected under the Law of Moses. Like Simeon, she is eld-
erly, which is another suggestion of powerlessness, but also of wisdom. Wise people can see beneath appearances, can "know the difference" (Serenity Prayer) between physical poverty—Jesus' parents
can't afford the deluxe sacrifice—and spiritual wealth.

This special vision of the two wise old people is spelled out in
Simeon's prayer. He speaks of this apparently ordinary baby as "a
revealing light to the Gentiles, the glory of your people Israel." This
feast has for centuries been associated with light and in particular
with the blessing of candles. The light that began to grow at
Christmas (around the shortest day of the year in the northern hemisphere) is now forty days old (forty is a significant number in

Jewish-Christian thought). And it is a light for everyone—Gentile and Jew, old and young, woman and man.

What does this light reveal? As spiritual enlightenment generally does, it reveals hope. The passage from Hebrews spells out that hope: Jesus is "like [us] in every way." He knows from experience what our life is like. And so he is "merciful and faithful," he can "help those who are tempted" (literally, "run to our side when he hears us yell"). Knowing this can "free those who through fear of death had been slaves their whole life long."

Bill W. would agree about the pervasiveness of fear in human, and particularly in addicted, life: "This short word somehow touches about every aspect of our lives. It [is] an evil and corroding thread; the fabric of our existence [is] shot through with it" (BB, 67). Ultimately, all human fear is fear of death, or more precisely fear that we will die before "our instincts" are "satisfied" (12 X 12, 49). What we celebrate today is that, in the light of Jesus' wonderful humility in becoming like us, "we [can] commence to outgrow fear" (BB, 68). If we grow in "the favor of God" (Lk 2:40), we will have enough—we will be enough.

June 24

St. John the Baptist

Is 49:1–6; Acts 13:22–26; Lk 1:57–66, 80

(The First Reading is also used on the Second Sunday
in Ordinary Time, Cycle A.)

*". . . before [Jesus'] coming John had already proclaimed
a baptism of repentance to all the people of Israel"*
(Acts 13:24).

We have met John the Baptist several times before, especially on the Second and Third Sundays of each Advent. The Christian Scriptures cast him in the role of the Last Prophet, heralding the very imminent arrival of Jesus the Messiah. His clothes, his austere lifestyle, and his preaching "in the desert" all link him to the long line of stern prophets, like Jeremiah, in the Hebrew Scriptures.

I remarked in Advent Cycle B that Christmas would be a very different holiday if John, and not Jesus, had in fact been the Messiah. In this event, I think Christmas would be a lot like the holiday in Tim Burton's *The Nightmare before Christmas*: instead of ornaments and holly, we would be decorating with shrunken heads and skeletons, and we might be exchanging ghoulish presents like hair shirts, or grasshoppers dipped in honey.

Many people at the time thought John *was* the Messiah. In fact, John's ferocity squared with the usual concept, held for instance by Jesus' disciples, of what the Messiah would be like. Luke shows us John preaching to soldiers (3:14), and it is a lot easier to picture John in a Lawrence-of-Arabia pose, leading hot-blooded troops, than it is to picture the gentle Jesus, who kept warning his followers against violence.

The picture of John I have painted so far may make him seem like a fire-eating crank, someone like the abolitionist John Brown. Yet Jesus once asserted that John the Baptist was the greatest human being up to that time (Mt 11:11). This cuts both ways, of course; it tells us how important John was, but it also sheds a gloomy light on human beings. Is the wild-eyed John the best our species can produce?

Maybe so. Up to the time of Jesus and of the message of a loving God that Jesus announced, John was in fact a pretty good sample of better members of the human race—kind of "angry" at "people, institutions [and] principles" (BB, 64), a little fixated on violence, but extremely clear on how much we as a species need God.

For good or ill, we do in fact have a birthday celebration for John, but as my friend Tom Weston, S.J., has remarked it's literally at the opposite end of the year from Jesus' birthday. Around the time of Jesus' birth, the light begins to grow; around the time of John's birth, the light begins to dim. For all of us, as for John, Jesus "must increase" in us, while "deep resentment" (BB, 66) must "decrease" (Jn 3:30). Thank God that Jesus was the real "light to the nations," whose "salvation" has "reach[ed] to the ends of the earth" (Is).

June 29

Sts. Peter and Paul

Acts 12:1–11; 2 Tim 4:6–8, 17–18; Mt 16:13–19

(The reading from 2 Tim is also used on the Thirtieth Sunday
in Ordinary Time, Cycle C; the Gospel Reading is commented
on at the Twenty-First Sunday in Ordinary Time, Cycle A.)

"[Jesus said to his disciples], 'But who do you say that I am?'"
(Mt 16:15).

On this feast we honor the memory of two co-founders of Christianity,
Peter and Paul. Like Bill W. and Dr. Bob, the co-founders of A. A., the
"co-founders" of Christianity had very dissimilar personalities.

Paul was the idea man, like Bill W., brimming with notions
about carrying the message in a novel way. His letters, full of brilliant, difficult theology and a great deal of purplish prose, comprise
a large portion of the Christian Scriptures. His most revolutionary
concept was that salvation should be available to non-Jews, to
Gentiles, without their having to become Jews first, in whole or in
part. Peter was more like Dr. Bob—more conservative, more traditional. Paul tells us in his Letter to the Galatians that he once had to
scold Peter for "relapsing" into the Jewish practice, in which they
had both been reared, of not eating with Gentiles.

Peter and Paul, like Bill and Dr. Bob, are clear instances of the
fact that spiritual groups are often comprised of "people who normally would not mix" (BB, 17). But, as the saying goes, it takes all
kinds of people to carry a saving message. Anyone who has ever
attended a 12-Step meeting can testify to this; and Christian communities are often healthier, the more heterogeneous they are.

Our Scripture Readings today shed an interesting light on the
qualifications for leadership in the Christian community. As in A. A.,
Christian leaders "do not have to be specially distinguished among

[their] fellows" (12 X 12, 124): like quite a few members of A. A., Peter and Paul served some jail time. Peter is sprung from jail without benefit of counsel in the First Reading; Paul is depicted as either in jail or awaiting trial in the Second. Nor does one have to be a ray of sunshine to be a Christian leader: the reading from 2 Timothy omits a passage in which Paul complains about being left alone in court, and lists the names of some people he thinks ought to get theirs for abandoning him.

No; to be a Christian leader you only have to answer one question: "Who do you say that I [Jesus] am?" (Mt 16:15) Peter gets the top post, for all his personal flaws, and despite having only a fisherman's job qualifications, because he answers correctly, "You are the Messiah." In fact, as the sequel shows, he is only half-right: Jesus *is* the Messiah, but not at all the kind of Messiah Peter expects and desires. Jesus literally would rather die than have anyone else get hurt, even his worst enemy.

In other words, "true ambition," among those who would follow Jesus as well as in A. A., "is not what we thought it was. True ambition is the deep desire to live usefully and walk humbly under the grace of God" (12 X 12, 124–25; see Mic 6:8).

August 6

The Transfiguration

Dn 7:9–10, 13–14; 2 Pt 1:16–19; Mk 9, 2–10

(Part of the First Reading overlaps with the First Reading for the Feast of Christ the King, Cycle B; the Gospel is also used the Second Week of Lent, Cycle B.)

"So we have the prophetic message more fully confirmed. You will do well to be attentive to this as to a lamp shining in a dark place, until the day dawns and the morning star rises in your hearts"
(2 Pt 1:19).

This feast commemorates the same event that we remember the Second Week of Lent (see also Meditation 32 in *A 12-Step Approach to the Spiritual Exercises*). There, in the context of Lent, it reminds us that Jesus' upcoming death on Good Friday is not the last word on him. Here, on this feast at the height of summer, it has a different flavor. Instead of focusing on how much pain is involved in "carrying the message," today's feast invites us to hope and to rejoice. Today, Mark's account of the Transfiguration is read with a section from Daniel, which comforts a persecuted people with the vision of a glorious future, and with a section from 2 Peter, which treats the Transfiguration as the memory of a glorious past, when "the first streaks of dawn appear[ed]." Recovery, which is another kind of transfiguration, is often described with similar imagery: "A new world c[o]me[s] into view," a world where we can "[stand] in the sunlight at last" (BB, 12).

However, despite the joy of this feast, the human propensity for rage, that "dubious luxury of [the] normal" (BB, 66), can never be completely forgotten. In this past century, human beings made decisions that will forever cast a shadow on this day. As if to underscore the fact that the reign of God is still a long way off, that "the morning star" (2 Peter) still hasn't yielded to full dawn; the Feast of the Transfiguration, 1945, saw the dropping of the first atomic bomb on human beings, in Hiroshima, Japan. The tremendous light and heat of a nuclear blast, obliterating the heart of that city and everyone in it, seem now like a parody of the "dazzling white" of Jesus' Transfiguration.

Perhaps this sad irony only underscores the high stakes that are involved in choosing between the hope of recovery, the hope that we can be different—and the despair that human beings can ever change, a despair that made us feel in our addiction "as though [we] lived in hell" (BB, 56). Finally, it is as simple as this: ". . . we had to fearlessly face the proposition that either God is everything or else [God] is nothing. God either is, or [God] isn't. What was our choice to be?" (BB, 53)

Despite our human worst, the Transfiguration still captures a hope for human beings that won't die. If we follow Christ, we believe in the kingdom he came to announce, "an everlasting dominion that shall not be taken away" (Dan). Our part in making that kingdom come is "to live usefully and walk humbly under the grace of God" (12 X 12, 125).

August 16

The Assumption

Rv 11:19; 12:1–6, 10; 1 Cor 15:20–26; Lk 1:39–56

(The Second Reading, from 1 Corinthians, is also used on the Feast of Christ the King, Cycle A. The Gospel overlaps with the Gospel for the Fourth Sunday of Advent, Cycle C.)

"The One who is powerful has done great things for me / And holy is God's name"
(Lk 2:49; my translation).

Today we celebrate a feast that has been around for a very long time in both Western and Eastern Christian churches—particularly Eastern, where the pageantry of a royal court has always played a large part in Christian worship. Admittedly, some Christians object to the Assumption because it has no specific scriptural grounding. But Roman Catholic theologians reply like this: believing that Mary is wholly with the God proclaimed by Mary's son is a special case of the scriptural belief that all Christians have this destiny.

I want to focus especially on Mary's song of praise in the Gospel today, since this is the only time it comes up in the Sunday feast day readings. It is called the *Magnificat*. It is a favorite prayer of Christians, especially in the evening.

Mary's Magnificat is a kind of collage of passages from the Hebrew Scriptures, especially the Song of Hannah in 1 Samuel; the theme of both these women's songs is that God is full of surprises. The biggest surprise, which God springs on human beings over and over again, is that God loves the lowly and raises them up, but doesn't care much for the pompous and the arrogant. (This is a favorite theme of the Gospel of Luke, in which the Magnificat appears.)

Twelve Step experience leads to a similar conclusion. An entire Step (7) is concerned mainly with humility ("lowliness" in Luke), as Bill W.'s commentary in the 12 X 12 makes clear. For 12 Steppers, "lack of humility" is a "crippling handicap" (12 X 12, 71). Addicts need humility as a "first step toward liberation," but "this is the barest beginning" (73). As we continue in recovery, "we now ought to be willing to try humility in seeking the removal of our other shortcomings . . ." (76). If we can remember Bill's advice, we can find ourselves finally filled up with "every good thing," a solution to the spiritual hunger that gnaws at addicts. We can be "raised" (Lk 2:52, 53), "[n]o matter how far down the scale we have gone" (BB, 84).

What we celebrate today is that the mother of Jesus was "raised" to God's side, in proportion to her humility, shown by her acceptance of God's will for her. Bill W. would agree—the "basic ingredient of all humility [is] a desire to seek and do God's will" (12 X 12, 72). Like Mary, we can hope that, "if we [keep] close to [God] and perform [God's] work well," if "we bec[o]me less and less interested in our-selves, our little plans and designs," we will be "reborn" (BB, 63).

September 14

The Holy Cross

Nm 21:4–9; Phil 2:6–11; Jn 3:13–17

(The Second Reading is also used on Palm Sunday, all three cycles, as well as on the Twenty-Sixth Sunday in Ordinary Time, Cycle A; the Gospel overlaps with the gospel passages for Trinity Sunday, Year A, as well as the Fourth Week of Lent, Cycle B.)

"Therefore [because of Jesus' acceptance of his cross] God also highly exalted him and gave him the name that is above every name"
(Phil 2:9).

Our readings on this feast invite us to consider the cross of Jesus as a sign that is "lifted up." Today's passage from John's Gospel links the cross to another saving sign that was "lifted up," the bronze serpent that Moses made to heal the people of Israel during their desert pilgrimage. The well-known passage from Philippians in the Second Reading speaks of Jesus being "lifted up" (the Greek words are similar) on the cross, after he reached hitting bottom, lower even than human—as low as a slave.

It's important for people who want to follow Jesus Christ to grasp the real meaning of the cross as a sign. In its form as a sequence of hand gestures, this sign has been reduced to a cliché in movies and on TV—a character who makes the sign of the cross must be a (dim-witted) Catholic. On film this is often a comic touch, suggesting cowardice, or fatuous piety, like the mother of the priest in *Saturday Night Fever* who crosses herself whenever anybody says her son's name. Does it mean anything more?

Before Paul recites, in Philippians 2, this version of Jesus' fall and rise, he explains that he is trying to paint a picture of Christ's "attitude," so that the group to whom he is writing can grasp in exactly which direction their "whole attitude and outlook upon life [should] change" (BB, 84). In a word, the "attitude" of Jesus that they ought to imitate is humility. And humility in this context means precisely what one of the Promises suggests: "No matter how far down the scale we have gone, we will see how our experience can benefit others" (BB, 84). In accepting his cross, Jesus went as "far down the scale" as he could; but, as John's Gospel makes clear, his willingness turned defeat into victory, into "exaltation," being "lifted up." In the same way, when we see how our humbling experience benefits other addicts, we are "lifted up"; our spirits soar.

Far from being a foolish superstition, the sign of the cross announces that the person making it is willing to provide "[s]ervice, gladly rendered" (12 X 12, 124) to anyone who needs it, and thus to follow Jesus. This is the kind of service that Bill W. said would teach alcoholics "the full meaning of 'Love thy neighbor as thyself'" (BB, 153). Jesus told his disciples on the night before he went to his cross what "the full meaning of '[l]ove'" is: "No one has greater love than this, to lay down one's life for one's friends" (Jn 15:13).

November 1

All Saints

Rv 7:2–4, 9–14; 1 Jn 3:1–3; Mt 5:1–12

"Beloved, we are God's children now; what we will be has not yet been revealed. What we do know is this: when he is revealed, we will be like him . . ."
(1 Jn 3:2).

In one of his poems, the Catholic monk Thomas Merton calls November "the days to remember the dead." Death is in the air at this time of year: in parts of the northern hemisphere where seasons change, nature is dying; the church year is coming to an end as well. In the Catholic Church, the first two days of November are devoted to memories of the dead, the first day as All Saints, the second as All Souls.

Both saints and souls are people on the spiritual path who have died. What's the difference between them? Traditionally, saints were those people whom the Church over time had come to think of as having been so holy that they must be with God—or, in any case, so holy that their lives would be well worth imitating by the living. In short, they were the people 12 Steppers call winners, as in the slogan "Stick with the Winners." Souls, on the other hand, were considered to be in an interim state. Souls were apprentice saints, whose "defects of character," as yet too well-remembered by the living, were still being "removed."

It may just be my impression, but I think the distinction between saints and souls has blurred a bit over the past few decades, especially with the death of Mother Teresa. In any event, I have known people who seemed to me unofficial saints. Some of them were Jesuits: I think of Father Leo E., a man of the Beatitudes, who showed mercy and acted as a peacemaker in a large and cantankerous city parish that he often compared to Mount St. Helens—likely to blow at any moment. I remember Cecil K., a 12 Stepper, who was willing to have heart surgery in his old age because, like St. Paul, he thought God might want him to carry the message a while longer. And I think of folks in many ways quite ordinary, like Evatt S., who was extraordinary only in his goodness. You can probably make a similar list.

At the beginning of Ordinary Time in Church Year A, Jesus speaks the Beatitudes, providing the platform for the kingdom he has come to announce, the reign of Abba. The same gospel passage is read on this feast. We end every church year in November—Gratitude Month in A. A.—by fondly remembering those we have known who lived the Beatitudes, and who have, we trust, inherited the kingdom.

November 2

All Souls

Wis 3:1–9; Rv 14:13; Jn 11, 17–27

"But the souls of the righteous are in the hand of God,
and no torment will ever touch them. . . . 'Yes,' says the Spirit,
'they will rest from their labors, for their deeds follow them'"
(Wis 3:1; Rv 14:13).

As I mentioned in the preceding meditation, the Catholic Church sets aside the first two days in November as occasions to remember those who have gone before us. On November 1 we thank God for All Saints (people whom we sense have made it all the way home). On November 2 we are grateful for All Souls (people we feel are somehow still on the Road). The Roman Church offers many suitable readings for today; I have chosen these three because I'm especially fond of them.

In countries like Mexico, All Souls is the Dia de los Muertos, the Day of the Dead, a festive occasion when families decorate the graves of loved ones or leave at their tombs gifts that those loved ones enjoyed during life (including bottles of booze). In such cultures, where death isn't as feared or as sanitized as it is in the United States, the family will have a picnic in the cemetery; their dead loved ones are still very much part of the family.

Here in the United States, death is a lonelier affair. We may resist memories of those we have loved who have died, because they naturally lead us to think about our own deaths. What lies on the other side of death is, of course, an "outside issue" for 12 Steppers—it's a case of death as we understand death. There is no such thing as 12-Step orthodoxy on this point (or any other, in fact). Still, I think that those of us who have been "reborn" through practice of the Steps (see BB, 63) possess an important clue about what death might mean.

This makes sense to me: a Power that can bring us back from a deathly illness is worthy of trust in the matter of our deaths as well (see the Thirty-Second Sunday in Ordinary Time, Cycle C for another commentary on this). We can prudently "turn our will and our lives"—and the end of our lives—"over to the care of" such a Power.

Or you might want to ponder these words of Bill W.: when we feel "new power flow[ing] in," early in recovery and later, and as we improve our "consciousness of [God's] presence, we beg[i]n to lose our fear of today, tomorrow or the hereafter" (BB, 63). A friend of mine, a recovering priest, had the privilege of being present at the deathbed of a man who for decades had been a member of both A. A. and Al-Anon. The man's last words—and probably the last words that can be said on the subject of this meditation—were "Thank God."

November 9

The Dedication of the Church of St. John Lateran

2 Chr 5: 6–10, 13–6:2; 1 Cor 3:9–13, 16–17; Lk 19:1–10

(This gospel passage is also used on the Thirty-First Sunday
in Ordinary Time, Cycle C.)
"All who saw it began to grumble and said,
'He '[Jesus] has gone to be the guest of one who is a sinner.'. . .
Then Jesus said to him, 'Today salvation has come to this house . . .'"
(Lk 19:7, 9).

This feast celebrates the dedication of a church building in Rome, the cathedral of St. John Lateran. This is the pope's cathedral as bishop of Rome (as opposed to St. Peter's, which is more the center of the Catholic Church precisely as "catholic," that is, "spread all over the world"). The feast offers an opportunity to reflect on and give thanks for the places where we meet to share "experience, strength, and hope" (BB, xxii, from the Preface to the third edition).

It sometimes strikes me as ironic when I hear people at a 12-Step meeting sharply criticizing Christian denominations. True, they may well have suffered considerably at the hands of people who claimed they were hurting them "in Christ's name." But what is ironic is that these 12 Steppers are often attacking Christians in the basement of a Christian church. Many Christian communities have shared their basements and their parish halls with 12 Steppers, and have charged only a nominal rent in exchange for use of space, heat, and light. It's not so true anymore, but some churches even let the recovering people yellow the curtains with cigarette smoke, so as "not to make too hard terms with those who [were] seek[ing]" (BB, 46) recovery through spiritual principles.

"The spiritual life is not a theory" (BB, 83)—but the spiritual life is not a contest, either. It doesn't make much sense to try to figure out who prays better, or who is more spiritual or closer to God, the people in the pews upstairs or the 12 Steppers on the folding chairs downstairs (in any case, there is frequently a lot of overlap). It's more helpful to ask what it is that makes any space holy, whether it's a church or a dingy 12-Step meeting hall.

The entrance hymn for the celebration of the dedication of a church has for centuries been "This Is a Place of Awe." It refers to Genesis, chapter 28; these are the words that Jacob says after he spends a night wrestling with an angel, who is a messenger from God (or, in another tradition, God's self). A holy place, then, is a place where one feels awe because spiritual struggle has occurred, all through a dark night until dawn came, and with the dawn, God's blessing. Or a holy place is a place where the stories of these struggles are shared. Our world is full of such places; they come in many guises. When you find yours, don't forget to say "Thank you."

Fourth Thursday in November

Thanksgiving

Is 63:7–9; 1 Cor 1:3–9; Mk 5:18–20

"[The newly sane man wanted to follow Jesus] But Jesus refused, and said to him, 'Go home to your friends, and tell them how much the Lord has done for you, and what mercy he has shown you'"
(Mk 5:19).

For a bonus meditation, I offer these reflections on Thanksgiving, the feast of gratitude that has been celebrated for centuries in the United States. There are different options for the readings to be used today; I have chosen three, including particularly this reading from Mark's gospel. As I suggested in Meditation 10 of *A 12-Step Approach to the Spiritual Exercises*, this gospel story has always seemed to me a striking allegory of addiction and recovery.

As an alcoholic, I identify strongly with this possessed man, from the land of the *goyim*. When his compulsion was on him, not even chains were "strong enough to subdue him." His life was so unmanageable that he had to live in complete isolation, in the cave-tombs, the most non-kosher, unclean place imaginable. All he could do in his powerlessness was "cry out and bruise himself with stones." He couldn't hurt other people, and especially loved ones, any more, but he could still destroy himself by slow inches. And he felt like he was more than one person—"Legion." How else could he account for all "the destruction [which] fell on the dining-room furniture or his own moral fiber" (12 X 12, 33)?

So much for "what [he] was like" (see BB, 58). Something happens—the possessed man meets someone with the power he lacks. And what is he like after? There sits the man, "clothed" and restored to sanity (Step 2). Note that he very naturally asks Jesus if he should leave home and follow him, but the answer, unexpectedly, is "No." Instead, in the words quoted above, Jesus tells the man to go home and "carry the message" (Step 12).

Bill W. would, I think, have fully embraced the principle at work in Jesus' advice to the "recovered" man. Bill D., the third member of A. A. (after Bill and Dr. Bob), tells the story of a conversation Bill W. had with Bill D. and his wife, Henrietta, when Bill D., "the man on the bed," was fresh out of the hospital and newly sober. Bill D. was wondering about "a release, a happiness, a something" that the first two members had, but which he felt he still lacked. Bill W. explained, ". . . [T]he Lord has been so wonderful to me, curing me of this terrible disease, that I just want to keep talking about it and telling people." Bill D's comment: "I thought, . . . 'I have the answer'" (BB, 191). The special "happiness" comes from "telling people" "how much the Lord in mercy has done for you."

On this American feast, let's make this "golden text" our own, in the spirit of the man who left the caves for good and went home to his family. And, in the words of an ancient Mass text, let us "pray that we may remain always in thanksgiving."